Early adolescence, a critically important developmental phase, has been neglected in terms of its potential to prevent educational and health problems. *Preparing Adolescents for the Twenty-First Century: Challenges Facing Europe and the United States* attempts to address this neglect by focusing on cross-national perspectives and linking fundamental research on adolescent development to the challenges of preparing young people for adult life. Serious examination is given to increasing the positive influence of education in promoting literacy for a high-technology economy, healthy lifestyles, and responsible citizenship.

Preparing adolescents for the twenty-first century

Preparing adolescents for the twenty-first century

Challenges facing Europe and the United States

Edited by

Ruby Takanishi
Foundation for Child Development

David A. Hamburg
Carnegie Corporation of New York

CAMBRIDGE
UNIVERSITY PRESS

PUBLISHED BY THE PRESS SYNDICATE OF THE UNIVERSITY OF CAMBRIDGE
The Pitt Building, Trumpington Street, Cambridge CB2 1RP, United Kingdom

CAMBRIDGE UNIVERSITY PRESS
The Edinburgh Building, Cambridge CB2 2RU, United Kingdom
40 West 20th Street, New York, NY 10011-4211, USA
10 Stamford Road, Oakleigh, Melbourne 3166, Australia

First published 1997

Printed in the United States of America

Typeset in Palatino

Library of Congress Cataloging-in-Publication Data
Preparing adolescents for the twenty-first century : challenges facing
Europe and the United States / edited by Ruby Takanishi, David A.
Hamburg.
p. cm.
ISBN 0-521-57065-4 (hardcover)
1. Adolescence – Congresses.   2. Teenagers – Education – Congresses.
3. Teenagers – Health and hygiene – Congresses.   4. Health promotion –
Congresses.   5. Life skills – Congresses.   6. School-to-work
transition – Congresses.   7. Cross-cultural studies – Congresses.
I. Takanishi, Ruby.   II. Hamburg, David A., 1925–   .
LB1135.P74   1997
305.23'5 – dc20   96–26087
                                                                              CIP

*A catalog record for this book is available
from the British Library.*

ISBN 0 521 57065 4 hardback

For Laszlo Nagy
Who cares deeply about the future of the world's youth

Contents

Contributors

Stephen Brand, Center for Prevention Research and Development, Institute of Government and Public Affairs, University of Illinois, Urbana, IL, U.S.A.

Robert Felner, Center for Prevention Research and Development, Institute of Government and Public Affairs, University of Illinois, Urbana, IL, U.S.A.

Nancy Flowers, Center for Prevention Research and Development, Institute of Government and Public Affairs, University of Illinois, Urbana, IL, U.S.A.

Beatrix A. Hamburg, The William T. Grant Foundation, New York, NY, U.S.A.

David A. Hamburg, Carnegie Corporation of New York, New York, NY, U.S.A.

H. Craig Heller, Program in Human Biology, Stanford University, Stanford, CA, U.S.A.

Donald Hirsch, International Consultant, London, United Kingdom

Klaus Hurrelmann, Research Center for Prevention and Intervention in Childhood and Adolescence, University of Bielefeld, Bielefeld, Germany

Anthony W. Jackson, Carnegie Corporation of New York, New York, NY, U.S.A.

Deborah Kasak, Center for Prevention Research and Development, Institute of Government and Public Affairs, University of Illinois, Urbana, IL, U.S.A.

Mary L. Kiely, Program in Human Biology, Stanford University, Stanford, CA, U.S.A.

Andreas Klocke, Research Center for Prevention and Intervention in Childhood and Adolescence, University of Bielefeld, Bielefeld, Germany

Ray Marshall, Lyndon B. Johnson School of Public Affairs, University of Texas, Austin, TX, U.S.A.

Peter Mulhall, Center for Prevention Research and Development, Institute of Government and Public Affairs, University of Illinois, Urbana, IL, U.S.A.

Henri Nadel, Department of Economics, University of Paris, 7, France

Eugeen Roosens, Department of Social and Cultural Anthropology, Katholieke Universiteit Leuven, Leuven, Belgium

Ruby Takanishi, Foundation for Child Development, New York, NY, U.S.A.

Foreword

Preparing Adolescents for the Twenty-First Century is the fourth volume of the Johann Jacobs Foundation's Conference Series. Like the previous ones, this volume promotes our Foundation's basic aim: to support young adolescents in becoming healthy and productive adults capable of making valuable contributions to society. This goal is accomplished through financial support of basic research on human development, the elaboration of educational and policy programs, and the furtherance of reliable research-based intervention strategies from which all adolescents can benefit.

This interest of the Johann Jacobs Foundation was particularly well served by two recent conferences. The first was held at our Marbach Castle Communication Center on the topic "Frontiers in the Education of Young Adolescents" (November 3–5, 1994). The second took place in Geneva, Switzerland (February 3–5, 1995), on "Schools as Health Promoting Environments." At both conferences, many interesting and original views were expressed regarding the difficult contexts in which young adolescents are negotiating on the often tortuous path to adulthood.

Not long ago, young people were often considered privileged, handed all the benefits of the consumer society on a silver tray. At the same time, other observers fretted about youth, making them feel guilty for misdeeds and reprehensible behavior for which they were not responsible. It is widely recognized that today's youths face completely different and incomparably more complicated challenges than those that confronted previous generations, including the prospect of a lower standard of living than their parents enjoyed.

Young people need to learn new skills and competences. They have to know how society functions, and they have to be good at problem solving, have a strong sense of self-efficacy, and possess sound communications skills.

This volume addresses a wide audience, including scholars, behaviorial scientists, educationalists, specialists from public health, and experts on school effectiveness, but also the general public interested in the welfare of youth. All share a willingness to help the new generation come of age confidently.

I would like to convey my gratitude to the main organizers of the two conferences, particularly David A. Hamburg from the Carnegie Corporation of New York and Ruby Takanishi from the Carnegie Council on Adolescent Development. Let me also thank the speakers, discussants, and other participants of both conferences, who all contributed to the success of a joint venture to improve the life chances of youth worldwide.

Klaus J. Jacobs
Chairman of the Board
Johann Jacobs Foundation

Preface

As we approach the twenty-first century, innovative approaches to preparing young people for adult life are much more urgent than ever. The global marketplace and the telecommunications revolution are spurring increasing interdependence among nations, as well as demanding the exchange of ideas and experiences about crucial human investment strategies among countries. These changing circumstances present vast challenges to national capacities for adaptation as each country searches for ways to produce well-educated, healthy, and productive youth. The European countries and the United States share common interests: How can our different educational systems attempt to meet the developmental needs of young adolescents, and how can these systems – curricula, instructional approaches, school organization – better prepare adolescents for adult life than they are now doing?

In the early 1980s, *A Nation at Risk* stimulated yet another wave of educational reform in the United States. In 1989, the Carnegie Council on Adolescent Development, an operating program of Carnegie Corporation of New York, issued *Turning Points: Preparing American Youth for the 21st Century*, a wide-ranging examination of the educational experiences of 10- to 15-year-old American adolescents. This report led to a Carnegie Corporation–sponsored Middle Grade School State Policy Initiative that has supported the reform of middle grades education in at least 15 states. International studies of education and health are also recently available, most noteworthy being the current activity around the Third International Study of Educational Achievement, to be released in the fall of 1996, and related multinational studies, such as the Third International Mathematics and Science Study (TIMSS). The Organization for Economic Cooperation and Development (OECD) has become more active in the education area as well.

This book, which is based on presentations made at a November 1994 conference in Marbach, Germany, and a February 1995 follow-up conference in Geneva, Switzerland, builds on the considerable ongoing research in Europe and the United States. The Marbach conference focused on the frontiers in the education of young adolescents in European countries and the United States. Education was broadly conceived to include the linkage of education with health and science education – specifically a life sciences curriculum for the middle grades – the engagement of families and other sources of social support in the learning and development of young adolescents, and life skills training. Attention was also paid to the increased diversity of ethnic groups in the United States and Europe and the preparation of adolescents for living in pluriethnic societies.

At the Geneva conference, about 100 participants, largely from all parts of Europe, met to discuss the growing movement of schools as health-promoting environments, which was one of the topics at the Marbach meeting. This meeting was a collaborative effort among the Johann Jacobs Foundation, Carnegie Corporation of New York, and the World Health Organization–Geneva. A major focus of examination was the experience of the European Network of Health-Promoting Schools, an initiative of the European Regional Office of the World Health Organization.

The book also reflects the highly productive collaboration between the Carnegie Council on Adolescent Development and the Johann Jacobs Foundation. The Council, which has since 1986 focused on the early adolescent period (ages 10 to 15), has sought to show how pivotal institutions – schools, health systems, community and youth organizations, families, and the media – can better meet the requirements for healthy development during adolescence amid widespread social, economic, cultural, and technological transformations. Established in 1988, the Johann Jacobs Foundation is a Swiss charitable trust dedicated to helping adolescents become actively contributing members of their societies in Europe and throughout the world.

Preparing Adolescents for the Twenty-First Century is unique in several ways. First, its principal focus is on the period of early adolescence, from ages 9 or 10 to 14 or 15 years, a developmental phase that has been vastly neglected in terms of its potential to prevent educational and health problems. Early adolescence should definitely be of interest, as the trend lines for child and adolescent indicators exhibit similar patterns in both Europe and the United States. Second, the volume takes a cross-national perspective to the demands of raising well-educated, healthy adolescents for the next century. Third, the book describes the theory, design, and implementation of comprehensive education and health approaches during adolescence, as well as the available research and evaluation studies to determine their effectiveness and needs for changes in these approaches. In the United States particularly, and increasingly abroad, there is a movement away from targeted, single-problem-focused intervention to more comprehensive, developmentally informed approaches to the education of adolescents and the promotion of their health. Finally, the book concludes by drawing together cross-cutting themes and identifying common ground where the European and American experiences intersect. It is at these crossroads that important lessons may emerge to benefit nations on both sides of the Atlantic.

This book is the fourth volume in the Johann Jacobs Conference Series. The three previous volumes have examined youth unemployment, psychosocial disorders during adolescence, and self-efficacy. This volume attempts to link fundamental research on adolescent development to the challenges of preparing young people for adult life in the next century. Serious examination is therefore given to increasing the positive influence of education in promoting literacy for a high-technology economy, healthy lifestyles, and responsible citizenship in societies with diverse racial, ethnic, and religious groups. It will therefore be a resource for behavioral and social scientists, educators, health care providers, and related policymakers and administrators who plan and implement programs for adolescents in the United States and Europe. For individuals interested in cross-national perspectives on the development, education, and health of adolescents, this book offers descriptions of programs that hold promise and have been implemented successfully in the United States and Europe.

We are deeply grateful to Klaus Jacobs, chairman of the board of the Johann Jacobs Foundation, for his support and sustained commitment to the issues addressed in this volume. In planning the Marbach conference, we worked with outstanding colleagues. A planning group with representatives from both sides of the Atlantic was involved in selecting the topics and presenters for the conference. The group included Klaus Hurrelmann, Henri Nadel, Laszlo Nagy, William Julius Wilson, and Carnegie Corporation staff Anthony W. Jackson, Elena O. Nightingale, and Vivien Stewart. For the February conference, our colleagues included Klaus Hurrelmann, Ilona Kickbusch, and Fred Paccaud.

The staff of the Carnegie Council developed strong, productive working relationships with Laszlo Nagy, then president of the Jacobs Foundation, and with Judith Kressig. We express our heartfelt appreciation to both of them, and to Linda S. Schoff, Timothy J. McGourthy, and Jenifer Hartnett, for their outstanding administrative and research assistance and attention to the details that are essential in conference planning and preparing a book for publication. Allyn M. Mortimer became involved in assisting us with the editing of the book in the middle of completing the Council's concluding report. Julia C. Chill competently prepared the entire volume for final delivery to Cambridge University Press. Among all of us, this was truly a collaboration of mutual respect and aid that promises to continue well beyond this effort.

> Ruby Takanishi, Executive Director
> Carnegie Council on Adolescent Development
> Carnegie Corporation of New York
> Washington, D.C.

> David A. Hamburg, President
> Carnegie Corporation of New York
> New York, New York

> February 1996

1. Meeting the essential requirements for healthy adolescent development in a transforming world

DAVID A. HAMBURG

The problem of world transformation provides a vital context for viewing adolescent development. It is a very large canvas on which to paint. Yet we must try to understand it because adolescence is, in some ways, very different than it was in our long evolutionary past.

The turn of the twentieth century is a useful benchmark. In 1900, there were hardly any automobiles or household telephones; motion pictures were barely getting under way. There were no household radios, no airplanes, no televisions, no computers. What a difference a century makes! Indeed, now even the changes within a decade are dramatic by evolutionary and historical standards. Never before have such rapid and complex transformations occurred as in our lifetime.

The recent changes driven by technological opportunities have had a huge impact on the economy, on communities, and on families. We have rocketed into a new way of life within a couple of generations. And these changes have had powerful effects on the experience of growing up. Today's children are in a very different situation than their parents or grandparents – in some ways better, in some ways worse. We need to clarify what is better and what is worse – and how to shift the balance from worse toward better.

The human child is an ancient creature, shaped by many millennia of biological evolution in ways that pose critical requirements for adequate development. These essential requirements have to be met if the child is to grow and develop, to thrive and learn, and to pursue a vigorous, constructive, adaptable life. Such requirements have always been difficult to meet, but if met, they provide profound advantages to our species – ways of learning and adapting and creating that are unparalleled in the annals of life on earth.

1

During the past few decades, the social conditions of child and adolescent development have changed drastically. Now, these ancient creatures must grow up in very different circumstances than ever before. Along with unprecedented opportunities, we have stumbled into unforeseen formidable obstacles. So we must find different ways to meet the essential requirements for effective child and adolescent development – not only through the family, but also through a set of pivotal institutions that have a strong bearing on the outcomes.

An evolutionary perspective

Let us briefly put adolescent development into evolutionary perspective. Simple forms of life have existed on earth for several billion years. Nonhuman primates have been on earth for more than 50 million years. Apes have been present for about 20 million years. Our own particular species is a very recent entry, about 100,000 years old. During all those millions of years, our ancestors – prehuman, almost human, and distinctly human – lived in small, face-to-face groups in which they learned the rules of adaptation for survival and reproduction. They used very simple tools to cope with the problems of living and probably struggled to obtain more control over their own destiny. For the most part, they were vulnerable to the vicissitudes of food and water supplies, weather, predators, other humans, and whatever nature might bring.

Their world began to change with the development of agriculture about 10,000 years ago. But the most pervasive, momentous changes occurred with the Industrial Revolution only two centuries ago, and above all with its effective implementation in the twentieth century.

Each advance in this dramatic sweep carried with it some side effects, largely unforeseen in most cases. A new development that is socially useful can also have inadvertent side effects that are risky or damaging. The way we live today is, in important respects, a novelty for our species.

Such problems as excessive population growth, drastic impacts of urbanization and industrialization, widespread family disruptions, serious environmental damage, resource depletion, and the profound risks of weapons technology have emerged since the Industrial Revolution, especially in the twentieth century. In a moment of evolutionary time, the human species has transformed its physical, biological, and social environments. Many of the changes are within the memory of living adults. Yet natural selection built human organisms over millions of years in ways that suited earlier environments. It is an open question and a matter of concern how well we are suited to the environment we have created so suddenly. To some extent, we are an old species in a new habitat.

Before getting to adolescence, we should think for a moment about ancient infants in a high-tech world. Can we meet the needs of very young children? What are the fundamental building blocks of child and adolescent development (Hamburg, 1992)? The years of infancy and toddlerhood have always been crucial in human adaptation. They provide the fundamental opportunity to learn the basic elements about ourselves, about each other, about the world around us, and about ways to cope and to solve problems of living (Cole and Cole, 1989).

Let us briefly consider the problem of prolongation of immaturity – years of helplessness and great vulnerability. What kind of adaptive gain could possibly overcome the disadvantages of prolonged helplessness? The principal gain probably is that this very long, protected time can be utilized for learning, adapted to the specific conditions of a given environment, whatever those conditions may be. A very diverse array of environments may be adapted to through the shaping of behavior in the long, protected interval of immaturity.

How does the human child and adolescent acquire the skills necessary for survival and reproduction? Overwhelmingly, the years of growth and development are spent in social relations with others of the same species – among nonhuman primates as well as humans (Hamburg, 1963). These relations offer protection, modeling, feedback, attachment, guidance, and encouragement. Such survival skills as obtaining food and water as well as avoiding predators have long been acquired in a social context, largely through the sequence of observation, imitation, and practice. A critical aspect of this learning occurs during infancy and involves mother–infant attachment. Secure early attachments are essential for primate and human development (Bowlby, 1988). Experimental research has demonstrated that development goes drastically awry when infants are deprived of the opportunity to develop an attachment to a dependable caregiver early in life.

On the other hand, rearing by a caring adult leads to strong attachment and provides a secure base from which the infant can explore the larger social and physical worlds. This is richly documented in studies of nonhuman primates in natural habitats (Smuts, Cheney, Seyfarth, Wrangham, and Struhsaker, 1986). Thus, throughout the long evolution of our species, societies have been built on the basic evolutionary requirements of survival and reproduction, and individuals have had to learn rules of adaptation compatible with these requirements (Lancaster and Hamburg, 1986).

Our ancestors lived for many millennia in hunting-and-gathering societies – long after they had acquired fully human biological characteristics. These early societies were characterized by the small size of their communities, typically between 20 and 50 people. In these simple societies, the occupations of children's parents were clearly visible throughout childhood. At an early age, boys joined the men in their regular activities and girls joined the women. Thus, both sexes prepared for the tasks of adulthood. A great deal of attention to the child from parents and older siblings was the rule, much of it in shaping the attitudes and skills essential for everyday life. In this way, children and adolescents participated extensively in their small society as age and circumstances permitted and, in doing so, they learned the skills necessary to sustain life.

In modern societies, the lives of children and adults are worlds apart. Contemporary American children are largely ignorant of how their parents make a living. Furthermore, by the time they become adults, many of their parents' jobs will have disappeared, made obsolete by some new technology. Thus parents are trying to hit a moving target in preparing children for adulthood.

Over many millennia, in the simple societies of human origins, the basic integrative force has been the family. The kin group historically served many functions: political, economic, educational, religious, and psychological. As societies grew in size and complexity, changes were inevitable. They have occurred drastically in recent decades.

Historically, several circumstances have been helpful in meeting essential requirements for healthy child development: (1) an intact, cohesive, nuclear family, dependable under stress; (2) a relationship with at least one parent who is consistently nurturing, loving, enjoying, teaching, and coping; (3) easy access to supportive extended-family members; (4) a supportive community, whether it be a neighborhood or a religious, ethnic, or political group, but some larger group beyond the family that is helpful; (5) experience with child rearing during the years of growth and development, in effect an ongoing education for parenthood; (6) an emerging perception of opportunities during childhood with a tangible basis for hope of an attractive future; and (7) some predictability in the adult environment that permits gradual preparation to cope with it and take advantage of its real opportunities. But lately these great historic desiderata have been jeopardized, and we are in a stressful time of major transitions. These drastic changes have had a notable effect on adolescent development.

In the past three decades – a moment of human history, let alone evolution – the change in regular patterns of contact between American children and their adult relatives is remarkable. These changes are less drastic in Europe so far, but the trends are similar. Not only are mothers home much less, but there is also little evidence of increased time by fathers at home to compensate. Especially for women, there is a difficult integration of work and family. Overall, the time parents spend with children in the United States has declined by about one-third in the past 30 years. Moreover, only about 5% of American children see a grandparent regularly, a much lower level than in earlier times.

Powerful institutions of society, such as business and government, have done little to facilitate parental availability for children or to strengthen the competence of families in the rapidly changing circumstances of the late twentieth century. European policies and practices are, so far, more effectively child centered. These problems are compounded by high mobility, massive flows of immigration, drastic mixing of cultures, and erosion of strong neighborhood ties and other social supports, as well as high divorce and separation rates. So we now live in a time of major family disruption, manifested in a variety of ways, and involving considerable jeopardy to child and adolescent development. It is a stimulating era but also a stressful one.

What is special about adolescence?

Adolescence is a time of upheaval, one of the greatest in the entire life span. Biological changes are pervasive, especially in hormones, brain, and behavior. Recent years have seen the discovery of adolescence in nonhuman primates. This opens a window on some basic attributes of adolescence that are part of our biological heritage. For example, chimpanzees manifest major changes in behavior associated with the pubertal growth spurt and hormonal changes. In males, there are sharp increases in aggressive, exploratory, and sexual behavior. In females, the most striking increases are in sexual and exploratory behavior, but above all in the migration to another group. That is, they leave the group of origin and join another group for the long term – a complex and difficult transition.

The drastic changes in secretion of sex hormones during early adolescence have profound effects. They have an impact on every tissue in the body, most notably the reproductive system but also the brain. In male chimpanzees, the change from childhood levels of circulating testosterone to adult levels occurs within 1 year. Such rapid shifts produce the growth spurt that is so characteristic of early adolescence. This growth spurt is most striking in the development of reproductive organs but involves the whole body. The human adolescent is a fascinated and sometimes horrified observer of these dramatic changes, asking in one way or another, "What does it all mean?"

So adolescence in humans as well as nonhuman primates is a time when profound changes occur in physiological and biochemical systems and behavior. The basic machinery of these neuroendocrine coordinations of puberty is of ancient origin in human ancestry. Yet historically recent events have drastically changed the experience of adolescence, in some ways making it more difficult than ever before.

1. *The lengthening period of adolescence.* In the past two centuries, control of infection and better nutrition in technologically advanced cultures have lowered the average age at which menstruation begins. At the same time, the social changes occurring during those centuries have postponed the end of adolescence and of dependence until much later. This elongated period of adolescence introduces much uncertainty. There is at least a decade of transition between childhood and adulthood.

2. *The disjunction between biological and social development.* Although the human organism is reproductively mature in early adolescence, the brain does not reach a fully adult state of development until the end of the teen years, and social maturity lags well behind. Young adolescents make many fateful decisions that affect their entire life course, even though they are immature in knowledge, social experience, and cognitive development.

3. *Difficulty in foreseeing the years ahead.* In early adolescence now, there is probably more ambiguity and complexity about what constitutes preparation for effective adulthood than was ever the case before. The version of adult life seen on television creates only a shadowy image of adult experience, a mix of reality and fantasy.

4. *The erosion of family and social support networks.* Throughout most of human history, small societies provided durable networks, familiar human relationships, and cultural guidance for young people, offering support in times of stress and the skills necessary for coping and adaptation. In contemporary societies, such social support networks have eroded.

5. *The easy access by adolescents to potentially life-threatening substances, weapons, and activities.* Although these activities may appear to young people to be casual, recreational, and tension-relieving, their effects often endanger themselves and others.

In the face of such drastic biological, social, and technological changes surrounding adolescence that have taken place since the Industrial Revolution, and especially in this century, there are basic human needs in adolescence that are enduring – indeed, crucial – to survival and healthy development. These are fundamental requirements for healthy, constructive, problem-solving adolescent development. Adolescents must (1) find a place in a valued group that provides a sense of belonging; (2) identify tasks that are generally recognized by the group as having adaptive value and that thereby earn respect when skill is acquired for coping with the tasks; (3) feel a sense of worth as a person; (4) establish reliable and predictable relationships with other people, especially a few relatively close relationships – or at least one; (5) find constructive expression of the curiosity and exploration that strongly characterize adolescence; (6) find a basis for making informed, deliberate decisions, particularly decisions that have lifelong consequences; (7) accept respectfully the enormous diversity of modern society, the individual differences among adolescents in size, shape, color, and rates of body and behavior change; and (8) find ways of being useful to others.

There are a variety of major indicators showing that, in many contemporary societies, we are failing to meet these fundamental requirements for large numbers of adolescents. The historical recency of drastic sociotechnical changes has outrun our understanding and institutional capacity to adapt. There is an urgent need to improve our capacity to deal with adolescent problems. That is why the Carnegie Council on Adolescent Development's basic focus is on meeting the essential requirements for healthy adolescent development through a variety of pivotal institutions in a world transformed, so that it will be possible to grow up inquiring and problem solving, healthy and vigorous, decent and constructive.

The central challenge of early adolescence

The early adolescent years, ages 10 through 14, see the formation of behavior patterns relevant to education and health that have lifelong significance (Hamburg, 1974). Many dangerous patterns are readily observable: becoming alienated from school, even dropping out; starting to smoke cigarettes, drink alcohol, and use other drugs; starting to drive automobiles and motorcycles in high-risk ways; not eating an adequate diet or exercising enough; risking early pregnancy and sexually transmitted diseases; and, in some ways worst of all, beginning to use weapons, even highly destructive ones.

Initially, adolescents explore these new possibilities tentatively. Experimentation is typical of adolescence. Before damaging patterns are firmly established, there is a vital opportunity to prevent lifelong casualties (Hamburg, 1992; Hechinger, 1992; Millstein, Petersen, and Nightingale, 1993). This opportunity is frequently missed in most communities now, all too often with tragic results.

To meet the essential requirements for healthy adolescent development, we must help adolescents to acquire constructive knowledge and skills, inquiring habits of mind, dependable human relationships, a reliable basis for earning respect, a sense of belonging in a valued group, and a way of being useful to others. These basic needs can be met by a conjunction of pivotal institutions: family; school; community-based organizations, including religious ones; the health-care system; and the media. The Carnegie Council on Adolescent Development has tried since 1986 to highlight ways in which the current inadequacy of these institutions for this purpose can be overcome.

Key concepts for inclusive, effective education

Research has shown the value of several concepts that are applicable to the middle grade schools – the main locus of education in early adolescence (Carnegie Council on Adolescent Development, 1989). In brief, they are:

1. Developmentally appropriate education – meshing the content and process of learning with the interests and capacities of the child in each phase of development.
2. Schools of small units, created on a human scale – very important and very inexpensive (e.g., school within school/houses).
3. Sustained individual attention in the context of a supportive group – a pervasive theme of educational reform, going beyond impersonal warehouses.
4. Students learning to cooperate in class, with an eye on future work and decent human relations – for example, through techniques of cooperative learning and through supervised community service.

5. Stimulation of curiosity and thinking skills – especially through the life sciences in upper elementary and middle grade schools.
6. Linkage of education and health – each nourishing the other.

As a young adolescent experiences puberty, there is a natural tendency to ask questions about one's own body. In effect, how shall I use my body? Any responsible education must answer that basic question with a substantial life sciences curriculum that gives young adolescents accurate information about their own bodies, including the effects of various high-risk behavior patterns. But information is not enough.

How can a young adolescent make good use of accurate and personally meaningful information? Life skills training can become a vital part of education in schools and community organizations, so that adolescents can learn how to make informed, deliberate, and constructive decisions rather than ignorant, impulsive, and destructive ones. Such training can also enhance their interpersonal skills, their ways of relating decently to others, learning from their experiences, even unpleasant ones – for example, how conflicts can be resolved without violence. This is especially important in multiethnic communities and an interdependent world economy. Skills can be built to establish dependable friendships and participation in problem-solving groups. But even this is not enough.

People need people, especially to weather the inevitable difficulties of growing up, the stresses of education, and the turbulent search for ways to protect personal health and the health of loved ones. To the extent that contemporary families are unable to meet these needs, specially designed social support interventions can be exceedingly helpful.

Thus, a life sciences curriculum linked with life skills training and social support interventions can provide the vital information, skills, and motivation necessary to meet the essential requirements for healthy adolescent development – even in poor communities. Moreover, this conjunction of information, skills, and motivation for personal development, indeed for survival, can be provided not only in schools but also through the participation of other pivotal institutions that powerfully shape the transition from childhood to adulthood: especially the health care system and community organizations that reach out to youth.

But there is still a serious unmet need for accessible health care (U.S. Congress, Office of Technology Assessment, 1991a, 1991b, 1991c). It may be met at the school or near the school. In any event, it must be arranged in such a way that it is clearly recognizable to middle grade students, that the care is available, within reach, and adapted to the distinctive needs of adolescent development (i.e., user-friendly). Another important perspective is that of making the entire school a health-promoting environment, as manifested in the World Health Organization–EURO's network of health-promoting schools.

The Carnegie Council on Adolescent Development published a report on community-based organizations entitled *A Matter of Time: Risk and Opportunity in the Nonschool Hours* (Carnegie Council on Adolescent Development, 1992). This report is about alternatives to current dangers. Alternatives to what? To growing up alone, to growing up on the street, to growing up with television and violence, to growing up with immature peers and drugs. To make the adolescent transition successfully, young people need respectful contact with responsible, caring adults. And they need an array of stimulating, constructive opportunities throughout their waking hours – both in school and beyond. So often, both parents are at work and the home is empty for many adolescents after school. There are thousands of youth-oriented organizations across the United States. The opportunities for reaching young people are immense.

But these organizations do not reach many of the young people who most need support and guidance, especially poor children and adolescents. And many programs for youth are provided for only an hour or two a week, which is not intensive enough to meet essential needs for healthy adolescent development. Many programs, too, are run by well-meaning adults who are untrained in dealing with young adolescents and their distinctive attributes. And contact fades as children move beyond childhood into adolescence. So this field needs more outreach, more time, more training and recognition of youth workers, and more focus on young adolescents. For all of this, community organizations need more funds from both the private and public sectors.

In essence, these organizations function best when they stimulate the interest of young people by whatever means are appropriate. They provide attractive settings – whatever is a magnet for young adolescents: food, music, sports, and friendly people. Then they build education and health functions into their operation.

Evidence shows that these organizations can connect young adolescents with reliable adults who provide social support and guidance, life skills training, and constructive alternatives to drug use, gang involvement, and premature, unprotected sex. These organizations offer young adolescents opportunities to make useful contributions to the community, to earn money, to build a sense of worth, and to make durable friendships. Thus, the strengthening of community organizations constitutes one of the frontiers for adolescent development in the next decade.

Conclusion

If we can find ways to meet the essential requirements for healthy adolescent development, we can build the foundation for a long, healthy life characterized by vigor, curiosity, learning, adaptability, and decency throughout its course. Health and education are closely linked in this process. Investments in health and education can be guided by research in biomedical and behavioral sciences (Feldman and Elliott, 1990) in ways likely to prevent much of the damage now being done to children and adolescents, thereby contributing substantially to a dynamic economy and a flourishing democratic society in the next century. But we have to find out how to meet the essential requirements for child and adolescent development through pivotal institutions, family and beyond, in a world that is still in the process of transformation. This is a fundamental challenge of great practical significance.

References

Bowlby, J. A. (1988). *A secure base: Parent–child attachment and healthy human development.* New York: Basic Books.

Carnegie Council on Adolescent Development, Task Force on Education of Young Adolescents. (1989). *Turning points: Preparing American youth for the 21st century.* Washington, DC: Author

Carnegie Council on Adolescent Development, Task Force on Youth Development and Community Programs. (1992). *A matter of time: Risk and opportunity in the nonschool hours.* Washington, DC: Author

Cole, M., and Cole, S. R. (1989). *The development of children.* New York: W. H. Freeman.

Feldman, S. S., and Elliott, G. R. (Eds.). (1990). *At the threshold: The developing adolescent.* Cambridge, MA: Harvard University Press.

Hamburg, B. A. (1974). Early adolescence: A specific and stressful phase of the life cycle. In G. V. Coelho, D. A. Hamburg, and J. E. Adams (Eds.), *Coping and adaptation* (pp. 102–124). New York: Basic Books.

Hamburg, D. A. (1963). Emotions in the perspective of human evolution. In P. Knapp (Ed.), *Expression of the emotions in man* (pp. 300–317). New York: International Universities Press.

Hamburg, D. A. (1992). *Today's children: Creating a future for a generation in crisis.* New York: Times Books.

Hechinger, F. M. (1992). *Fateful choices: Healthy youth for the 21st century.* New York: Hill and Wang.

Lancaster, J., and Hamburg, B. A. (Eds.). (1986). *School-age pregnancy and parenthood: Bio-social dimensions.* Hawthorne, NY: Aldine de Gruyter.

Millstein, S. G., Petersen, A. C., and Nightingale, E. O. (Eds.). (1993). *Promoting the health of adolescents: New directions for the twenty-first century*. New York: Oxford University Press.

Smuts, B. B., Cheney, D. L., Seyfarth, R. M., Wrangham, R. W., and Struhsaker, T. T. (1986). *Primate societies*. Chicago: University of Chicago Press.

U.S. Congress, Office of Technology Assessment. (1991a). *Adolescent health: Volume 1: Summary and policy options* (OTA Publication No. OTA-H-468). Washington, DC: U.S. Government Printing Office.

U.S. Congress, Office of Technology Assessment. (1991b). *Adolescent health: Volume 2: Background and the effectiveness of selected prevention and treatment services* (OTA Publication No. OTA-H-466). Washington, DC: U.S. Government Printing Office.

U.S. Congress, Office of Technology Assessment. (1991c). *Adolescent health: Volume 3: Crosscutting issues in the delivery of health and related services* (OTA Publication No. OTA-H-467). Washington, DC: U.S. Government Printing Office.

2. Adapting educational systems to young adolescents and new conditions

ANTHONY W. JACKSON

"If someone had purposely designed the worst possible institution for educating young adolescents, they could not have done better than the American junior high school." This sweeping conclusion was expressed by Deborah Meier, noted American secondary school principal, during deliberations of the Carnegie Council on Adolescent Development's Task Force on the Education of Young Adolescents.

In June 1989, the Task Force produced *Turning Points: Preparing American Youth for the 21st Century*, a wide-ranging examination of the educational experiences of 10- to 15-year-old youth. *Turning Points* applied current research about the characteristics, needs, and development of young adolescents to an assessment of the effectiveness of the services health and community organizations provide to schools. Using language more temperate than Meier's but voicing similar sentiments, the Task Force found that "a volatile mismatch exists between the organization and curriculum of middle grade schools [junior high, intermediate, or middle schools] and the intellectual, emotional, and interpersonal needs of young adolescents" (Carnegie Council on Adolescent Development, 1989, p. 32).

Turning Points was an attempt to define that volatile mismatch and to offer a plan of action for transforming middle grade schools into learning environments suited to the needs of young adolescents and equal to the challenges of a rapidly changing world. The report's release was followed quickly by an initiative stimulated by the Carnegie Corporation of New York to implement the recommendations in states and schools across the United States.

Drawing upon and, where possible, updating concepts and findings presented in *Turning Points*, this chapter briefly reviews Carnegie-sponsored efforts to adapt educational systems to young adolescents and to new conditions. The first section briefly outlines the challenges of early adolescence for American youth, challenges that for some lead to an increased risk of problems as adolescents and as adults. The second section then contrasts the problems found in the traditional junior high school to the principles and methods described in *Turning Points* for educating young adolescents to promote intellectual development, physical and mental health, and good citizenship. The final section reports encouraging preliminary results from the first 4 years of the Carnegie-sponsored initiative.

The challenges of early adolescence

Early adolescence for American youth is a vortex of change. Young adolescents go through puberty, a period during which growth and development is more rapid than in any other phase of life except infancy. Over a period of 4 to 5 years, young people experience dramatic changes in height, weight, and body configuration, and they acquire the capacity to reproduce.

Concurrent with this biological maturation are changes in adolescents' intellectual capacities. From early adolescence on, thinking begins to involve abstract rather than merely concrete representation; to become multidimensional rather than limited to a single issue; to become relative rather than absolute in the conception of knowledge; and to become reflective and self-aware (Keating, 1990).

As a result of their increased capacity for thinking and decision making, adolescents have greater opportunities for self-determination in many areas of their lives and face greater risks than younger children. They have more control, for example, over how vigorously they apply themselves in school, the kinds of friends they have of both genders, and the extent to which they adopt such perilous behaviors as smoking, using alcohol or other recreational drugs, and engaging in early or promiscuous sexual activity. Unfortunately, the tendency of young adolescents to focus on the here and now rather than on the long-range consequences of their actions puts them in substantial danger of making errors in judgment (Feldman and Elliot, 1990).

Promotion from elementary school to junior high or middle school also represents a dramatic shift for young adolescents. In this transition, they move from the stability of a relatively small elementary school in which a student generally has one teacher and remains within a class of perhaps 25 to 30 children for an entire school year to a middle grade school of perhaps 1,000 or more students in which each student has as many as six or seven classes, each with a different teacher. Each class is comprised of a different group of students and meets for less than an hour each day, a structure that severely attenuates the possibility of intensive intellectual discourse or the development of sustained, supportive relationships with adults or peers.

Despite the many new pressures and challenges of adolescence, most American youth emerge from this period relatively unscathed, prepared for a productive adult life. Yet according to one estimate, as many as one-quarter of girls and boys aged 10 to 17 in the United States – some 7 million youth – may be extremely vulnerable to the negative consequences of multiple high-risk behaviors, many of which first present themselves to youth during the middle grade school years (Dryfoos, 1990). For these highly vulnerable youth as well as for their less vulnerable peers, the nature of their experience in middle grade school may substantially influence the trajectory of their adolescent and adult lives.

Turning Points: Transforming the education of young adolescents

At the heart of the Carnegie Council on Adolescent Development's *Turning Points* is a set of eight principles for transforming the education of young adolescents. The principles were created by integrating current research knowledge with the considered opinions of eminent researchers, educators, policymakers, and advocates for children and youth. The eight principles are as follows:

1. Large middle grade schools are divided into smaller communities for learning.
2. Middle grade schools transmit a core of common knowledge to all students.
3. Middle grade schools are organized to ensure success for all students.
4. Teachers and principals have the major responsibility and power to transform middle grade schools.
5. Teachers for the middle grades are specifically prepared to teach young adolescents.
6. Schools promote good health; the education and health of young adolescents are inextricably linked.

7. Families are allied with school staff through mutual respect, trust, and communication.
8. Schools and communities are partners in educating young adolescents.

The next few sections of this chapter explain the contexts and goals of each principle in greater detail.

Creating communities for learning

Many American middle grade schools are large, impersonal institutions. Opportunities for teachers to develop the sustained personal relationships with students that are essential to teach them well and to provide guidance during the sometimes turbulent period of early adolescence often are nonexistent. In the largest, most alienating urban junior high schools that house over 2,000 students in various states of suspended anonymity, conditions virtually guarantee that the intellectual and emotional needs of youth will go unmet.

One way of dividing unacceptably large schools into human-scale communities of learning is to create schools-within-schools, or "houses" within the school, and then divide these subunits into smaller "teams" of teachers and students. These teams consist of as few as two teachers, but more often three or four, and the students they instruct.

In effective middle schools, such teams are considered the core structure for organizing teaching and learning. Teaming brings together teachers of different subjects to share responsibility for the same students and create a common interdisciplinary curriculum. Joint planning enables the teachers to provide consistent expectations for their students and enables the students to strive to meet clearly understood standards of achievement. Teaming also allows teachers to share perspectives on a student's behavior and to intervene before minor problems escalate.

For students, teaming provides an environment conducive to learning by reducing the stress of anonymity and isolation (Arhar, Johnston, and Markle, 1989). Learning often takes place best when students have opportunities to discuss, analyze, express opinions, and receive feedback from peers (American Association for the Advancement of Science, 1989). Teaming also creates an integrated learning environment that encourages students to grapple with ideas that may span several academic disciplines and to address problems with solutions that reflect understanding, not memorization.

Teaching a core of common knowledge

Much of learning and the development of solutions to complex problems lies in the ability to integrate disparate bodies of information. Yet in many middle grade schools, the curriculum is so fragmented by subject area that a student's daily schedule seems more like academic pinball than like a planned set of learning experiences. Students have virtually no opportunity to make connections among ideas in different intellectual disciplines.

Even within individual classes, middle grade students often are not challenged intellectually, reflecting the persistent misapprehension that young adolescents generally are incapable of critical or higher-order thinking. Current research provides encouraging evidence that higher-order thinking among adolescents is attainable and that attempts to stimulate such engagement, if carried out systematically, do offer considerable promise (Keating, 1990).

When teachers are given sufficient common planning time, the team approach allows them to organize the curriculum and instruction around integrating themes that cut across academic disciplines. Such interdisciplinary or thematic instruction can help students understand relationships between seemingly unrelated ideas. At the same time, there is a danger that thematic teaching may trivialize these relationships if it is used only to emphasize superficial links between subject areas rather than substantive connections among fundamental concepts. For this reason, it is critical to consider the *content* of the middle grade curriculum as well as its integration.

Efforts to define the appropriate content of the middle grade curriculum – what young adolescents should know and be able to do – currently are under way at the federal, state, and local levels across the United States. In most instances, this work is part of a larger effort to develop curriculum frameworks or "content standards" for all elementary and secondary education. The California State Department of Education, for example, has created curriculum frameworks for instruction in English and language arts, foreign language, health, history and social sciences, mathematics, physical education, science, and visual and performing arts. Most states and many educational organizations are mounting similar efforts.

A persistent theme in content development work is that *less is more*. That is, the current emphasis in the curriculum on covering a large quantity of information must yield to an emphasis on the depth and quality of understanding of a limited number of major concepts in each subject area. A primary task for middle grade educators, especially teaching teams, is to identify the most important principles and concepts within each discipline and to concentrate on integrating these main ideas to create a meaningful interdisciplinary curriculum.

Because young people must be healthy to learn, and because risks that threaten healthy development are so prevalent in early adolescence, the core middle grade curriculum must combine knowledge from the traditional academic disciplines with information about adolescent physical and emotional development and about the dangers of illicit drugs, alcohol, and tobacco. Moreover, young people need training in skills that help them resist engagement in risky behaviors; these skills are often referred to as *life skills*. In-depth reviews of these critical aspects of adolescent education are the subject of other chapters in this volume.

Ensuring success for all student⌐

One of the most troubling aspects of middle grade schools – and of American education in general – is the inequitable distribution among youth of opportunities to learn. For example, because financial resources for education are largely based on property-tax revenues, middle grade schools in states with high tax rates and high property values can have from three to four times more money per student to sustain and improve the educational program than do schools in states with low tax rates and low property values (Odden and Kim, 1992). Although intuitively one would assume that greater resources equal greater learning opportunities, research had failed to demonstrate this link until recently (Hedges, Laine, and Greenwald, 1994). Considerable controversy remains over the nature and strength of the relationship (Hanushek, 1994).

No controversy exists, however, about whether learning opportunities differ for adolescents in the high and low tracks of their middle grade schools, regardless of the school's overall level of resources. Arranging classes into high and low tracks and placing students in one or the other based on their past academic achievement is almost universal in American middle grade schools (McPartland, Coldiron, and Braddock, 1987).

Tracking was implemented to reduce the heterogeneity of students in a class, thus enabling teachers to adjust the level of instruction to match students' knowledge and skills. In theory, students in both the high and the low tracks would master a rich and engaging curriculum suited to their abilities. In practice, however, tracking is one of the most harmful school practices in existence. Wide disparities are common between the high and low tracks in the quality of instruction and the competence of teachers. These disparities result in a progressive diminution of academic achievement for students kept in the lower track for prolonged periods of time (Oakes, 1985).

Because racial and ethnic minority youth disproportionately are placed in lower academic tracks (Goodlad, 1984), tracking often reinforces racial isolation in schools, perpetuates racial prejudice among students, and increases alienation from school among lower-achieving students (Slavin, 1995). The consequences are especially damaging during early adolescence, when young people's impressions about the worth of those racially and culturally different from themselves begin to become entrenched.

Middle grade educators can do little to remedy broad financial inequities among schools, but they can adopt effective methods other than tracking to teach students of diverse ability. A recent review of promising approaches to "untracking" schools suggested the following ideas (Wheelock, 1992):

1. Provide all students with the thinking skills and enrichment activities often offered only to those labeled "gifted" and "talented."
2. Communicate high expectations for all students through school routines and classroom techniques that result in increased student effort and higher achievement for all.
3. As a first step toward eliminating all tracking, eliminate the bottom levels of the ability grouping hierarchy (courses labeled *basic* or *general*), and expose everyone to grade-level textbooks, activities, and expectations while providing extra support for those who need it.
4. Use cooperative learning and other innovative teaching approaches to deepen academic learning for all students while promoting self-esteem.

Research on cooperative learning has shown that in mixed-ability learning groups, high achievers deepen their understanding of material by explaining it to lower achievers, who, in turn, receive immediate tutoring from their peers (Johnson, Maruyama, Johnson, Nelson, and Skon, 1981; Newmann and Thompson, 1987; Slavin, 1983). Cooperative learning has been shown to help students learn course material faster, retain it longer, and develop critical reasoning power more rapidly than by working alone (Skon, Johnson, and Johnson, 1981). Cooperative learning also requires students to get to know and work with classmates of different ethnic, racial, and cultural backgrounds, setting the stage for students to meet the requirements of adult work life and of citizenship in a multicultural society (Slavin, 1984).

Empowering teachers and administrators

Currently, teachers and administrators at all levels of elementary and secondary education, including middle schools, are severely limited in their ability to make decisions about their own practice. They are bound by tradition, by their own educational experiences, and by the specific rules and regulations of state and local educational agencies. Yet these same people increasingly are being asked to develop and implement innovations that will produce high levels of achievement among a much larger proportion of students than is currently the norm. In experiments across the country, compensation and professional rewards for teachers are being linked to the attainment of better outcomes by their students. These studies indicate that to produce such gains, school staff members must have greatly increased decision-making authority on important matters, beyond being consulted about such matters (Hornbeck, 1991).

Subschool structures in middle grade schools are one important means to shift decision-making authority to school staff. Working in teams, teachers can exercise creative control over how curricular goals are to be reached. Collectively, teachers can choose instructional methods and materials for classroom use, identify and develop curricular themes, schedule classes, and design authentic assessment instruments to measure student performance.

Some decisions about the educational program inevitably will involve more than one team or subschool within the middle school. For this reason, middle schools also need new methods for shared decision making across the institution. One solution is to create a building governance committee that involves the entire school community – teachers, administrators, support staff, parents, students, and key neighborhood representatives – in decisions affecting the school. Through the building governance committee, key stakeholders in the school community can initiate, plan, monitor, and evaluate change efforts during the transformation of a traditional junior high school into a progressive middle school. By its very nature, the committee systematically fosters interaction among school constituencies, interaction that promotes the trust and respect essential to the process (Comer, 1980).

Preparing teachers for the middle grades

Currently, most teachers in middle grade schools are not specifically educated to teach young adolescents before entering professional service. Although there are a few graduate education programs that prepare middle grade teachers, most teachers are educated either as elementary or as secondary school teachers.

Compared to elementary grade teachers, whose training and practicum experience are focused on the kinds of students they actually teach, middle grade teachers often feel less effective, especially with low-performing students (Eccles et al., 1993). For example, in one study, middle grade mathematics teachers reported being much less confident of their teaching efficacy than elementary grade teachers in the same school district, even though the middle grade teachers were more likely to be specialists in the subject than the elementary school teachers (Midgley, Feldlaufer, and Eccles, 1989).

To prepare teachers effectively for the middle grades, it is vital to create educational programs that help them to teach as part of a team, to design and assess meaningful interdisciplinary curricula, to participate in decisions that promote continuous school improvement, and especially to understand adolescent development. Induction of new teachers also needs to be addressed carefully, perhaps by pairing novice teachers with mentor teachers during the first year of professional service (Arends, 1990).

Also, middle grade teachers, like all other teachers, need meaningful opportunities to upgrade their knowledge and skills, opportunities that go beyond the "workshop menu" that currently defines professional development for teachers. Such occasions for in-depth inquiry and dialogue might involve teachers' participation in subject-specific teacher networks, school–university collaborations designed to support school reform, or schoolwide professional communities that provide time for reflective dialogue on specific challenges and on ways to overcome them (Little, 1993; Newman, 1994).

Reengaging families in the education of young adolescents

Despite the clearly documented beneficial effects of parental involvement on students' achievement in and attitudes toward school, parental involvement of all types declines progressively during the elementary school years. By middle grade school, the home–school connection has been significantly reduced and in some cases is nonexistent (Epstein, 1986).

For their part, many middle grade schools do not encourage, and some actively discourage, parent involvement at school. Particularly in low-income and in racial and ethnic minority neighborhoods, parents often are considered to be part of the problem of educating young adolescents rather than an important potential educational resource. With their sometimes painful memories of their own school experience, many parents in such communities become deeply alienated from their young adolescent's school (Comer, 1980).

Research on parent involvement in the middle grades, although limited, suggests several avenues through which better home–school relations can be fostered. Epstein and Connors (1992), for example, outline six such strategies for involving parents: (1) providing basic information to parents regarding adolescents' needs; (2) communicating information about school programs and students' progress; (3) providing guidance to parents on how to help with homework and with other learning activities; (4) involving parents as volunteers in the school; (5) including parents in school governance committees; and (6) creating partnerships among the school, parents, and community organizations that share responsibility for children's development.

Involving parents in decision making through the building governance committee is a particularly useful way of engaging them in important school matters. Parents involved in planning the work of the school feel powerful, develop confidence in their relations with school staff, and are more likely to attend school activities, a practice that signals to their young adolescents the importance of school. In low-income communities, parents' cooperative work with school staff members on a governance committee can help bridge the schism that often exists between families and schools (Epstein and Connors, 1992).

Improving academic performance through better health and fitness

Middle grade schools often need, but do not have, the support of health and social service agencies to address young adolescents' physical health, mental health, and social needs. Left unattended, these needs interfere with adolescents' ability to learn. As was mentioned in the first section of this chapter, young adolescence is the doorway to an increasingly risky environment. Many youth today first experiment with tobacco, alcohol, and illicit drugs during early adolescence. For example, in 1993,

77% of eighth-grade students had already begun drinking alcohol, and 45% had begun smoking (Johnston, O'Malley, and Bachman, 1994).

More than 40% of teenagers are sexually active by the time they are 16 years old (Alan Guttmacher Institute, 1994). These youth run the risk of unintended pregnancy and of contracting sexually transmitted diseases, including acquired immunodeficiency syndrome (AIDS). Each year, about 25% of sexually active adolescents become infected with a sexually transmitted disease (Alan Guttmacher Institute, 1994).

Mild to severe mental health problems are widespread among young adolescents, yet adolescents often do not receive the services they need. About one in five adolescents aged 10 to 18 suffer from a diagnosable mental disorder. Suicide is now a major cause of death among older adolescents: The suicide rate among 15- to 19-year-olds in 1988 was double the rate in the early 1970s (U.S. Congress, Office of Technology Assessment, 1991). Yet 70–80% of all youth in need may not receive any mental health services or may receive inappropriate services (U.S. Congress, Office of Technology Assessment, 1986).

Schools should not be responsible for meeting every need of their students. But when the need directly affects learning, as it does in the area of health, it is in the school's and community's best interest to link education to prevention and treatment. Infusing the core curriculum with health and life skills education is one important approach noted earlier. A second strategy is developing health-promoting school regulations and customs, such as an absolute intolerance of violence, a complete ban on smoking, and a policy of serving only nutritious foods. A third key component is the integration of health and social services with the educational program.

Efforts to link services for adolescents to middle grade schools have taken several forms: school-based health centers (located on school grounds), school-linked health centers (located "off campus" but near the school), ties to community-wide health centers that serve adults and children, and arrangements with adolescent service providers in hospitals or health maintenance organizations. The most prevalent approaches are school-based and school-linked centers, and these have emerged as extremely promising approaches to ensuring student access to health and counseling services (Millstein, 1988). The vast majority of the 615 existing school-based or school-linked centers serve high school youth, but 165 of these centers serve middle school age youth (Advocates for Youth, 1994).

Most visits to school-based or school-linked centers are for physical examinations, acute illnesses, and minor emergencies. Serious conditions are detected in about 25% of the adolescents who use the centers (Advocates for Youth, 1994). Many centers report high rates of depression, and nearly every site reports a high incidence of sexual abuse (Advocates for Youth, 1994).

Connecting schools with communities

For adolescents, the nonschool hours are extremely important in shaping their development. This time period can afford opportunities for healthy relaxation and for intellectual and social development, or it can lead to unproductive and risky behaviors. How youth spend this time depends, in part, on whether they have access to organized activities. More than 17,000 organizations offer community-based youth programs after school, on weekends, or during vacation periods (Carnegie Council on Adolescent Development, 1992), yet 29% of all young adolescents are not reached by these programs (U.S. Department of Education, 1990).

Rather than socializing with peers or adults and learning new life skills, many youth are at home alone after school. Nearly 27% of all eighth graders report spending 2 or more hours at home by themselves each day; youth from the lowest-income families report regularly spending 3 or more hours alone at home (Carnegie Council on Adolescent Development, 1992).

Middle grade schools can work with community organizations to create a unified system of youth development opportunities that recognizes all participants' common goals while respecting their inherent differences and strengths. Such a system might involve joint planning, coordination of resources, and the initiation of new services for youth based on a joint assessment of their needs (Advocates for Youth, 1994). Coordination between schools and community organizations can provide important opportunities for adolescents to engage in youth service or *service learning* – supervised activity helping others in the community or in school. Such service learning opportunities help students become active, caring citizens.

Implementing *Turning Points* reforms in policy and practice

In 1990, a year after the release of *Turning Points*, Carnegie Corporation of New York began the Middle Grade School State Policy Initiative

(MGSSPI), a program of grants to states (usually the state department of education) to stimulate statewide changes in middle grade educational policy and practice. Designed as a top-down, bottom-up reform strategy, the initiative has the following goals:

1. Promote widespread implementation of the eight *Turning Points* reform principles through changes in state policies that encourage local schools to adopt promising practices;
2. Stimulate the development of schools serving those most in need – educationally disadvantaged youth – that produce intellectually prepared, healthy young adolescents.

The initiative provided $60,000 in planning grants to 27 states, which were selected based on proposals that were sent by nearly all the states. Since 1991, the initiative has focused its support on 15 of these states through a series of 2-year grants ranging from $50,000 to $180,000 in 1991 and from $190,000 to $360,000 in 1993. All Carnegie Corporation grants are matched by an equal commitment of resources by the recipient.

Since 1990, the 15 states in the Carnegie initiative have enacted changes in a wide range of state policies affecting middle grade education. They also have provided many opportunities for practitioners across the state to increase their capacity to educate young adolescents well.

Each of the states also chose to work directly with a group of schools interested in implementing the *Turning Points* recommendations. Initially, these schools were drawn from a range of socioeconomic conditions. In 1993, however, the Carnegie Corporation stipulated that each state must focus substantial attention on a group of schools in disadvantaged urban communities. These schools were called *systemic change schools*.

What follows is a brief discussion of these states' work in four areas critical to the fundamental reform of middle grade schools: (1) support of the school change process; (2) professional development; (3) curriculum, instruction, and student assessment; and (4) health education and services. Much of the information included here is drawn from a recent survey of the states conducted by the Carnegie Corporation and the Council of Chief State School Officers. The Council, the professional organization of all state superintendents of education, has provided technical assistance to states involved in the initiative since its inception. The survey asked states to describe their work to improve state policies and to modify the practices of the state education agency (and other state agencies) to provide greater support to the systemic change schools or other middle grade schools in disadvantaged communities.[1]

The school change process

Turning Points delineates the elements of an effective middle grade school but does not attempt to describe a process for implementing its recommendations. Each of the states, therefore, has developed its own methods for promoting change at the local level. Several states have developed a systematic process of self-assessment, experimentation, and evaluation to guide schools through the process of reform. The following is an example of the application of such a process in a large, urban, traditional junior high school.

In the state's MGSSPI project, every participating middle grade school has engaged in a formal Middle Grade School Development Process. The process involved school staffs in self-study, which has led to the development of specific plans for improvement.

As a typical example of the implementation of the Middle Grade School Development Process, take the Thomas Jefferson School. Jefferson is a large urban school with almost 100% minority enrollment. In 1992, the middle-level program was a typical junior high school program. None of the recommendations in *Turning Points* was being implemented.

At the beginning of the 1992–1993 school year, the middle-level staff received an orientation to the recommendations in *Turning Points* from the state education agency (SEA) staff. Shortly after that, the state's Middle Grade School Survey was administered to the whole staff. The staff then examined and discussed the results. This inquiry set the stage for further analysis and intensive planning by an all-volunteer team of staff members.

To obtain time for staff involvement in self-study, the school administration asked the district central office to excuse its middle grade teachers from all preplanned districtwide professional development activities. The half days that were made available were used throughout the school year to plan activities and to engage in professional development activities including analysis of the characteristics of young adolescents, cooperative learning, adviser–advisee programs, curriculum integration, and multiple intelligences.

During 1993–1994, dramatic changes began to occur in the middle-level program of the school. For the first time, the middle-level staff became organized into interdisciplinary teams, and grades 5–8 were changed from homogeneous to heterogeneous grouping. Midway through the year, an authentic assessment program based on Howard Gardner's multiple intelligences theory was implemented in the sixth grade, and in the latter half of the year an advisory program for all students began. The MGSSPI staff and student surveys were also administered during the year, and the staff has used the results of these assessments (of *Turning Points* practices) to develop additional plans for change in the 1994–1995 school year.

States' efforts to promote school change have yielded many important lessons about the difficult process of reforming traditional junior high schools. The school principal, for example, is pivotal to successful school transformation, yet few principals receive any training in managing the process of change in schools. Moreover, even those principals who enthusiastically support change often find it difficult to adapt traditional leadership styles to a new environment.

As an example, prior to the MGSSPI at a school, the principal had begun the transition to a middle school concept, and he saw the Carnegie project as an excellent opportunity to continue his school change efforts. Despite his enthusiasm about the improvement process, it became clear that its success depended on his ability to change his autocratic management style because the envisioned whole-school change would require broad ownership by many constituencies. This challenge was both a personal and a professional one, but he would receive the support of his staff (who liked and respected him) and the assistance of the state project directors.

Other factors critical to the process of change are the establishment of site-based planning and decision-making committees broadly representative of the school community, including parents and students; commitment by a critical mass of the school faculty to fundamental reform (states routinely require agreement of at least three-quarters of the faculty); support of the local school district, especially in the use of time for planning and reflection; a "coach" external to the school to facilitate the change process and to broker additional resources; and the ability to collect school program data in a way that can be usefully related to outcomes for students.

One state particularly noted the traditional failure of middle schools to use their available data to guide them toward new solutions. If there has been an embarrassing lacunae in the whole middle-level reform process, it has consisted not in a failure to gather diagnostic data on school programs but in failure to use the data constructively. Local schools collect a lot of student performance data, but these are almost never used effectively to make decisions about change. Part of the reason is that school personnel have little time to study the data or to answer the question "How can this information be used?"

Perhaps the greatest barrier to fundamental school change is simply the lack of time for the complex, sustained interactions among school staff members that the process requires and a similar lack of time for discussion with faculty members in other reforming schools. There is consensus among the states that time within the normal work day of school staff is required for these interactions. Several states have attempted to develop policies that would provide such time, but these efforts have met with only limited success because an additional financial investment is required. Many states, therefore, have used available discretionary resources, including Carnegie support, to "buy time" for faculty members engaged in reform. Overnight retreats and week-long summer institutes appear to be more productive than after-school meetings.

Professional development

States' efforts to guide schools through a process of change are a powerful form of professional development for school staff involved in the process. In addition, states have used a wide variety of other methods to build practitioners' capabilities. For example, many states have developed networks of reforming schools. These networks provide staff members with myriad opportunities for interschool visits and peer coaching, as well as opportunities to pool resources to obtain either materials or the services of outside consultants.

Because they facilitate pragmatic, practitioner-to-practitioner learning, networks are rapidly emerging as a primary means of supporting professional development. States are finding, however, that the most effective networks are those in which the state not only helps build the capacity of member schools to coach each other, but also provides sustained, concentrated assistance to a select number of "mentor" schools that assume a leadership role in providing information and coordinating the collaborative work of schools within the network. One state describes the activities of its mentor school network as follows:

> State support for professional development is handled primarily through the mentor school network. Every year, the state gives each of its 60 mentor middle schools $9,000 to use for professional de-

velopment. Of that amount, $4,000 is allocated for the mentor school to send its staff members anywhere to receive professional development. The intent is to enhance the leadership capacity of the mentor schools so that they not only grow in knowledge themselves, but become increasingly able to lead schools within their network. The mentor school can use the remaining $5,000 to assist other network schools, either by providing campus-to-campus technical assistance or by collaborating with other mentor schools to produce regional training workshops. Each mentor school usually sponsors two to four workshops or staff development conferences during the school year. These events specifically target the expressed needs of the attending campus professionals.[2]

The states' experience suggests that the most effective professional development has the following characteristics: It involves the entire school faculty whenever possible; it reflects the expressed needs of teachers and involves them in every phase from planning to evaluation; it provides opportunities for in-depth inquiry and support for experimentation; it uses a variety of approaches to adult learning; and it is regarded as part of the daily work of teaching, not an add-on. Professional development, say the states, should also produce an important, demonstrable outcome that improves instructional practices in the school.

Schools' efforts to create high-quality professional development programs are sometimes hampered by resistance from faculty who are not used to intensive, sustained inquiry or to relying on themselves and their peers (rather than on outside consultants) to generate solutions to problems. States also note the particular problems of urban middle grade schools: "[T]he climate in many urban schools does not support such efforts. Union contracts that preclude after-school faculty meetings, when combined with the fortress mentality of embattled union officials, make it difficult for schools to get beyond issues of working conditions to the loftier goals of school reform."[3]

Predictably, the lack of human and financial resources prevents broad-scale development of high-quality professional development systems. Many states have chosen to invest limited dollars in partnerships with other educational organizations to expand the range of support offered, and in some instances they have helped create new institutions. For example, a number of states work closely with middle grade educators' professional organizations, and one state was instrumental in creating a new association that is now a key source of professional development opportunities within the state.

Other states have established mutually supportive links between middle grade schools and university education departments. In these partnerships, university faculty help support the inquiry process among middle grade practitioners, and the middle grade school provides a dynamic setting for prospective teachers' practicum experiences.

Lack of resources is not the only barrier to high-quality professional development. Many states find it difficult to break away from their traditional roles as monitors and regulators of schools, and are neither equipped nor inclined to facilitate directly high-quality professional development in schools. The ability of state (and local) education agencies to make this shift to direct involvement in change is crucial to the systematic reform of elementary, middle, and high school education.

Curriculum, instruction, and student assessment

Each of the 15 MGSSPI states is establishing or revising its curriculum guidelines, as is virtually every state in the nation. State curriculum frameworks are nearly all defined by academic disciplines. At least among states in the Carnegie initiative, however, these state frameworks strongly encourage interdisciplinary instruction, and many provide examples of how knowledge from different subject areas can be meaningfully related. To further support interdisciplinary instruction, one state's school accreditation system – the system by which schools are held accountable for providing high-quality education – specifically calls for schools to define learning objectives for students that require the integration of knowledge from various subject areas.

At the school level, the creation of thoughtful interdisciplinary curricula and learning strategies is time-consuming and intellectually challenging, requiring a significant effort by the interdisciplinary teaching team. Teachers may fear that important concepts from their subject of specialization will be lost within an integrated approach, or that they will be unable to satisfy state and local requirements to "cover" masses of information. Responding to these concerns, some states have provided substantial training to teaching teams so that the integrating themes they produce, along with the related learning activities, are intellectually challenging and personally relevant for students.

States are also concerned about the potential pitfalls of curriculum integration. One state noted the potential difficulties of the undertaking as follows:

The Division of Middle School Education is concerned about the move to interdisciplinary curriculum because there is not enough high-quality staff development and guidance for schools in this area. The result is that a number of teachers think that they are doing interdisciplinary instruction when they are actually just packaging their instruction in topical units. Too often, the topical approach to curriculum is superficial and contrived, and it leaves large gaps in skill and concept development.[4]

Despite the difficulties, many states describe examples of effective interdisciplinary instruction in middle grade schools, including some remarkable schools serving disadvantaged adolescents. Here is one example:

Washington Middle School focuses on interdisciplinary project learning and portfolio assessment. Its humanities program, which combines language arts and social studies, builds curriculum around concepts that are important in students' lives, for example, power and authority, individual and group responsibility, and conflict.

This past year, the school's humanities curriculum was built around the following overarching questions: What is courage? What does it mean to be a hero? Why do individuals take action to change and improve the world around them?

To explore these questions, students focused in-depth on the Holocaust, the Civil Rights Movement, and other periods of sharp conflict, as well as historical and present-day issues in the local community. The curriculum strongly emphasized primary source material, oral history, journal writing, process and peer review writing, small-group and individual project construction, media use, and other interactive approaches.

The classes also studied acting and the writing of plays. The last months of the school year were spent creating a student-written and acted play that highlighted the concepts and themes studied. The play was performed for the school, parents and other middle school students, and educators across the city.

All students are required to maintain a portfolio containing draft and finished written work, photographs of three-dimensional projects (such as sculptures), videotapes of all presentations and exhibitions, and art work. At the end of the year, students assembled their portfolios, created a table of contents, and wrote a cover essay explaining their portfolio's contents and reflecting on their learning for the year. Students presented their portfolios to a panel consisting of one or two prominent people from outside the school and the teacher. The portfolio and presentation were rated according to a developed scale.

Washington Middle School continues to have the highest scores of any middle school in the city on state tests and the California Achievement Test. The school also has the largest waiting list of families wishing to enroll their children.[5]

Washington Middle School exemplifies the seamless integration of curriculum, instruction, and assessment. There is, however, substantial variation in the degree to which work on state curriculum frameworks is aligned with the development of new state assessment measures. This disjuncture, in turn, mirrors the lack of integration between groups responsible for curriculum and assessment development in some state education agencies. This lack of coordinated effort continues despite the fact that states consistently conclude that clearly defined learner outcomes are a prerequisite for authentic assessment of student performance.

Several states face substantial political hurdles in the development of new assessment systems. One state provides the following troubling, albeit extreme, example:

The education community has been very pleased with the [new state test] because they viewed it as a more accurate reflection of what students were learning and should learn. Many politically conservative parents, however, strongly objected to the assessment. They didn't like certain selections of literature on the reading part, and they took the position that some questions on the reading and writing portions infringed upon students' rights to privacy.

Specifically, students were asked to read a certain selection and give their opinions of it. No answers were right or wrong. The assessment gauged how well the students supported whatever position they took.

Some parents reasoned that this approach might cause students to challenge their parents' value system. Rumor amplified these concerns. . . . Many parents in conservative areas of the state refused to let their children take the exam.[6]

Despite these setbacks, the state continues to develop a statewide performance-based assessment system.

Health education and services

Perhaps one of *Turning Points'* unique contributions is its recognition of the inextricable link between adolescents' health and intellectual development. Middle grade students must be healthy to learn well. In disadvantaged communities, too often the reverse is true: Adolescents' poor health and exposure to multiple risks severely impede learning.

There appears to be an encouraging trend among the 15 states to re-examine the health curriculum and instruction for adolescents, often under the impetus of the Carnegie middle grade initiative. For example, states are infusing knowledge about health promotion and disease prevention into new curriculum frameworks and standards. Many states have formed cross-agency task forces or committees to coordinate state-supported health education and the delivery of health services, and some have created permanent, high-level interagency structures to promote collaboration. To organize their work, several states have used a framework for comprehensive school health developed by Lloyd Kolbe of the Centers for Disease Control and Prevention.

Middle grade school-based or school-linked centers, campus wellness centers, or some other mechanism to provide students greater access to health services have been established in a majority of MGSSPI states. There is a strong consensus that these efforts have already provided important benefits. A state describes one school's experience:

During the 1993–94 school year, the associate principal directed efforts to establish a School Health Advisory Council which would have representation from key people in the local educational agency and from the community health and social services agencies. . . . One important accomplishment was the establishment of a partnership between the school and the Wilma Rudolph Community Health Center which is located nearby. This relationship has resulted in improved health services already during the current school year. One benefit is that the children themselves have learned how to access the services of the Center. For example, students with infant children used to have to miss school whenever they traveled across town to pick up publicly-provided food for their babies. Now, they are able to visit the health center nearby to obtain food and, therefore, do not miss any school time. Likewise, parents used to take their children out of school for a full day for doctor's appointments. This year, children had appointments at the health center and, therefore, missed little time from school. . . . The relationship has also resulted in numerous children being identified as being in need of eyeglasses. The Center assisted families to obtain the glasses with public funds.[7]

The lack of adequate funding for adolescent health services is a barrier for all the states involved in the MGSSPI initiative. Many states have cobbled together streams of financial support from a variety of sources, including the federal Medicaid program, which states are becoming increasingly sophisticated in tapping. Middle grade educators and health care providers alike hope that additional funds for school-based or school-linked health services will be available through national health reform legislation, if and when it comes.

Preliminary data on school effects

To document the impact of the implementation of *Turning Points* recommendations in designated systemic change schools, a national evaluation of the MGSSPI was begun in 1993 under the direction of Robert Felner, director of the Center for Prevention Research and Development at the University of Illinois. Baseline data were collected in the spring of 1994 from nearly all the schools and are now being analyzed.

PIML longitudinal study

Although results from the MGSSPI evaluation are not yet available, Felner has since 1990 been collecting information on a group of middle grade schools in Illinois that have been implementing the *Turning Points* recommendations, first as part of a program funded by a federal grant and now as part of a self-supporting network of reforming schools. This initiative, called Project Initiative Middle Level (PIML), is being conducted by the Association of Illinois Middle Schools (AIMS). PIML is a separate initiative from the MGSSPI project in Illinois but is closely linked to it. Evaluation of PIML was initially supported with federal funds; since 1992, Carnegie Corporation has supported this work.

As in the national MGSSPI evaluation, data collected for the PIML study are primarily drawn from surveys of teachers, administrators, and students in the reforming schools. These carefully constructed surveys, which exceed conventional standards for reliability and validity, ask the adults and young people in the school to provide information on the extent to which the structures and experiences recommended in *Turning Points* actually occur. The implementation data then are compared to two outcome measures: student achievement scores on the state-administered Illinois Goals Assessment Program test, and students' self-ratings on the Revised Children's Manifest Anxiety Scale and the Self-Esteem Questionnaire.

In the following chapter, Felner and his colleagues present the findings thus far from their PIML study, a 5-year longitudinal evaluation of a network of 52 PIML schools that are at various stages of implementing the *Turning Points* recommendations and principles.

Notes

1. The responses of state MGSSPI directors are confidential so as to promote candor in their analysis of the state's strengths and weaknesses. Therefore, state names are omitted and the names of individual schools have been changed. All quotations are from an October 1994 Council of Chief State School Officers' internal document, "A Synthesis of State Responses on Increasing the Capacity to Create and Sustain Reform."
2. Ibid., p. 70.
3. Ibid., p. 121.
4. Ibid., p. 139.
5. Ibid., pp. 123–124.
6. Ibid., p. 145.
7. Ibid., pp. 155–156.

References

Advocates for Youth. (1994). Unpublished data. Washington, DC.

American Association for the Advancement of Science. (1989). *Science for all Americans: A Project 2061 report on literacy goals in science, mathematics, and technology.* Washington, DC: Author.

Arends, R. I. (1990). Connecting the university to the school. In B. Joyce (Ed.), *Changing school culture through staff development* (pp. 129–140). Alexandria, VA: Association for Supervision and Curriculum Development.

Arhar, J. M., Johnston, J. H., and Markle, G. C. (1989).The effects of teaming on students. *Middle School Journal, 20*(3), 24–27.

Carnegie Council on Adolescent Development, Task Force on Education of Young Adolescents. (1989). *Turning points: Preparing American youth for the 21st century.* Washington, DC: Author.

Carnegie Council on Adolescent Development, Task Force on Youth Development and Community Programs. (1992). *A matter of time: Risk and opportunity in the nonschool hours.* Washington, DC: Author.

Comer, J. P. (1980). *School power: Implications of an intervention project.* New York: Free Press.

Dryfoos, J. G. (1990). *Adolescents at risk: Prevalence and prevention.* New York: Oxford University Press.

Eccles, J. S., Midgley, C., Wigfield, A., Buchanan, C. M., Reuman, D., Flanagan, C., and MacIver, D. (1993). Development during adolescence: The impact of stage–environment fit on young adolescents' experiences in schools and in families. *American Psychologist, 48*(2), 90–101.

Elliott, G. R., and Feldman, S. S. (1990). Capturing the adolescent experience. In S. Feldman and G. Elliott (Eds.), *At the threshold: The developing adolescent* (pp. 1–13). Cambridge, MA: Harvard University Press.

Epstein, J. L. (1986). Parents' reactions to teacher practices of parent involvement. *Elementary School Journal, 86,* 277–294.

Epstein, J. L., and Connors, L. J. (1992). *School and family partnerships in the middle grades.* Baltimore, MD: Johns Hopkins University, Center on Families, Communities, Schools and Children's Learning.

Goodlad, J. I. (1984). *A place called school.* New York: McGraw-Hill.

Alan Guttmacher Institute. (1994). *Sex and America's teenagers.* New York: Author.

Hamburg, D. A. (1992). *Today's children: Creating a future for a generation in crisis.* New York: Times Books.

Hanushek, E. A. (1994). Money might matter somewhere: A response to Hedges, Laine and Greenwald. *Educational Researcher, 23*(4), 5–8.

Hedges, L. V., Laine, R. D., and Greenwald, R. (1994). Does money matter? (A meta-analysis of studies of the effects of differential school inputs on student outcomes). *Educational Researcher, 23*(3), 5–14.

Hornbeck, D. W. (1991). New paradigms for action. In D. Hornbeck and L. Salamon (Eds.), *Human capital and America's future* (pp. 360–389). Baltimore: Johns Hopkins Press.

Johnson, D. W., Maruyama, G., Johnson, R., Nelson, D., and Skon, L. (1981). Effects of cooperative competitive, and individualistic goal structures on achievement: A meta-analysis. *Psychological Bulletin, 89,* 47–62.

Johnston, L. D., O'Malley, P. M., and Bachman, J. G. (1994). Incidence of use of various types of drugs by grade: Eighth graders. *The Monitoring the Future Study.* Ann Arbor: University of Michigan, Institute for Social Research.

Keating, D. (1990). Adolescent thinking. In S. Feldman and G. Elliott (Eds.), *At the threshold: The developing adolescent* (pp. 54–89). Cambridge, MA: Harvard University Press.

Little, J. W. (1993). Teachers' professional development in a climate of educational reform. *Educational Evaluation and Policy Analysis, 15*(2), 129–152.

McPartland, J. M., Coldiron, J. R., and Braddock, J. H., II. (1987). *School structures and classroom practices in elementary, middle, and secondary schools.* Baltimore: Johns Hopkins University, Center for Research on Elementary and Middle Schools.

Midgley, C., Feldlaufer, H., and Eccles, J. S. (1989). Change in teacher efficacy and student self- and task-related beliefs during the transition to junior high school. *Journal of Educational Psychology, 81,* 247–258.

Millstein, S. G. (1988). *The potential of school-linked centers to promote adolescent health and development* (working paper). Washington, DC: Carnegie Council on Adolescent Development.

Newman, F. M. (1994). *School-wide professional community.* Issue Report, 6. Center on Organization and Restructuring of Schools. Madison: University of Wisconsin, Center for Education Research.

Newmann, F. M., and Thompson, J. A. (1987). *Effects of cooperative learning on achievement in secondary schools: A summary of research.* Madison: University of Wisconsin, National Center on Effective Secondary Schools.

Oakes, J. (1985). *Keeping track: How schools structure inequality.* New Haven, CT: Yale University Press.

Odden, A., and Kim, L. (1992). Reducing disparities across the states: A new federal role in school finance. In A. Odden (Ed.), *Rethinking school finance: An agenda for the 1990s* (pp. 260–297). San Francisco: Jossey-Bass.

Skon, L., Johnson, D., and Johnson, R. (1981). Cooperative peer interaction versus individual competition and individualistic efforts: Effects on the acquisition of cognitive reasoning strategies. *Journal of Educational Psychology, 73*, 83–92.

Slavin, R. E. (1983). When does cooperative learning increase student achievement? *Psychological Bulletin, 94*, 429–445.

Slavin, R. E. (1984). Team assisted individuation: Cooperative learning and individualized instruction in the mainstreamed classroom. *Remedial and Special Education, 5*(6), 33–42.

Slavin, R. E. (1995). Enhancing intergroup relations in schools: Cooperative learning and other strategies. In W. Hawley and A. Jackson (Eds.), *Toward a common destiny: Improving race and ethnic relations in America* (pp. 291–314). San Francisco: Jossey-Bass.

U.S. Congress, Office of Technology Assessment. (1986). *Children's mental health: Problems and services – A background paper.* (OTA Pub. No. OTA-BP-H-33). Washington, DC: U.S. Government Printing Office.

U.S. Congress, Office of Technology Assessment. (1991). *Adolescent health. Volume 1: Summary and policy options.* (OTA Publication No. OTA-H-468). Washington, DC: U.S. Government Printing Office.

U.S. Department of Education, Office of Educational Research and Improvement, National Center for Educational Statistics. (1990). *National education longitudinal study of 1988: A profile of American eighth graders* (pp. 50–54). Washington, DC: U.S. Government Printing Office.

Wheelock, A. (1992). *Crossing the tracks: How "untracking" can save America's schools.* New York: New Press.

3. The impact of school reform for the middle grades: A longitudinal study of a network engaged in *Turning Points*–based comprehensive school transformation

ROBERT FELNER, ANTHONY W. JACKSON,
DEBORAH KASAK, PETER MULHALL, STEPHEN BRAND,
AND NANCY FLOWERS

Educational policymakers and practitioners are today under a constant barrage of calls for reform to produce better student performance. Efforts to improve schooling in the United States are not new, and have waxed and waned over the decades in their urgency and level of public support. The impetus for reform emerged with renewed vigor in the last two decades, fueled by reports such as *A Nation at Risk* (National Commission on Excellence in Education, 1983) and, more recently, by the national "Goals 2000" legislation. Driving current reform efforts are concerns about the changing, more competitive world economy and dramatic increases in the number of low-income and racial and ethnic minority children in schools, children whom American schools have too often failed to educate well (Carnegie Council on Adolescent Development, 1989; Carnegie Forum on Education and the Economy, 1986; William T. Grant Foundation, 1988). A consensus has emerged that there can be little hope of addressing the increasing levels of social inequity and social problems that confront us daily unless all students receive the quality education necessary for participation, opportunity, and success in to-day's world.

Into this mix of calls for reform and shifts in the social context in which schools must operate have come a wide array of reform recommendations. Some are linked to the belief that market forces can improve schools, emphasizing such strategies as the privatization of school management and voucher plans. Other school reform efforts have emerged from case studies of individual schools in which heroic or idiosyncratic efforts have led to remarkable outcomes. Often recommendations that stem from these studies emphasize issues of leadership, as well as the involvement of parents, teachers, and local community leaders in school governance.

Collectively, these calls for reform have led to broad definitions of goals and frameworks for change that appear to have facilitated broad support for reform (Murphy, 1993). But once the need for reform is acknowledged, it becomes evident that this very diversity of approaches to change has been a barrier to developing the knowledge base required for guiding *systematic* and thereby more effective reforms in policy and practice. Thus, although comprehensive, systematic change is the goal, a lack of comprehensive, testable models for reform has led to such a broad array of loosely related conditions labeled *systematic reform* that any implication that systematic reform is occurring is incorrect. (Murphy, 1993).

To address these issues, the Project on High Performance Learning Communities, in partnership with Project Initiative Middle Level (PIML), has been studying what is now a network of more than 70 schools in Illinois. For the past 6 years, we have studied these schools as they undergo the process of restructuring from a more traditional organization toward implementing the recommendations of the Carnegie Council's report, *Turning Points: Preparing American Youth for the 21st Century*. This report, more so than perhaps any other, provides a holistic, integrated model of education for 10- to 15-year-old youth.

The work to implement its recommendations began with a pilot effort involving a smaller set of schools during the 1990–1991 school year. The schools in the study are all members of PIML and are drawn from the broader membership of the Association of Illinois Middle Schools (AIMS). Schools must apply to join PIML and are admitted as members only after meeting a number of rigorous criteria. Not the least of these criteria is a written commitment from the district and school (supported by more than 80% of its teachers) to shift from more traditional junior high school structures and practices to those that are consistent with the recommendations of *Turning Points*.

Some of the schools are admitted to PIML as demonstration schools. These schools team up with less advanced "partnership" schools to provide technical assistance, ongoing exchange of visits, and intensive training across teacher–administrator teams in structured workshops and conferences. The demonstration schools must make the same commitment as the partnership schools to continue their implementation efforts, to provide for visits to their schools by their partner schools, and to participate in on- and off-site consultation and staff development with those partner schools. In 1995, the PIML network became an intensive subset of schools within the broader network of Illinois middle schools supported through Carnegie Corporation's Middle Grade School State Policy Initiative (MGSSPI) (see the previous chapter).

The Project on High Performing Learning Communities is built on the recognition that despite the strong appeal of the recommendations of *Turning Points* and the state-level plans that have resulted from MGSSPI efforts, the degree to which implementation of these or any other current restructuring and reform efforts will produce the desired results is not clear. There are many theoretical and empirical studies pertaining to the development and education of young adolescents (see Beyth-Marom, Fischhoff, Jacobs, and Furby, 1989; Epstein and MacIver, 1990; Falco, 1988; Felner and Adan, 1988; Hein, 1988a, 1988b; Millstein, 1988; Nightingale and Wolverton, 1993; Schine, 1989). There are also several notable qualitative case studies that typically focus on one or several schools undergoing restructuring or the implementation of *Turning Points*–related recommendations (see Lipsitz, 1984; Murphy, 1993; Oakes, 1990). There is, however, a dearth of empirical research, especially intensive longitudinal studies, on school restructuring that focuses clearly on the impact of these changes or informs its design and implementation.

Murphy (1993) argues that very little of the current understanding of restructuring efforts has come from studies of what is actually happening in districts, schools, and classrooms that are in engaged in the reform of schooling. His conclusion that "There is a notable paucity of empirical studies and research on school restructuring" (p. 4) has been echoed by other researchers (Prestine, 1991; White, 1992). Similarly, Lee and Smith (1994) state that despite the wealth of conceptual discussions of school reform, "only one study, in a single school district (Jefferson County, Kentucky) has evaluated the effects of school restructuring on student outcomes" (p. 5). To address these limitations, Murphy emphasizes the need for studies of ongoing efforts at restructuring, stating, "as popular and appealing as restructuring is, information about the [nature/process] and [their] effects . . . remains conspicuous by its absence" (p. 20).

It has also been suggested that the structural elements of school reform, especially as they relate to recommendations for middle grades' education, have been largely accomplished, adequately understood, and accepted. Among these authors, Mergendollar (1993) argues that change in instructional and curricular practices in schools has moved forward far more slowly than change in structural areas, such as the development of schools-within-schools and teacher–student teams, and that data pertaining to instructional changes that can inform policy and practice changes are seriously lacking.

Both our own work and the research literature (see Murphy and Hallinger, 1993, for review) strongly support the view that there is a paucity of evaluative information on changes in pedagogy. However, neither the research literature nor our own findings to date support the contention that structural changes have been institutionalized to the degree that we no longer need to give them further consideration. For example, preliminary findings in our parallel study of the middle grade schools that are participating in the MGSSPI show that even relatively "mature" and highly motivated middle schools (i.e., schools that have been teaming and attempting the implementation of practices consistent with *Turning Points* for several years or more) have not realized the full extent of structural issues and changes that would be consistent with the recommendations of *Turning Points*. As Jackson (1990) notes, although a common response to *Turning Points* has been "we are already doing that, . . . few of the recommended actions, although frequently proposed, are actually practiced in schools" (p. 1).

A national study by Epstein and MacIver (1990) provides additional findings supportive of this view. These researchers found that the majority of the national sample of schools participating in their study have neither teacher-based advisory (or similar) programming nor team structures in which common planning time is afforded to teachers on a daily basis. The authors state, "The bottom line is, however, that at this time most schools do not use interdisciplinary teams, including about 60% of middle schools and 75% of schools with other organizations [that have middle grades in them]" (p. 30).

There is a clear need, then, for additional research that directly addresses the process of middle grade restructuring and its impact. Although a more well-developed research base does not, by itself, ensure more successful reform efforts, without such a foundation the progress and fruits of reform efforts will continue to be disappointing. The urgent need for such research felt by those concerned with the reform of education for young adolescents is clear in Mergendollar's (1993) comment: "A past characteristic of middle grades reform that has slowed change is that it has been powered more by rhetoric than by research. . . . reform cannot be left to rhetoric alone. Research is needed to validate, guide, and extend it" (pp. 444–445).

In this chapter, we describe the evolution and current status of one effort to evaluate a comprehensive, integrated set of recommendations for transforming the education of young adolescents. Specifically, we sought to assess and evaluate the process of implementation of the recommendations of *Turning Points* for middle grade reform, as well as their impact on students' academic achievement, socioemotional development, and behavioral adjustment. Of particular concern was the exploration of the association between the levels of implementation of the reforms that participating schools attained and relevant student outcomes.

As we will explain in greater detail, the research is also designed to provide reliable data to reforming schools that can facilitate decision making and planning at the site level. Such data are required for effective decisions pertaining to school management and to develop strategic plans for school improvement. Moreover, schools must have systematic, objective data on student achievement outcomes in relation to the reforms they are attempting, as well as data on the degree to which changes that are implemented are consistent with the *Turning Points* recommendations. The latter data will enable schools to understand the nature of any changes they do (or do not) obtain and to create greater congruence between intended and actual changes.

Research questions

The evaluation research on which this chapter is based focuses on several core questions, including the following:

1. As participating schools move from more traditional structures, norms, and instructional practices to increasing levels of comprehensiveness and fidelity in their implementation of *Turning Points* recommendations, are there parallel changes in students' levels of health, well-being, and socioemotional functioning; academic achievement and progress; experiences of the school climate and functioning; levels of resources and support from important others inside and outside of the school setting; and involvement with parents and the community?
2. Consistent with the goal of *Turning Points* that no child should be left behind, a central concern of our work is the way in which racial and ethnic minority adolescents, those from economically disadvantaged families, and those experiencing other risk conditions (e.g., living in

high-crime/low-employment communities) are affected by the *Turning Points* recommendations. Hence the study asks, in what ways, within and across participating schools, do variations in the levels and forms of the implementation of the *Turning Points* recommendations relate to outcomes for groups of students at varying levels of risk for academic difficulties and other problematic developmental outcomes?

3. An issue related to the differential impact of *Turning Points* recommendations on adolescents at risk is, how may the implementation and effect of the recommendations vary as a function of differences in school settings and community contexts? It is critical to consider these contextual interactions when interpreting the patterns of relationships found between school changes and student outcomes. For example, we have observed that large schools with high concentrations of low-income children are often among the first to attempt to implement reforms. Yet because there are often acute problems of poor student performance in such schools (the impetus for initiating reforms in the first place), a strictly cross-sectional correlational analysis that fails to control for context variables would suggest that increases in *Turning Points* practices are associated with poorer student outcomes! For these and related reasons, long-term longitudinal studies are critical to understand fully the patterns of relationships between implementation of *Turning Points* recommendations, student characteristics, context variables, and student outcomes. This chapter reports on the first phase of one such effort.

Conceptual and measurement models

To truly understand a school reform effort, the measurement model and assessments in that research need to provide data about the actual levels and patterns of implementation. MacIver and Epstein (1993, p. 530) note that "few middle grades schools have implemented many of the practices recommended for the education of early adolescents and even fewer have implemented them well." Cuban (1992) and others (e.g., Mergendollar, 1993) argue that structural changes that have been at the core of most middle grade reform recommendations may do little to change the fundamental experiences of students. These authors argue that structural changes, such as the creation of teacher teams, implementing advisory periods, and making scheduling modifications that allow for longer and more intensive class periods are "too distal to improve students' learning and attitudes." Further, these critics argue that there is often too little linkage between the implementation of these structural changes and actual changes in the practices and experiences of teachers and learners.

For these reasons, it is clear that an evaluation research design that simply assigns schools to categories of "implemented" or "nonimplemented" or to some "experimental schools" condition versus a "control" condition will not be informative. The reality of school reform does not lend itself to such dichotomous categories. Changes in schools are not simply either/or. Rather, reform is an evolutionary and developmental process. Thus, when considering the differences between groups, it is critical to know that the researcher's distinction between schools is meaningful, reflecting real differences in the levels and forms of what is occurring in these settings. It should also be understood that these issues are endemic to scientific research. Even classical experimental design requires that there be "manipulation checks" and assessments of the impact of various levels and combinations of exposure to the independent variables if the investigators are to assert plausibly that the results obtained are attributable to the experimental manipulations.

In evaluation research on school reform, the manipulation check can and should be the systematic assessment of the degree to which the intended transformations have occurred. If measured carefully, variation in the level of implementation can provide the opportunity to answer important questions about the degree of change and the patterns of interaction between these changes that are required to obtain the desired results. Given the limited resource contexts in which schools operate, it is critical to clarify these complex relationships between and among the comprehensive set of *Turning Points* recommendations, as well as the point at which additional resources or changes yield decreasing returns.

Hence, we included direct assessments of changes in the teaching and learning process and context at multiple levels (e.g., school, grade/team, classroom) in our measurement model and instruments. We also started with an open stance concerning the potential importance of the structural changes that have been at the core of the recommendations of middle grade reformers. That is, we sought to evaluate whether, and if so how, these structural changes by themselves produced important changes in student outcomes and/or changes in the teaching and learning process that we and others recognize as being central to improved student performance.

Given the central focus of this work on the development of a more systematic model for reform, we sought to consider these and implementation variables in ways that were more conceptually driven than in most prior work. Therefore, in considering both the impact and nature of the structural variables of concern, as well as all other implementation variables assessed, we were concerned with the degree to which each of the measured variables added to the manifestation of one or more of the eight overarching conceptual goals of *Turning Points*. For example, rather than simply focusing on whether or not one school is "teaming" in a checklist fashion, we sought to understand the defining features of teams that related to differential levels of the attainment of "small communities for learning" – one of the eight core recommendations of *Turning Points*.

Furthermore, we sought to determine the influence of such team structural variables and operational norms as team size (numbers of both teachers and students), student:teacher ratios, stability of teams, frequency and duration of common planning periods, and length of time teaming or the experiences of students and teachers of the school as a smaller, more orderly, predictable, and supportive community for learning, the attainment of other reforms (e.g., changes in instruction), and, ultimately, student achievement.

The core of the evaluation is a compressed longitudinal design. Such a design relies on obtaining observations of sets of schools that are at different levels of maturity in the reform process and following them over time. This enables us to evaluate the impact of shifts in levels of implementation in less time than would be required if all schools in the study were just starting the process. Hence, across a period of 6–7 years, we can evaluate the impact of all levels of changes that might take 10 years to assess if all schools began the process at the same (low) level of implementation. Further, such a design allows for several replications over time. That is, because we are adding cohorts of schools to the analyses, we can test whether subsequent cohorts show patterns of change similar to those of cohorts that precede them.

Figure 3.1a depicts our conceptual and measurement model at the most general level. As will be described, each element of the model is assessed from at least two converging independent sources. Figure 3.1a shows the basic assumptions of the PIML efforts, as well as of *Turning Points* in terms of hypothesized pathways of influence. Of critical concern for understanding the importance of each of the recommendations of *Turning Points* are (1) the degree to which the implementation of each recommendation separately contributes to the attainment of the changes in school and student outcomes and (2) the degree to which, as schools implement increasing numbers of the recommendations of *Turning Points*, additive and other combinational effects are obtained. As the

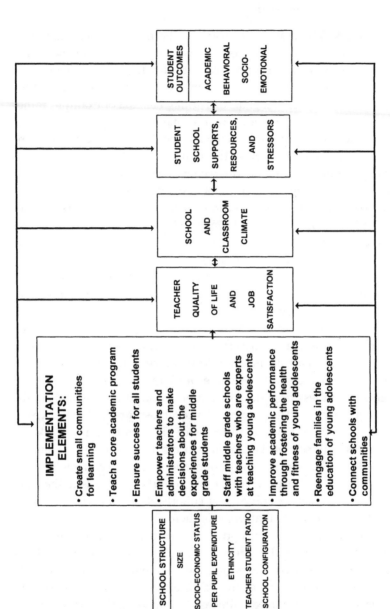

Figure 3.1a. Pathways of influence between middle school implementation elements and student outcomes, middle school logical model: major assessment domains.

model shows, each of the elements of the pathway will be considered as having both direct and mediated influences on the outcomes of concern. Further, the longitudinal nature of the current study allows for consideration of the reciprocal relationships that are inherent in these pathways. As teachers become more invested in students, student adjustment should improve. In turn, this improvement should influence the feelings of teachers about students.

Figure 3.1b shows a model in which the *Turning Points* recommendations for implementation are replaced by a representative but not comprehensive set of the ways in which the assessment of implementation elements were operationalized. All other elements of this model remain the same. Table 3.1 presents a representative list of variables assessed in each of the key measurement domains and *Turning Points* dimensions.

Finally, Figure 3.1c shows a slightly revised version of the model, based on our findings thus far, in which we show the sequence of implementation elements that best reflects the most successful of the school transformation efforts. This model shows that both our assumptions and emergent data indicate that those schools that make key changes in leadership processes and staff values about the importance of the recommended practices (what Oakes, Quartz, Gong, Guiton, and Lipton, 1993, would call *normative* and *political* changes), as well as critical shifts in the operational norms and structures of the school (Sarason, 1982), implement changes faster and more intensively.

Inherent in the measurement model are the three primary domains for assessment that any adequate evaluation of an educational program or policy reform needs to contain (Felner, 1994; Price and Smith, 1985):

1. *Assessment of the context in which the intervention occurs* to understand the ways in which situational factors may systematically distort or otherwise affect program implementation;
2. *Process evaluation* to determine the degree to which each of the *Turning Points* recommendations has been implemented (its intensity or "dosage"), as well as the comprehensiveness of implementation. These assessments are important to determine: (a) that the actual program elements are present and (b) that systematic variation on these process dimensions relates to differing levels of student, staff, and parent/ community outcomes.
3. *Outcome/impact assessments.* As shown in Figure 3.1a–c, there are several levels and forms of impacts that should accrue from the implementation of the structural and organizational aspects of the *Turning*

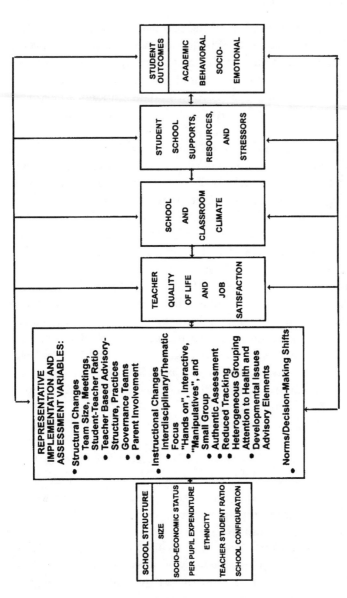

Figure 3.1b. Hypothesized pathways of influence of school restructuring based on *Turning Points*: representative implementation variables and major assessment domains.

Points recommendations. Some of these variables (e.g., changes in staff/teacher job functions and roles) are influenced by and have influence on other implementation elements. Other variables, such as student achievement, are more truly outcome variables reflecting the cumulative impact of many aspects of implementation.

Before proceeding, it is worth noting that one of the reasons PIML and the Project on High Performance Learning Communities selected *Turning Points* as the key set of recommendations for our reform efforts is that it is one of the very few reform proposals that yields testable, systematic, and comprehensive recommendations for change that are necessary for both effective school reform and sound research.

Samples

Overall, schools participating in the PIML network represent the full range of geographic, demographic, and size characteristics of all schools in Illinois, including urban, suburban, and rural schools. For example, the sample involves schools that have populations approaching 2,000 students and those with fewer than 200 students. The full range of student characteristics is also represented, with the student populations ranging from primarily economically disadvantaged and/or from African American, Hispanic, or other racial and ethnic minority backgrounds, to heterogeneous student populations, to those that are highly affluent and/or predominately European American.

Data analyses and report of baseline findings

Before we discuss the findings, we ask that the reader consider our results as preliminary for a number of reasons. First, we have only recently completed our third year of large-scale data collection. Second, Oakes and Guiton (1994) and others have noted that 3 years or less is not an adequate period for schools to implement successfully all of the recommendations of *Turning Points* or other school reform efforts.

Schools, once they enter PIML, typically spend the first year in the project planning for the actual start of the restructuring process and participating in in-service and AIMS/PIML institute activities. During the second year of their participation, the vast majority of partnership schools move forward rapidly in their efforts to implement teaming,

Table 3.1 Turning Points *recommendations and representative variables*

1. *Turning Points* goal: *Creating small communities for learning*
   - Structure, level, intensity, and quality of interdisciplinary teams and activities, including joint planning time
   - Degree to which students are grouped in teams throughout the school day, team sizes, student:teacher ratios, common planning time, schools within schools
   - Level of implementation and utilization of adviser-advisee/and other mentoring advisory-focused programs
2. *Turning Points* goal: *Teaching a core of common knowledge*
   Teaching practices that focus on:
   - Critical thinking
   - Integrative curriculum connections and themes
   - Experiential learning opportunities
   - Comprehensive health education
   - Life skills development and education
   - Computer skills
   - Innovative grading/assessment practices
   - Promotion of cultural diversity
3. *Turning Points* goal: *Ensuring success for all students*
   - Use of heterogeneous ability grouping in classroom practices and teaching
   - Use of cooperative learning and similar techniques
   - Cross-age and same-age peer tutoring practices
   - Flexibility of class scheduling, teaching of cross-topic integrated lessons
   - Expansion of learning opportunities to include experiential, nontraditional, culturally diverse, and real-world topical coverage
4. *Turning Points* goal: *Empowering teachers and administrators*
   - Degree to which teachers report that teams have independence in decision making
   - Degree to which teachers report having autonomy in making decisions concerning curricula and other practices in their classrooms (e.g., using flexible block scheduling)
   - Levels of involvement of teachers in decision making impacting overall school practices
   - Degree to which teachers feel that they are recognized for their accomplishments and are able to utilize their skills and knowledge in the classroom
   - Degree to which building advisory teams have been established that are representative of teacher, community, and other appropriate groups
   - Whether teacher leaders have been established for each team and/or other organizational subunits and have decision-making authority, resources, and support
5. *Turning Points* goal: *Preparing teachers for middle level*
   - Level of training that teachers have received specific to middle school practices and young adolescents, training needs of teachers, teacher perceptions of practices that are congruent with such training as important to middle level education

Table 3.1 (*cont.*)

6. *Turning Points* goal: *Improving academic performance through better health and fitness*
   • Implementation, level, and intensity of comprehensive school health educational curriculum
   • Presence of a school-based health coordinator
   • Levels of coordination and formal affiliations with local health and counseling centers; presence of a school-based health clinic or health services
   • Implementation of school policies that promote healthy behaviors
   • Opportunities for physical education and exercise that are integral to the school day
   • Direct (e.g., mediation programming; safe access efforts with law enforcement; programming that teaches cooperation and acceptance of diversity and ethnic/racial tolerance) and indirect (e.g., school climate change) efforts to reduce violence and conflict

7. *Turning Points* goal: *Reengaging families in the education of young adolescents*
   • Level of parental involvement and participation in school governance
   • Extent, regularity, and nature/focus of team/teacher–parent communications (some schools do not yet have teams, depending on the level of implementation)
   • Degree to which parents provide support/stimulation and emphasize educational achievement at home

8. *Turning Points* goal: *Connecting schools with communities*
   • Extent to which students are taught about and involved in youth service activities, community programming and services
   • Levels of community support for educational enrichment and innovation through formal and informal programmatic/collaborative efforts by social and human service organizations centered on the middle grades school
   • Enactment and range of school–community partnerships

common planning time (most with 5 days per week), and teacher-based advisory structures.

Our preliminary data indicate that the first year of implementation may be one of considerable disruption (as is true for most organizations going through dramatic changes, whether educational institutions or not). It may take an additional year or two for the organizational changes to become institutionalized, for teacher norms to reflect acceptance of the assumptions that underlie the restructuring, and for changes in teaming and classroom practices to begin to emerge. It must also be recognized that if, for example, a school has grades 6–8 in its middle grades program, it may be 5 years or more before a cohort of students is exposed to a fully realized middle grades program.

Given these caveats, it is critical to understand, considering the fol-

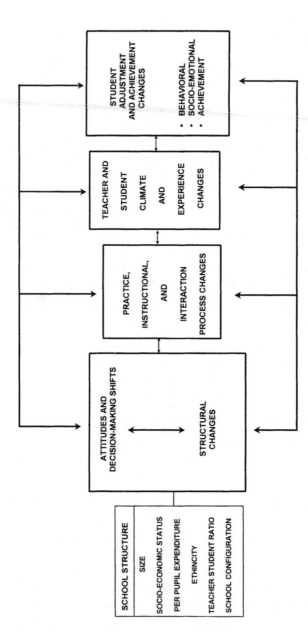

Figure 3.1c. Pathways of influence between *Turning Points*–based middle school implementation elements and student outcomes: altered sequencing. Model based on current findings.

lowing analyses, that those schools in the "most fully implemented" group are typically some distance from being "fully implemented." Indeed, we and the schools know that they still have a long way to go. This is one reason that we hope to follow our cohorts over a much longer period of time. Hence, in the following analyses where we compare schools at varying levels of implementation, it must be clear that the comparisons are among schools at *relative* levels of implementation. To anticipate the findings somewhat, however, it does appear that our most fully implemented schools are dramatically different and better places for students to learn and teachers to teach than those at lower levels of implementation.

Preliminary findings and issues for the future

The analyses of the data thus far have taken a variety of forms, ranging from correlational, hierarchical regression, and structural modeling approaches to those that deal with the data in a less linear fashion. As we explore our data in these different ways, we are learning a great deal, not only about our own data but also about issues that may require attention in analysis plans that are employed in future studies of school restructuring.

One of the major overarching findings is the importance of considering the comprehensiveness and level of implementation (LOI) of the *Turning Points* recommendations. There are a number of ways in which the effects of scope and intensity are manifested, ranging from the impact of the presence or absence of critical elements on the levels of implementation of other recommendations to the degree to which each element contributes directly to differential student achievement, physical health, and mental health. Consideration of a few of the findings that illustrate these points may be helpful here.

School and cross-school analyses

One key set of analyses involves cross-sectional comparisons across schools that have attained different levels of implementation of overall middle school practices, including some schools that have not attempted to change and that thus serve as traditional comparison schools. The central question of these analyses is the extent to which schools that have attained different levels of implementation show concomitant differences in student achievement, behavior, health practices, and socioemotional

Table 3.2. *Summary of 1991–1994 PIML data collection*

Year of data collection	Number of participating schools	Number of participating students	Number of TCRSs collected	Number of participating administrators
1991	11	4,548	4,794	11 administrators
1992	31	15,762	14,347	29 administrators
1993	44	23,258	21,542	34 administrators
1994	52	25,434	24,865	44 administrators
				28 assistant administrators

adjustment for all students and for targeted subgroups (e.g., students who are economically disadvantaged; students during the transition year coming from differing types of feeder school configurations).

A related set of analyses is concerned with changes within schools (and sets of schools) in their practices over time and the way that these changes impact subsequent functioning of the inhabitants of the schools (i.e., teachers, students, administrators, targeted subgroups, and parents of students).[1] Let us briefly turn to a representative set of the findings of these analyses.

In the initial year of the study (1990–1991), there were 11 schools in the sample. During the 1991–1992 school year, the number of schools was increased by 20 to a total of 31, and we obtained second-year data on the 11 original schools. Although the number of schools now in the sample has reached 52, the results to be presented pertain to the 31 schools that were a part of PIML in the 1991–1992 school year. Analysis of data involving the larger sample is ongoing.

Employing data we had obtained about the 31 schools concerning key structures and resources, decision-making patterns, teacher norms, and instructional patterns, each school was classified into one of three LOIs based on what we have labeled the *Carnegie Index of Middle School Trans-formation*. Briefly, schools classified as being in the highest level of implementation ($N = 9$) were those that had accomplished the majority of structural changes "at high levels," that is, in ways that most reflected their underlying principles. For example, schools in which teams had four or five common planning periods per week, had relatively small numbers of students on the team (i.e., not more than 120), had relatively low teacher:student ratios (i.e., one teacher per 20–25 students), where advisories occurred with relatively high frequency (e.g., four or five times per week), and where teacher: student ratios in advisories were approximately 20–22 or less were judged as having more fully implemented the *Turning Points* goal of creating "small communities for learning." In addition, those schools showed critical changes in the school context and in the teaching and learning processes. Schools that showed patterns of instruction, decision making, and teacher norms consistent with the educational practices that attended to the developmental issues of adolescents also were generally included in the highest group.

Schools in the initial "partial" group were those that had implemented at least some of the key structural changes at high levels but were not yet showing the levels of instructional and contextual changes that were typical of the high group. Typically, the schools in this group ($N = 12$) had made the structural changes either more recently or at lower levels than those in the most fully implemented group. Finally, schools in the "low implementation" group included both those that were not making changes and those that had recently joined PIML but had yet to make significant progress on any implementation front.

In considering the findings that follow, the reader is reminded that the assignment of schools to a LOI group was done on the basis of their relative similarity (within groups) and relative difference (across groups), not on the basis of some absolute scale. Moreover, in assigning schools to groups and, more specifically, in establishing boundaries between groups, we also considered sociodemographic characteristics of the schools to maximize comparability of the groups. As a result, there were three sets of schools that, although clearly differing in level of implementation, are demographically comparable in terms of size, percentage of free/reduced-priced lunch students served (an indication of family income), and per pupil expenditures.

Figure 3.2 shows the average achievement scores in reading, mathematics, and language arts that were obtained by schools in each of these groups. These schools include more than 15,000 students and nearly 900 teachers. The state mean score on each of these achievement dimensions is 250, with a standard deviation of 50. The data show that across subject areas, adolescents in highly implemented schools had higher achievement than those in nonimplemented schools and substantially better than those in partially implemented schools. Average achievement scores shown in this and later charts are a composite of sixth- and eighth-grade scores. The states' achievement tests are constructed so that scores across grade levels are comparable and can therefore be averaged to create a single schoolwide composite. It is important to note, however, that com-

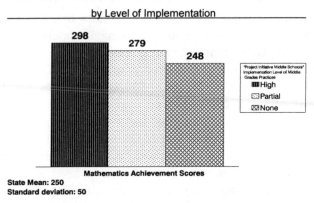

Mathematics Achievement Scores
by Level of Implementation

298 279 248

"Project Initiative Middle Schools"
Implementation Level of Middle
Grades Practices

▥ High
▨ Partial
▧ None

Mathematics Achievement Scores

State Mean: 250
Standard deviation: 50

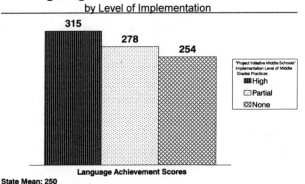

Language Achievement Scores
by Level of Implementation

315 278 254

"Project Initiative Middle Schools"
Implementation Level of Middle
Grades Practices

▥ High
▨ Partial
▧ None

Language Achievement Scores

State Mean: 250
Standard deviation: 50

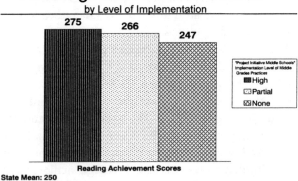

Reading Achievement Scores
by Level of Implementation

275 266 247

"Project Initiative Middle Schools"
Implementation Level of Middle
Grades Practices

▥ High
▨ Partial
▧ None

Reading Achievement Scores

State Mean: 250
Standard deviation: 50

Figure 3.2. Student achievement test scores by schools' level of implementation of *Turning Points* recommendations.

bining sixth- and eighth-grade scores into a single index is a more conservative test than using only eighth-grade scores, which some would argue represents a truer assessment of the power of the conditions that appear to influence achievement. Reflecting longer exposure to these conditions, differences between groups when only eighth-grade scores are used are substantially larger than with the combined sixth/eighth-grade index.

A critical feature of our design is that we have attempted to obtain multiple convergent measures on aspects of both the implementation of reforms and outcomes. Hence, for these initial LOI analyses, a number of other student outcomes were considered, including additional indicators of achievement. These indicators included the percentage of students who are performing at grade level and scores in subsets of schools that administer the Iowa Test of Basic Skills or the California Test of Basic Skills. Generally, these additional indicators show strong association with the state-level scores.

We also examined different domains of student outcomes as they related to the level of implementation that schools had obtained. These include teacher ratings of student behaviors, as well as student self-reports of behavior, depression (fear, worry) anxiety, and self-esteem. Figures 3.3 and 3.4 show representative findings employing these data.

As can be seen in Figure 3.3, the patterns of teacher reports of student behavioral problems, including aggressive, moody/anxious, and learning-related behavior problems, are highly correlated with the patterns noted earlier within achievement data but in the desired *opposite* direction. That is, in the most fully implemented schools, teachers report far lower levels of student behavior problems than do teachers in less implemented and nonimplemented schools. Similarly, teachers in the partially implemented schools still perceive students as showing fewer behavioral problems than those in the least implemented schools.

Figure 3.4 shows the results of the same analyses for student self-reports of a representative set of the domains of socioemotional function that were measured.[2] These data show patterns that are highly convergent with the achievement and behavioral outcomes. Specifically, the three graphs indicate that students in the more fully implemented schools are less fearful, for example, about being victimized; are less worried about something bad happening at school and about the future; and have higher levels of self-esteem. Students in the partially implemented schools show better outcomes than those in the nonimplemented

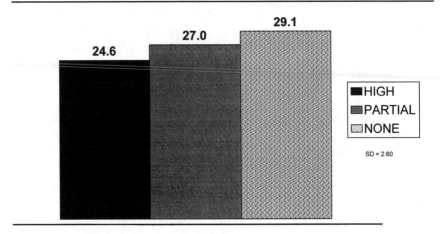

Figure 3.3. Teacher ratings of student behavioral problems by level of implementation. Total of reported aggression, moody/shy, and learning difficulties (lower values indicate better scores; all group differences are significant).

schools, but ones that are not as good as those in the most fully implemented schools. Because the groups of schools are comparable with regard to important school and community context variables, it is not the case that youths in nonimplemented schools differ systematically from those in partially and highly implemented schools in the degree to which, for example, their fearfulness might be justified by unsafe conditions in the neighborhood.

Clearly, across quite different types and sources of data (e.g., achievement tests, teacher reports, student self-reports), there are distinct differences between schools that have attained different levels of implementation of the *Turning Points* recommendations. Such patterns are important indicators of the reliability and validity of the multiple outcomes.

Nevertheless, the data are limited by their cross-sectional nature. The core of the current evaluation is a long-term longitudinal study in which we are tracking schools as they move *through* different levels of implementation. We will then consider the association of such changes in implementation within schools as they relate to shifts in intermediate variables and, ultimately, to student achievement and related outcomes.

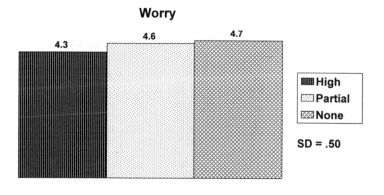

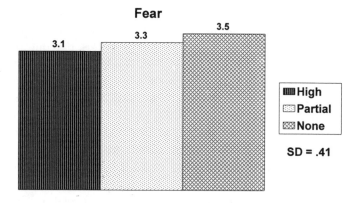

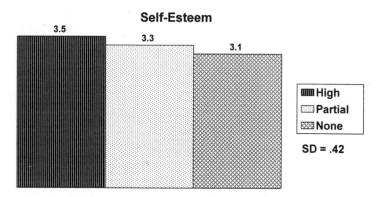

Figure 3.4. Student self-reports of adjustment by level of implementation. Scores are average item responses to allow for comparability across scales. All scales have 1–5 item response choices.

The focal question here is, do student performance and adjustment improve as the level and quality of implementation increase over time?

Schools in the longitudinal analyses are categorized according to degree of implementation. These categorizations, however, have been expanded to consider both the level of implementation obtained, as in the cross-sectional analyses, and the rate of change over the past year. Consequently, level 5 includes schools that were nonimplemented or only marginally so in the previous year and had made no changes during the current one. By contrast, level 4 includes those schools that were nonimplemented or only marginally implemented in the previous year but, over the intervening year, had initiated planning processes and had begun to make some structural changes that, although important, will require further refining to be truly effective. For example, level 4 schools include those that had moved to teams of 130–150 or more students, with teachers having perhaps one or two planning periods, and where the planning did not yet reflect any instructional changes. By contrast, level 1 schools include those that had attained the highest levels of structural changes, had implemented key changes in instruction and decision making, and, importantly, were showing continuing refinements in these latter critical areas of teaching and learning processes and practices. The latter activity, again, shows that even our most fully implemented schools have considerable room to improve, particularly in areas of instructional change and in the extent to which *Turning Points* recommendations are embraced by all teachers within the school.

The first set of analyses considered the simple correlations between changes in degree of implementation across 1- and 2-year periods, as well as changes in reading and mathematics scores. As schools move up in their level of implementation of *Turning Points* recommendations from 1991–1992 to 1992–1993, the 1-year correlation of such changes with increases in eighth-grade reading scores was .51 ($p < 001$) and with increases in eighth-grade math scores was .30 ($p < 001$). Similar patterns were found for two-year changes in implementation level and achievement scores (from 1991–1992 to 1992–1993), with correlations of .53 and .35, respectively (both $p < .001$). It is encouraging to note that longer-term analyses, if anything, yielded findings that were as strong and stable as or stronger than those of shorter-term change analyses.

Patterns similar to those with achievement score gains were also found when we examined indicators of students' experiences of school climate, student adjustment, and health indices. These data complement the cross-sectional data described earlier, showing that whatever the preexisting levels of student outcomes in these areas, as schools move through degrees of implementation of the *Turning Points* recommendations, there appear to be associated gains in key areas of student behavior and socioemotional adjustment.

We also examined the relative magnitude of the gains that were associated with differences in degrees of implementation. For these data we have 4 years of observations of changes in achievement scores (i.e., from the school year 1990–1991 through 1993–1994 – these data are available even for schools that joined after 1990–1991) and attained changes in LOI from 1991–1992 on. We considered both 1- and 2-year changes in achievement scores in math and reading (these are the most consistently available data for all schools) across LOI change and attainment categories. In all analyses of both 1- and 2-year data, there were large, meaningful differences between schools that had reached the highest levels of implementation or those that had made the most progress toward high levels of implementation, and those schools in which little implementation had occurred and where relatively smaller LOI changes were made.

To illustrate the general pattern of these findings, Figure 3.5 shows the combined average gain in reading and math scores across two sets of changes obtained by schools in each category across 2 years (i.e., 1990–1991 to 1992–1993 and 1991–1992 to 1993–1994). LOI attainment and change scores are based on 1994 and prior data, as 1994–1995 implementation data were not yet fully available for these analyses. As can be seen in Figure 3.5, the average gain in math/reading achievement scores across two 2-year periods in the most fully implemented schools (level 1 described earlier) was nearly 21 points (recall that 25 points is a full half standard deviation on these scales). Schools that had attained high levels of (i.e., comprehensive) implementation structurally, but had done so most recently and thus had rather moderate change in the core teaching and learning processes (labeled category 2 – "highly implemented, more recent"), showed average achievement gains of more than 15 points. Those schools that were not yet highly implemented but had shown several categories of LOI gain (labeled category 3 – "partial implementation, greater improvement") had average gain scores of nearly 12 points. By contrast, schools in category 1, "intermediate levels of implementation – little refinement" (i.e., where little improvement had recently occurred) showed average gains of less than 3 points, and those schools that had made little or no movement toward implementation showed declines in student achievement.

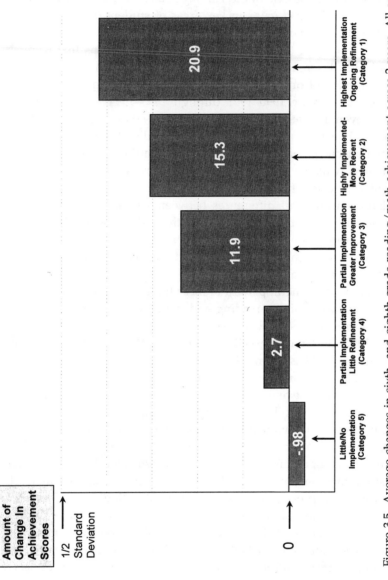

Figure 3.5. Average changes in sixth- and eighth-grade reading/math achievement across 2 years. All scores are the combination of the average gains in sixth- and eighth-grade math and reading achievement scores in participating schools across two 2-year periods (i.e., 1990–1991 to 1992–1993; 1991–1992 to 1993–1994).

Taken together, these findings are extremely encouraging and show the potential impact of *Turning Points* recommendations on the achievement and adjustment of adolescents. Yet, as teachers and administrators in our category 1 schools would quickly point out, these highly implemented schools are far from fully transformed, particularly in terms of actual changes in classroom instruction. Hence, if we consider that our most fully implemented schools are only partway there, then the potentially positive impact of the comprehensive transformation of a school to reflect the recommendations of *Turning Points* appears to be well beyond what we have already obtained. This is an issue we will explore further in our future efforts. What will happen if schools fully implement *Turning Points* recommendations? How do we get there, and what have we learned about the current process that can help? It is with a brief consideration of these issues that we close.

The case for comprehensive implementation

Perhaps the most important lesson about implementation from this ongoing research is that successful reform must be comprehensive and integrative, with careful attention to the sequencing of some *Turning Points* elements upon which other elements can be added. There are clear patterns of interdependence among the implementation elements that may require additional attention by those involved in school reform efforts if we are to fully realize the benefits of middle grade restructuring.

One of the clearest patterns that has emerged in our data is the difference between a checklist-based implementation of structural changes and idea-driven implementation. The latter attempts to reflect the underlying constructs and issues in the *Turning Points* recommendations. Take the *Turning Points* recommendation of "Creating small communities for learning" as an example. If one employs a checklist approach, as typified in many sets of recommendations for middle grades reform (see Mergendollar, 1993), a school might ask itself whether or not it has team teaching or interdisciplinary instruction. Unfortunately, being able to "check off" these practices becomes an end in itself, with little regard to why they should be implemented or in what forms and levels they need to be present to contribute to a more effective teaching and learning process.

Across our Illinois, MGSSPI, and other samples, schools that say they are teaming may have teams that range from those with 60–70 students and 2 or 3 teachers to those with over 240 students and 9 to 12 teachers.

Student:teacher ratios on a team may range from less than 20 to more than 40. Additionally, levels of common planning time, which appear to be a critical element of small learning communities, vary from no common planning time, to the shared use of individual planning times, to daily common planning time, in addition to individual planning time, for each teacher on every team.

There are considerable differences in the costs of these implementation options. Policymakers, as well as school administrators who must make decisions about expending resources, need to take these differences into account. Our findings reveal a number of patterns that, if they hold, make the case against attempting middle grades school restructuring "on the cheap."

We have found that each of the dimensions of teaming noted previously (e.g., team size, student:teacher ratio, amount of common planning time) appears to have a significant association with the degree to which other elements of *Turning Points* reforms may be accomplished. Our findings indicate that lower levels of each of these variables are associated with (1) the failure of teams to implement critical teaming activities that focus on curriculum integration, coordination, and collaboration around student needs/assignments; this appears to be true both cross-sectionally and longitudinally, where large team sizes and the absence of sufficient common planning time relate to relatively slow implementation or non-implementation of critical teaming practices; (2) a more negative school climate as reported by students; (3) student and teacher reports of elevated levels of student mental health and behavior problems; and (4) poor student achievement. Indeed, it appears that in cases where schools attempt to implement these practices but do so poorly (e.g., one or two common planning times per week, interdisciplinary instruction without common planning time, large teams), there may be no effect or even negative effects, especially on teacher attitudes and student performance.

It also appears that the patterns of change and impact are neither linear nor interdependent. Going from 1 day per week of common planning time to 2, or moving from 200 to 180 student teams seems to matter little. Rather, there appear to be critical levels below or above which changes make little difference. Teams that exceed approximately 120 students, that have fewer than four common planning periods per week, and that have student:teacher ratios beyond 24–26, tend to show little impact on instructional practices or student well-being.

It should also be clear that deficits in any of these elements place severe limits on what is yielded by the others. Thus, small teams of students may improve students' reports of their level of support and feeling of connectedness to schools somewhat, but unless teachers have adequate amounts of common planning time, actual instruction does not appear to change. Indeed, changes in actual classroom practices that are in keeping with *Turning Points* recommendations (e.g., use of small group instruction, interdisciplinary instruction) appear, not surprisingly, to be significantly associated with changes in team activities. Thus, one can begin to see the way in which the desired changes are nested within each other. These findings underscore the statement by Sarason (1982) that if we are to avoid the "predictable failure of educational reform," we must understand that schools are complex, integrated systems. Therefore we must address the full set of operational norms, regularities, and behaviors that may impact or undermine efforts at change.

The interdependence of the elements of reform is also suggested by the manner in which poor student outcomes that are likely to occur can be prevented. In a paper on the transition to middle grade schools, Felner (1994) reported that the patterns of relationships between higher levels of implementation and student achievement, mental health, and behaviors result, in part, from the preventive effects of middle grade structures. Small teams and teacher-based advisory programming in particular, especially when those teams are kept in their own areas of the building and away from older students, appear to enable students to make the transition to middle schools without the pronounced declines in socioemotional well-being and achievement that have been reported in some studies of students moving into middle schools and junior high schools (Simmons and Blyth, 1987).

It appears, then, that student achievement scores are higher in schools that have at least created small communities for learning, not because this one change dramatically improves student performance but because it prevents the decline in achievement that often occurs in traditionally structured schools. This is not a trivial finding. These predictable declines have, in the past, been linked to the full range of socioemotional problems among youth (e.g., school failure, dropping out, crime, depression, substance abuse, and teenage pregnancy and parenthood).

Middle grade reformers have sought not only to avoid the onset of new difficulties but also to enhance the developmental course of students. Our current sample contains a small but growing set of schools that have shown significant levels of implementation across virtually all

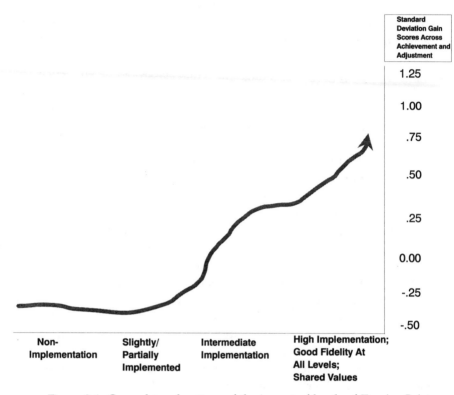

Figure 3.6. General trend pattern of the impact of levels of *Turning Points* implementation for higher-risk (e.g., minority and/or free/reduced-priced lunch) students.

Turning Points recommendations. Our findings suggest that it is only when schools begin to realize much more complete implementation of the full range of *Turning Points* recommendations that such enhancement effects accrue.

Illustratively in the important case of at-risk students, our results indicate that the majority of gains are not realized until implementation is quite mature and comprehensive. Figure 3.6 illustrates the potential importance of high levels of comprehensive *Turning Points*–based implementation for attaining both preventive and enhancement effects for students at great risk. This figure shows the average effect size (amount of change in an indicator relative to the standard deviation of that measure) across a set of achievement and adjustment indicators (e.g., classroom behavior, student school attitudes/bonding/climate ratings, sense of efficacy, deviant behavior) for students who are minorities and/or eligible for free/reduced-priced lunch as a function of the level of implementation of their school.

Consistent with much prior work, students in more traditionally structured schools show declines in achievement and adjustment indicators. It is not until substantial transformation has been accomplished (e.g., structural changes that are necessary for creating small learning communities, changes in norms and some instructional practices) that preventive effects (e.g., the absence of declines that would otherwise appear) are found for these at-risk students. Finally, and critically, the findings show that for at-risk students, broad-range enhancements in achievement and adjustment are not obtained until implementation is quite mature, comprehensive, and conducted with a high degree of fidelity.

Assuming that these patterns hold for future analyses as additional data are acquired, our findings should encourage policymakers to continue restructuring even though the results during the early stages are not all as expected. It should not be surprising that it takes fairly comprehensive and intensive levels of implementation for the suggested changes to produce major gains in all spheres of functioning of high-risk students. Often these students live in community environments that may be high in stress and low in opportunities and resources. However, our findings to date strongly support the view that quality schooling, well implemented, can make profound contributions to the achievement, mental health, and sociobehavioral functioning of students who are often left behind and for whom there is often a sense that school cannot make a difference in their lives. These data also argue for the effective use of resources in schools with high concentrations of at-risk students and, in some instances, for resources to be increased significantly to create the conditions that our research is showing are required for all young adolescents to be successful.

Notes

1. Univariate and multivariate correlation analyses, multiple regression procedures, multiple analyses of covariance (MANCOVA) and subsequent univariate analyses (ANCOVA), and structural equation modeling are the primary analytic procedures that serve as the bases for the results reported in this chapter. They have been conducted to test for nested settings effects at multiple levels (e.g., school, grade, team).
2. Scores in this figure have been put through a linear transformation procedure that involves converting the overall scale score to the average item-level score for each measure so that the scales could be displayed in equivalent ways.

Hence, on these scales, apparently small differences translate into larger and significant scale-score differences when converted back to full-scale scores.

References

Beyth-Marom, R., Fischhoff, B., Jacobs, M., and Furby, L. (1989). *Teaching decision-making to adolescents: A critical review* (working paper). Washington, DC: Carnegie Council on Adolescent Development.

Carnegie Council on Adolescent Development, Task Force on Education of Young Adolescents. (1989). *Turning points: Preparing American youth for the 21st century.* Washington, DC: Author.

Carnegie Forum on Education and the Economy. (1986). *A nation prepared: Teachers for the 21st century.* Washington, DC: Author.

Cuban, L. (1992). What happens to reforms that last? The case of the junior high school. *American Educational Research Journal, 29*(2), 222–252.

Epstein, J. L., and MacIver, D. J. (1990). *Education in the middle grades: Overview of national practices and trends.* Columbus, OH: National Middle School Association.

Falco, M. (1988). *Preventing abuse of drugs, alcohol, and tobacco by adolescents* (working paper). Washington, DC: Carnegie Council on Adolescent Development.

Felner, R. D. (1994). *Understanding the impact of "Turning Points" on the adjustment and educational experiences of young adolescents: A longitudinal study of the impact of school reorganization and restructuring.* Carnegie Corporation of New York funded proposal from the University of Illinois, Champaign, IL.

Felner, R. D., and Adan, A. M. (1988). The school transitional environment project: An ecological intervention and evaluation. In R. H. Price, E. I. Cowen, R. P. Lorian, and J. Ramos-Mckay (Eds.), *Fourteen ounces of prevention: A casebook for practitioners* (pp. 111–122). Washington, DC: American Psychological Association.

Hein, K. (1988a). *Issues in adolescent health: An overview* (working paper). Washington, DC: Carnegie Council on Adolescent Development.

Hein, K. (1988b). *AIDS in adolescence: A rationale for concern* (working paper). Washington, DC: Carnegie Council on Adolescent Development.

Jackson, A. (1990). From knowledge to practice: Implementing the recommendations of Turning Points. *Middle School Journal, 21*(3), 1–3.

Lee, V. E., and Smith, J. B. (1994). *Effects of high school restructuring and size on gains in achievement and engagement for early secondary school students.* Madison: University of Wisconsin, Center on Organization and Restructuring of Schools.

Lipsitz, J. (1984). *Successful schools for young adolescents.* New Brunswick, NJ: Transaction Books.

MacIver, D. J., and Epstein, J. L. (1993). Middle grades research: Not yet mature but no longer a child. *The Elementary School Journal, 93,* 519–533.

Mergendollar, J. R. (1993). Introduction: The role of research on the reform of middle grades education. *The Elementary School Journal, 93,* 443–446.

Millstein, S. G. (1988). *The potential of school-linked centers to promote adolescent health and development* (working paper). Washington, DC: Carnegie Council on Adolescent Development.

Murphy, J. (1993). Restructuring: In search of a movement. In J. Murphy and P. Hallinger (Eds.), *Restructuring schooling: Learning from ongoing efforts* (pp. 1–31). Newbury Park, CA: Corwin Press.

Murphy, J., and Hallinger, P. (Eds.). (1993). *Restructuring schooling: Learning from ongoing efforts.* Newbury Park, CA: Corwin Press.

National Commission on Excellence in Education. (1983). *A nation at risk: Imperative of educational reform.* Washington, DC: U.S. Government Printing Office.

Nightingale, E. O., and Wolverton, L. (1993). Adolescent rolelessness in modern society. In R. Takanishi (Ed.), *Adolescence in the 1990s: Risk and opportunity.* New York: Teachers College Press.

Oakes, J. (1990). *Multiplying inequities: The effects of race, social class, and tracking on opportunities to learn mathematics and science.* Santa Monica, CA: RAND Corporation.

Oakes, J., and Guiton, G. (1994). *Implementing systematic middle school reform with "Turning Points": Research goals, design, and methodology.* Unpublished manuscript. University of California, Los Angeles, School of Education.

Oakes, J., Quartz, K. H., Gong, J., Guiton G., and Lipton, M. (1993). Creating middle schools: Technical, normative, and political considerations. *The Elementary School Journal, 93,* 461–480.

Prestine, N. (1991, April). *Completing the essential schools metaphor: Principal as enabler.* Paper presented at the annual meeting of the American Educational Research Association, Chicago,.

Price, R. H., and Smith, S. S. (1985). *A guide to evaluating prevention programs in mental health* (U.S. Department of Health and Human Services Pub. No. ADM 85-1365). Washington, DC: U.S. Government Printing Office.

Sarason, S. B. (1982). *The culture of the school and the problem of change* (2nd ed.). Boston: Allyn and Bacon.

Schine, J. (1989). *Young adolescents and community service* (working paper). Washington, DC: Carnegie Council on Adolescent Development.

Simmons, R. G., and Blyth, D. A. (1987). *Moving into adolescence: The impact of pubertal change and school context.* Hawthorne, NY: Aldine.

White, P. A. (1992). Teacher empowerment under "ideal" school-site autonomy. *Educational Evaluation and Policy Analysis, 14*(1), 69–82.

William T. Grant Foundation. (1988). *The forgotten half: Non-college youth in America.* New York: Author.

4. Schooling for the middle years: Developments in Europe

DONALD HIRSCH

This chapter discusses seven key issues of how European school systems address, or fail to address, special needs of young adolescents, in particular of the kind identified in the American context by the Carnegie Council's report, *Turning Points: Preparing American Youth for the 21st Century*. The middle years are here defined as approximately ages 10 to 14. A background understanding of how various European countries structure educational provision for children in the middle years of schooling can be found in *Schooling for the Middle Years: Developments in Eight European Countries* (Hirsch, 1994).

Key issues

In 1989, the Carnegie Council on Adolescent Development published a report, *Turning Points: Preparing American Youth for the 21st Century*, demonstrating that schools attended by most young American adolescents were strikingly out of phase with the developmental, social, and academic needs of their students. The report advocated measures that would make schools into more sensitive "communities for learning," with a stable core of academic programs, measures to ensure success for all students, links with communities, and a focus on the specific problems of adolescents.

In many European countries, schooling in the middle years is similarly seen as a weak link in the educational system. Although the reasons are not always the same as those cited in the United States, there is much overlap. Most notably, the lack of a specific philosophy of education for the middle years has created difficulties, in particular for weaker students making the transfer from a protected elementary school to the "jungle" of the secondary school. At the center of this problem in Europe is the tendency to base middle grade education on the transmission of core knowledge considered necessary before entering senior high school, and in so doing to focus insufficiently on the personal, social, and intellectual development of individuals aged about 12 or 13.

Europeans, like Americans, have started to grapple with this situation, even if an ideal solution seems elusive. An important difference between the United States and most of the countries examined in this chapter is the ability of the latter to change educational structures systematically from the national level. So, whereas the movement to reform middle grade education in the United States has been a bottom-up approach (albeit with strong leadership from the state level), the recent introduction, for example, of a core curriculum in the Netherlands, of a more humanized pedagogy in the Czech Republic, and of greater help for students in difficulty in France have all been legislated from the center. Even in Germany and Switzerland, both federal countries, states tend to legislate the content and structure of schooling in greater detail than their American counterparts.

Every country's situation is different, yet a striking number of common issues and sometimes common approaches arise from an examination of their educational systems. The following seven issues in particular arise in relation to the middle years of schooling in European countries. The last of these, the issue of schools as health-promoting environments, relates to all levels of schooling but has particularly strong implications for early adolescence. This issue was the subject of a separate Johann Jacobs Foundation–Carnegie Corporation of New York conference in Geneva in February 1995. Its discussion here, at somewhat greater length than the other six issues, summarizes some key messages to emerge from the Geneva conference.

Issue 1: The status of the middle years: Extension of elementary, preparation for secondary, or a stage in their own right?

In Scandinavia, the term *primary* (or *basic*) *education* is applied to the first 9 years of schooling; in Denmark, most children have the same class teacher from age 7 to age 16. In most other Western European countries, children make a sharp break into secondary education some time between the ages of 10 and 12, and lower-secondary schooling takes place under the heavy shadow of upper-secondary education.

No country has come to formulate the education of children in the middle years mainly in terms of their own specific needs and characteristics. The example of France, which has made an effort to do so with a specific school for 11- to 15-year-olds (the *collège*), illustrates why not. The style of this institution has been strongly influenced by the competition to enter a prestigious upper-secondary school (the *lycée*); the teaching practices and curriculum of the *collège* mimic those of the academic *lycée*. Conversely, the Scandinavian schools could be accused of being influenced excessively by the elementary school style, cocooning pupils in too protected an environment. There have been repeated concerns about children unused to the more competitive atmosphere of secondary school finding it hard to cope when they graduate to that level at age 16.

In many respects, measures to introduce practices appropriate to the middle years stand more chance of succeeding in a predominantly primary than in a predominantly secondary school environment. Denmark has lengthened the period in which children prepare to make choices at age 16 to 3 years; Sweden has increased testing in the middle years. Perhaps the biggest potential problem is the subject competence of teachers in the primary school model, with less specialized teachers. Reservations about middle schools in England focus on doubts that they can provide specialized instruction of the same quality found in secondary schools. This may create a trade-off requiring a decision about educational priorities: Is it more important for a 13-year-old to be in a secure and friendly environment or to maximize the academic quality of his or her instruction?

Issue 2: Together or separate: Should the middle years be a common experience or adapted to different needs?

Unlike the United States, most European countries either separate children by ability sometime in the middle years or have done so in the relatively recent past. Germany, Switzerland, and the Netherlands still divide pupils into separate tracks at the end of primary school; these countries are starting to see the need to lengthen the period of common education.[1] But countries such as France, Italy, the Czech Republic, and Denmark that have abolished selection in favor of a completely common education in the middle years are starting to wonder whether they might have taken uniformity too far.

The problem is that at the end of the lower-secondary cycle, pupils still have to make important choices about multiple senior high school options. Where everybody has studied an identical curriculum, it can be hard for pupils to make a sudden decision about specialization. There are thus cautious moves in these countries to reintroduce an optional element into lower-secondary schooling.

This situation highlights the problem of two competing demands on schooling in the middle years: On the one hand, it must offer a curriculum that is appropriate to the developmental and learning needs of the young adolescent; on the other, it needs to orient pupils to a future phase of learning. Orientation – the preparation of pupils for a future choice of learning track – is a prominent theme in debates about European middle grade education because of the importance of making the right choices at the senior high school level. But it is also widely considered important for all children in the middle grades to round off their general basic education effectively rather than unduly anticipating the tracking that follows.

Issue 3: Equal success or equal opportunity to fail?

Although the term *opportunity to learn* is not generally used in Europe, concern over disadvantaged groups' ability to cope with the curriculum in the middle years mirrors this issue as it has been formulated in the United States. In Europe, the concern is not just with the growth of certain social phenomena that add to these difficulties (e.g., immigration, drug cultures), but also with the unpreparedness for a rigorous secondary school curriculum of a section of the population that has not hitherto been expected to cope with it. This causes failure as much in Germany, where more pupils are attempting the elite strands of a still-divided secondary school system, as in France, where the least able children find it hard to keep up with an academic-style common curriculum in a single school. In both cases, the failure does not typically lead to early dropout, as in the United States, but rather to repetition of grades, growing demoralization, disaffection with the system, and, ultimately, failure through dropout at a later academic level.

The common curriculum represents a well-founded attempt to raise all students toward the higher educational levels that are needed in modern society and work. But this effort will be translated into a common opportunity to learn only if attention is given to helping the large number of students who face both intellectual and social difficulties that threaten their ability to keep up. France has accepted that pupils leaving elementary school are not always fully prepared for a formal secondary curriculum, and plans to concentrate in the first lower-secondary year on identifying what pupils have learned and giving them individual help with any difficulties.

Cultural and linguistic diversity complicates this issue in most of Western Europe, which has become far more ethnically mixed due to recent immigration. There is not room in this chapter to deal with the many complex issues related to educating a multiethnic population – issues that are not confined to the middle years. But one problem of particular relevance to early secondary education that has arisen in several European countries is worth noting.

Special classes for linguistic and cultural minorities, if unaccompanied by efforts to make mainstream education more multicultural in approach, risk marginalizing the groups targeted for help. In France and Germany, genuine efforts have been made to assist educationally the large numbers of recent immigrants, but conservative, monocultural approaches to curriculum content remain relatively intact. In Scandinavia, tolerance and understanding has allowed resources to flow into mother-tongue tuition (especially in Sweden), but this has sometimes helped sustain ghettoes.

It is in early secondary education that exclusion from the mainstream starts to become a systematic and often irreversible disadvantage. This can be seen most clearly in the Netherlands, where, despite a genuine commitment to intercultural education (since 1984, a compulsory component of initial teacher training in the Netherlands existing nowhere else in Europe), 12-year-olds of foreign origin are assigned overwhelmingly to the lowest academic track, which is often a dead end. In Britain, the creation of a more genuinely multicultural mainstream is at least an aspiration in the dominant professional ideology, although still far from a reality. Perhaps ironically, after the limited success of native multiculturalism (e.g., the Welsh in Britain, the Alsatians in France) in the 1970s, and of immigrant multiculturalism in the 1980s, it is another force that in the 1990s might have the best chance of making national curricula less monocultural: the pluralism of European integration.

Issue 4: The organization of teaching and counseling: Qualified specialists or caring generalists?

It is a common experience to children in most European countries to switch from having a single class teacher in elementary school to having a different teacher for each subject in secondary school. In Denmark, the outstanding exception, specialized teaching builds up progressively over the years. Another country where the switch is less sudden is Italy, where even elementary schools are abandoning the practice of the single class teacher.

One aspect of European education that makes the switch to multiple teachers less harsh than it might otherwise be is the common curriculum. With every child studying the same subjects, a class of pupils is easily kept together and normally allocated a "home" teacher who interacts with the subject specialists about each child's progress. This often amounts in practice to what in the United States would be referred to as *team teaching*.

In many European countries, the concept of counseling or separate pastoral care plays a negligible role in the school system. Counseling is effectively deprofessionalized. It becomes the responsibility of either the class teacher or another teacher with special counseling responsibilities but not specific training as a counselor.

One merit of relying on this form of advice is demonstrated by the unsatisfactory nature in England and France of overstretched professional services detached from schools. The experience of career and counseling interviews provided by such services is that they often fail to relate directly to any help the child may be getting at an everyday level in school. Thus a well-integrated, mainly teacher-based form of guidance would seem the ideal, as long as it succeeds in identifying student difficulties. The size, organization, and environment of the school may be a more important influence than the formal nature of pastoral duties. Certainly a Danish teacher in a small school with small classes who has been teaching the same pupil for 9 years seems well placed to identify and cope with problems as they arise.

Issue 5: Academic instruction or educating the whole person?

In many countries the middle years of schooling are a time when a number of new pressures and requirements arise simultaneously. Not only must the student get used to the increased rigors of secondary school, but the curriculum is generally fuller than at any other stage. Foreign languages, particular social and natural science disciplines, and subjects such as technology and computer studies get added to the curriculum, and there is not yet an opportunity to specialize. At the same time, there is an evident need to raise the awareness of the young adolescent in less academic areas such as health, citizenship, and sex education. The pressures of adulthood are crowding in from every angle.

Several school systems have acknowledged the need for a better balance between academic instruction and the education of the whole person, but under pressure the former has a tendency to command more teaching effort than the latter. In England, teachers find it hard to do justice to the five "cross-curricular themes" such as health education when they have just acquired a 10-subject national curriculum for 11- to 14-year-olds with detailed attainment targets in each discipline. In the Netherlands, it took intensive parliamentary lobbying to get "social and life skills" into the lower-secondary curriculum – as the 15th compulsory subject, with just 3% of teaching time.

In practice, the degree to which teaching heeds the development of the individual rather than merely imparting knowledge is likely to depend on the teaching philosophy applied to the mainstream subjects rather than the addition of "social" ones. Several countries, including the Netherlands and England, are trying to move toward the development of useful skills as well as subject knowledge throughout the curriculum. In the Czech Republic, there is a concerted attempt to move away from didactic teaching and to create syllabuses that emphasize human moral qualities, democratic coexistence, and values such as tolerance.

Issue 6: Can schools be made "communities for learning"?

The environment of a school is influenced as much by national culture and local circumstance as by conscious policies to create a learning culture. Smaller schools in tightly knit communities start with a natural advantage. So do schools in countries where parents have a strong tradition of participating in school life, and where teachers feel valued and respected. But countries have also made specific attempts to encourage the creation of learning communities, for example by:

1. Giving greater autonomy to school leaders. This virtually universal trend in European countries can potentially enhance the sense of identity and mission of a school, although there is also a risk that in becoming a manager of resources, the principal's important role as educational leader is diminished.
2. Encouraging contacts in schools that go beyond the single-subject specialist teaching a 50-minute lesson. Cross-disciplinary work would seem a feasible option in the middle grades in European schools, where one group of children studies a common set of subjects. But curricula that define subject content and attainment targets in terms

of the traditional disciplines can make multidisciplinary work less likely. England's adoption of a national curriculum appears to have checked a growing enthusiasm for projects crossing subject boundaries.

3. Creating new links with parents and others in the community beyond the school. Many countries involve parents in formal advisory structures, but parental involvement on a day-to-day level seems a more important way of extending the educative mission of the school into the home. Most countries acknowledge the need for regular information for parents, but there are wide differences in terms of how readily outsiders are welcomed into classrooms. England and the Netherlands have a stronger tradition of involvement than France and Italy, where classrooms are still mainly regarded as places for professionals. In all countries there is a much greater involvement of parents at the elementary than at the secondary level, related partly to the more open timetable where there is a single multidisciplinary teacher. But conversely, involvement of businesses in school life is growing, in particular at the upper-secondary level in European schools. Middle grade schools could potentially fall between these two kinds of involvement, or alternatively could get involved in both of them.

Issue 7: Can schools become "health-promoting environments"?

Health education has rarely been more than an adjunct to the activities and curricula of schools. In some cases, students are told of certain prescriptions for healthy living and encouraged to avoid potentially harmful activities. What is less common is a school that goes beyond disseminating this information and makes a healthy ethos an integral part of all its activities. But there is now a growing movement of schools that aim systematically to become health-promoting environments.

The health-promoting school entails a two-way relationship between health and education. On the one hand, it aims to reduce health risks to children as they grow up, helping them to gain greater understanding of and control over their own health as they pass through adolescence and then into adulthood. At the same time, it aims to use health to enhance education. Children who are mentally and physically healthy, in a school with a healthy physical environment, a healthy staff, and a healthy ethos, are well positioned to learn effectively.

Health-promoting schools also involve the wider community beyond their walls, including health professionals and parents, in a joint effort to promote healthy lifestyles. This collaboration entails, most importantly, the involvement of children themselves in devising health-promoting strategies and in taking responsibility for their own health.

There is no single model of what a health-promoting school should look like. Yet it is possible to identify some essential features likely to be present in any school that has a comprehensive policy for health promotion, rather than merely adopting one or two measures in isolation. In particular:

1. The *content* of health-promoting activities should be wide-ranging, and should encourage an overall understanding of health rather than a list of dos and don'ts. It is possible to teach a lot about health to children of all ages through an imaginative science curriculum. Stanford University in California has developed a human biology curriculum geared to the developmental needs of children in American middle schools. It does so by offering 22 modules that teach children about themselves through hands-on learning, and allows them to draw connections between biological and behavioral phenomena. A curriculum for health promotion in its broader sense needs to address key life skills that empower young people to develop healthy lifestyles. These include communication skills, relation-building skills, stress management skills, and self-esteem. A project led by health authorities in Donegal, Ireland, helps secondary schools to develop such skills by providing resource materials appropriate for children at various ages. Young people entering secondary school need help with such things as the transition to a new environment, study skills, safety, hygiene, and self-esteem. For those in their final year, matters such as stress management, job hunting, and homemaking become more relevant.

2. The creation of health-promoting schools should enlist the *involvement* of as wide a range of people inside and outside the school as possible. A health-promoting school cannot be created merely by a principal's decree or by the enthusiasm of an individual science teacher. It needs to be created with the active and willing participation of all those with an interest in healthy schooling. This includes, in particular, the children themselves, but also the staff working at the school, other adults in the surrounding community including parents, and staff in various professional services.

3. These various people need to *cooperate* to ensure that their efforts blend into a single strategy rather than working in isolation. A reduction in teacher isolation can involve, on the one hand, better com-

munication among the various teachers of an individual student and, on the other, the development of cross-curricular projects. Both forms of cooperation involve a change in the cultural norms of schools, which vary from one country to another. Team teaching – the allocation of a relatively small group of pupils to a set of common teachers, who discuss their progress – is an important innovation in large, "factory" high schools in the United States but is a less necessary innovation in smaller, less anonymous schools of some European countries. Cross-curricular collaboration, on the other hand, contradicts the traditions of some European countries such as Germany, where the focus of teacher training and of teachers' self-concept is their subject discipline. In such systems, the teacher's norms are derived from the state or national curriculum devised outside the school more than from internal school initiatives. Yet in many European countries, notably France and Spain, this tradition is being challenged, and the change is increasingly being led by schools themselves rather than by a central inspectorate.

4. Health promotion must be integrated with the school's *long-term mission* as an organization. Research on school effectiveness has stressed the importance of a shared vision and goals within a school as influencing student outcomes. Not just examination results but also behavior, delinquency, and attendance have been shown to be influenced by elements of the school's ethos, including strong and participative leadership, unity of purpose, an orderly and attractive environment, and a commitment to developing staff in a "learning organization."

5. The *health perspective* should take its place alongside the educational perspective in bringing up young people. Considerations influencing the health and educational development of young people do not always point in identical directions. To pursue health objectives alongside educational objectives in schools, it will be necessary for community health professionals to work cooperatively with educators, considering the best overall interests of children rather than assessing their educational and health needs in isolation.

In Europe, the importance of links between health and education has typically been recognized more recently than in North America. But the ideal of the health-promoting school has now been formulated by 3 international organizations, and recognized by 28 countries and 500 schools attended by a total of more than 200,000 pupils. These are the participants in the European Network of Health Promoting Schools, a joint project of the World Health Organization, the Council of Europe, and the Commission of the European Communities. The aim of this network, initiated in 1992, is "to provide a coherent framework in which to foster and sustain innovation, to disseminate models of good practice and to make opportunities for health promotion in schools more equitably available throughout Europe." The network identifies core schools in each country, served by national support centers, as well as providing strategic support through an international planning committee.

The rapid growth in membership of the European Network of Health-Promoting Schools is an example of the potential power of the idea of health as a focus of school improvement. But espousing an idea is not the same as translating it into action. There is a real danger that *health-promoting school* will become a fashionable label rather than a mark of genuine commitment to promoting healthy living and healthy learning in all school activities.

It is important that any school seeking to promote health develop a clear strategy for action. The content of this strategy will relate to particular local circumstances, but it should address in particular five key issues: (1) the mustering of professional will; (2) the mustering of community effort; (3) involving students in the process; (4) integration with other curricular objectives; and (5) evaluation.

A tentative conclusion

The various attempts to reform the middle grades of schooling in European countries have not managed to resolve a fundamental dilemma. If these grades base their style and programs too heavily on the secondary school model, they risk neglecting the particular needs of young adolescents and creating courses that discourage them from learning. If, on the other hand, there is a distinctive model for the middle grades, will students be able to cope adequately when they pass on to the next phase, for which they have received little preparation?

This dilemma can perhaps be resolved only if there is a genuine change in ideas about the purposes of schooling and the nature of scholastic achievement. Most European systems still measure and value school achievement largely in terms of passing examinations in academic subjects, usually at some time close to the end of secondary education. The needs of young adolescents may include preliminary preparation for this task, but also include the development of confidence, skills, and attributes that will help them to learn and to develop in a balanced way toward mature adulthood. These are attainments that are less easily certificated and less consciously valued, but they are often prerequisites for successful and productive learning beyond the middle years.

There is now a growing acceptance of the rationale for transforming schools into healthy and health-promoting environments. But even those who see this logic may not always feel that it should be a high priority. Educators are being asked to do many different things simultaneously. There is pressure to improve the quality of teaching of basic subjects such as reading and mathematics; employers are calling for schools to create new kinds of skills appropriate to a modern workplace; schools are struggling to cope with truancy, dropout, and the alienation of young people from learning; they are having to confront new organizational tasks as responsibilities devolve from the governmental to the school level. Is this the time to take on yet another burden, the promotion of children's health?

It will be possible to give a high priority to strategies for health-promoting schools only if they are seen as helping to *resolve* these other issues rather than competing with them. If paying attention to the school's health in the widest sense is seen as an effective way of reducing dropout, improving learning, and shaping the school's organizational ethos, the health-promoting school will become an attractive strategy. It is therefore essential that its proponents make it clear to all concerned that this is a comprehensive approach to fulfilling a school's mission, rather than merely a means of promoting health education in a competing hierarchy of school subjects and activities.

Note

1. In this chapter, *tracking* is used in its American sense of dividing pupils by ability, whether into different schools or into groups within schools. In Britain, *streaming* is used to describe the practice of dividing pupils into different classes based on ability.

References

Carnegie Council on Adolescent Development, Task Force on Education of Young Adolescents. (1989). *Turning points: Preparing American youth for the 21st century.* Washington, DC: Author.

Hirsch, D. (1994). *Schooling for the middle years: Developments in eight European countries.* Washington, DC: Carnegie Council on Adolescent Development.

Johann Jacobs Foundation. (1995). *Annual Report 1995.* Geneva: Author.

5. The role of the school in comprehensive health promotion

KLAUS HURRELMANN AND ANDREAS KLOCKE

Introduction

Despite all advances in technology and medicine, the protection of the health of youth is at risk under present-day conditions. The widespread idea that children and adolescents have a particular vitality and good health seems to be challenged by the confirmed health impairments and health-threatening behaviors. Although it has been possible to successfully suppress the traditional, mostly infectious diseases, new kinds of health risks and diseases are being exhibited in this age group as well as health-threatening behaviors and lifestyles, which can be traced back, in part, to long-term strains on physical, mental, and social adaptation (Hurrelmann and Lösel, 1990; Lösel and Bender, 1991; Millstein, 1989).

The high incidence of psychosomatic complaints, chronic disease, and mental disorder, as well as behavioral health risks to which adolescents are exposed through drug use, careless behavior in driving automobiles, poor nutrition, insufficient physical exercise, unprotected sexual activity, and self-destructive and aggressive behavior, has shown a marked increase in recent years (Engel and Hurrelmann, 1989; Remschmidt, 1987; Weber, 1990). The causes of these many-sided phenomena of psychosocial risk and strain are found at least partially in living conditions, and in the conditions of the natural, social, and technological environments (Hurrelmann, 1989). Only too clearly, the results of research on the health of the young have shown that major factors of health impairment and health-threatening behaviors in children and adolescents are due to changed living conditions. Less stable family relationships, increasing achievement demands, consumer and leisure-time stress, and pluralized values provide external conditions that impede the development of a stable personality and an accompanying healthy lifestyle during adolescence (Engel and Hurrelmann, 1993; Nordlohne, 1992).

82

In this chapter, we will (1) give an overview of the state of adolescents' health and (2) elaborate on concepts and models of health promotion in schools, discussing modern interdisciplinary approaches.

Current health and health behaviors of children and adolescents

Many health impairments and health-threatening behaviors in childhood and adolescence are based on objectively threatening living conditions. The broad spectrum of risks that can be experienced by these age groups is related not only to ecological risks, but also to socially and emotionally stressful life circumstances in school, work, the family, and leisure time. The health of adolescents is very much shaped by these everyday strains. Furthermore, the health status and health behaviors of adolescents have to be seen in the context of maturing, finding one's own gender role, separating from parents, and engaging in peer-group activities. Thus, risky health behaviors reflect and can be interpreted as a reaction to the stressful transition from childhood to adulthood.

However, the latest survey data for Germany show that the vast majority of adolescents rate their health as "very good" or "rather good." These findings support the assumption that adolescence can be regarded as a very healthy phase of life. A closer look at the survey data provides a more complex picture.

The findings from Germany presented in this chapter are from the Health Behavior in School Aged Children (HBSC) Survey, a World Health Organization collaborative study (World Health Organization, 1994). The survey is carried out at schools and addresses students 11, 13, and 15 years of age. The project offers substantial information about the perceived health and health behaviors of school-age children. Besides providing basic scientific comparative knowledge about health in young people, the project encourages health promotion and health education at school and fosters health promotion policies in general. Data are gathered by regular surveys at schools in a growing number of countries.

In the 1993–1994 survey, 24 mainly European countries cooperated. German data are based on a quota sampling by age group, type of school, and region. The survey was conducted in spring 1994 in the federal state of North Rhine–Westphalia, offering good insights into the living and health conditions of western German adolescents. North Rhine–Westphalia is the largest federal state in Germany, with 18 million inhabitants.

If we look at the self-reported health (health status and psychosocial well-being) data, two main findings emerge (Table 5.1). The older the young people, the less healthy they regard themselves. This conclusion reflects growing strains and more risky health behaviors as they get older. The second finding shows gender differences. Boys rate their health status as significantly better than girls do.

The psychosocial well-being variables support these findings. These variables can be regarded as a measure of health in general. They show the same pattern: Boys are healthier than girls, and greater dissatisfaction may be observed with the process of aging. These findings highlight differences in the perceived health of adolescents by gender and age, which gives hints to gender- and age-specific life conditions. These factors need to be considered when implementing health-promoting programs. Although the vast majority of adolescents regard their health as good or very good, recent increases in chronic diseases and psychosocial disorders point toward growing stress in the everyday life of adolescents. Table 5.2 gives an overview of self-reported ailments and symptoms.

The list of eight items covers physiological and psychological complaints of adolescents from 11 to 15 years of age. Single items show variation with age; even more significant differences can be observed by gender. Girls report a much higher prevalence rate of symptoms than boys do. Correspondingly, they report higher use of prescribed drugs. These observed gender and age differences in health reflect societal sex roles, as well as an increasing need to manage developmental change in the process of aging. Health behaviors can be interpreted as coping with developmental problems and frictions, as well as serving as a functional tool to help an adolescent become integrated into a peer group and determine his or her own social role.

Next, we will focus on nicotine and alcohol consumption, the most widespread health-threatening behaviors in adolescence. In Table 5.3, smoking is presented by age group.

Smoking in adolescence is a major health concern because a large number of young people who smoke can be expected to continue smoking into adulthood. Smoking is therefore a primary concern of health education in schools. Our survey data show that by the age of 11, 16%, and by the age of 15, over half (60%) of all students questioned have tried smoking. Gender differences are less significant here. However, the proportion of daily smokers increases from 0.5% by the age of 11 to 18% by the age of 15. By the age of 11, those who smoke more or less regularly smoke up to 10 cigarettes per week; by the age of 15, they smoke much

Table 5.1. *Health status and psychosocial well-being among German adolescents in the North Rhine–Westphalia region (figures in percentages)*

Group	Very healthy	Quite healthy	Not very healthy	Very happy in life	Very often self-confident	Very often helpless	Very often lonely	Distribution of respondents (%)
11-year-olds	45	49	5	41	39	6	10	34
13-year-olds	36	58	6	26	30	6	12	34
15-year-olds	32	61	7	23	30	7	12	32
Boys	45	51	4	33	42	4	8	49
Girls	31	61	8	28	25	9	14	51
Total	38	56	6	30	33	6	11	100
								N = 3,324

Source: Health behaviour in school aged chlidren. (1994). A WHO Cross-National Survey. Copenhagen: World Health Organization–Europe.

Table 5.2. *Ailments and symptoms experienced more than once a week by German adolescents in the North Rhine–Westphalia region (figures in percentages)*

Group	Headache	Stomach ache	Backache	Feeling low	Irritability or bad temper	Feeling nervous	Difficulties in getting to sleep	Feeling dizzy	Distribution of respondents (%)
11-year-olds	14	10	7	6	18	11	20	8	34
13-year-olds	11	7	10	6	18	13	17	8	34
15-year-olds	13	6	12	7	17	14	14	9	32
Boys	7	4	8	4	15	11	15	5	49
Girls	19	11	11	9	20	15	19	11	51
Total	13	8	9	7	18	13	17	8	100
									N = 3,143

Source: Health behaviour in school aged chldren. (1994). A WHO Cross-National Survey. Copenhagen: World Health Organization–Europe.

Table 5.3. *Smoking habits of German adolescents in the North Rhine–Westphalia region (figures in percentages)*

	11-year-olds	13-year-olds	15-year-olds
Ever smoked	16.3	42.5	60.0
Smoke daily	.5	5.1	17.9
Smoke weekly	.4	3.6	7.3
Smoke < weekly	3.0	8.2	8.0
Do not smoke	96.1	83.0	66.8
			N = 3,307
Smokers who:			
Smoke 1–10 cigarettes/week	93.3	61.0	36.9
Smoke 11–20 cigarettes/week	6.7	17.1	17.1
Smoke 21–40 cigarettes/week	—	15.1	17.4
Smoke 41+ cigarettes/week	—	6.8	28.6
			N = 463

Source: Health behaviour in school aged children. (1994). A WHO Cross-National Survey. Copenhagen: World Health Organization–Europe.

more frequently. Nearly 30% reported smoking 40 or more cigarettes per week. Thus, by the age of 11, most smoking is occasional, but by the age of 15, it becomes more regular; almost 3 out of 10 in this age group can be regarded as smokers.

Alcohol consumption in childhood and adolescence is a second major area of prevention and intervention at schools. About 80% of all young people reported having tried an alcoholic beverage. Again, there is no significant difference between boys and girls in drinking behavior. Even in the youngest age group, two out of three reported that they have already tried an alcoholic drink. By the age of 15, almost all (92%) have tried an alcoholic drink. The percentage of young people who have been drunk at least once is 23%, but almost none of those in the youngest age group reported to have ever been drunk. By the age of 15, every second student (47%) has. In Table 5.4 we can see the proportion of young people who drink weekly and daily by different beverages.

Those who report drinking an alcoholic beverage daily are very few. More relevant is the number of students who drink weekly. Almost

Table 5.4. *Alcohol consumption among German adolescents in the North Rhine–Westphalia region (figures in percentages)*

	Beer		Wine/Sparkling Wine		Spirits/Liquor	
	Daily	Weekly	Daily	Weekly	Daily	Weekly
11-year-olds	0.7	1.1	0.3	0.9	0.5	0.3
13-year-olds	0.7	2.5	0.4	1.5	0.3	1.5
15-year-olds	1.3	18.4	0.5	4.9	0.3	6.8
Boys	1.2	9.3	0.3	2.0	0.4	2.8
Girls	0.7	5.6	0.5	2.6	0.4	3.0
Total	0.9	7.4	0.4	2.3	0.4	2.9

$N = 2,933$

Source: Health behaviour in school aged children. (1994). A WHO Cross-National Survey. Copenhagen: World Health Organization–Europe.

every fifth adolescent by age 15 reports drinking beer weekly. Wine and spirits are consumed in this age group weekly by 5 and 7%, respectively. By the age of 15, the number of young people who report drinking anything alcoholic regularly rises substantially. The proportion for the 11- and 13-year-olds is rather low.

The data for Germany, which can stand for most of the industrialized countries, show the following results. Although most young people consider themselves to be very or rather healthy and fit, there are substantial health problems. In addition to the more traditional ailments and diseases, we find a growing number of children and adolescents who report negative beliefs about their mental and social well-being. Here there are significant gender differences, which suggest that different approaches are warranted in implementing health-promoting programs at schools. Analysis of the data also shows that unhealthy behaviors, like alcohol consumption and smoking, are correlated. Thus, it is likely that there are groups of young people who have a more unhealthy lifestyle than others. This suggests that health-promotion programs at schools should be designed for lifestyle groups rather than for individuals; furthermore, they should cover the broader social background and circumstances of the groups in question.

Changes in the spectrum of diseases, and the fact that it is particularly behavior-related and socially induced life habits and lifestyles that predominantly determine the incidence of death and disease in Western industrial societies, have to be recognized in theory building: What is needed is not only an expansion of traditional (medical) explanations of the etiology of health impairments and disease, but also the development of innovative concepts and orientations to health prevention and maintenance.

The importance of children and adolescents as a target group for preventive measures is shown by the fact that almost 80% of the incidence of adult death and disease in Germany, with comparable statistics in other industrialized countries, is determined by a few, mostly behavior-related diseases (Kleiber, 1992). The roots of these diseases are often found in behavioral dispositions and lifestyles that frequently go back to childhood and adolescence. Therefore, childhood and adolescence take on a key function for adult health. It is estimated that approximately 50% of adult mortality is directly related to basically modifiable factors that are acquired, above all, during adolescence (Millstein, 1989). Many of the behaviors and lifestyles that determine the health of adults have their origins in the life phase when children and adolescents attend school. In addition, this life phase is decisive for the acquisition and consolidation of general value orientations and beliefs that affect broad areas of health in later life (Tones, Tilford, and Robinson, 1990).

Theoretical foundations and guidelines for promoting health in childhood and adolescence

Recent years have seen a marked increase in interest in improving the health of children and adolescents. Numerous health education programs and various individual activities have been developed to strengthen the health and health-related behavior of adolescents (Hesse and Hurrelmann, 1991). Discussion over the last 20 years about traditional methods of health education, which mostly operate through publicity campaigns, has clearly demonstrated the limited impact of such strategies. Available findings, particularly from the United States, show that although such programs increase knowledge, they do not lead to the establishment of correspondingly positive behaviors in adolescents (Connell, Turner, and Mason, 1985; Kolbe, 1985; Rundall and Bruvold, 1988).

A major reason for the relative ineffectiveness of traditional health education, which is based on teaching rational knowledge and giving warnings about risks, is their systematic exclusion of the social life (Franzkowiak, 1986; Jessor, 1984). The limited breadth of the traditional conception, particularly with regard to the promotion of health in children and adolescents, has also been shown by the failure to address the lifestyle of the young, which is characteristically directed less toward health-protecting behavior than toward the satisfaction of expressive and social needs.

In its fixation on the medical model of disease etiology, health education has additionally concentrated on the individual in a reductionist way and has mostly failed to address the ecological and social living conditions as prerequisites for the maintenance of health (Franzkowiak, 1993). As prior experiences have shown, to be effective, health education has to be embedded in structural measures that take into account the relationship between health and the environment, and that aim to improve the living conditions of children and adolescents (Anderson, Davies, Kickbusch, McQueen, and Turner, 1988; Coates, Petersen, and Perry, 1982).

From this point of view, various measures for improving living and environmental conditions for the young have been discussed in recent years under the heading of "health promotion" (Millstein, Petersen, and Nightingale, 1993). Health promotion aims to avoid and diminish health-threatening factors in the everyday world of young people. In this comprehensive conception, it includes strategies directed toward the behavior and conditions of life. Strategies support individuals, as well as institutions and organizations. Health promotion aims to recognize health-threatening factors and, at the same time, to develop policies to deal with these factors both individually and collectively (WHO, 1986).

Health promotion is conceived as a preventive intervention within an ecological and contextual framework that is directed toward the social, mental, and physical well-being of children and adolescents within the family, preschool, school, and leisure-time contexts. Recent concepts focus on the promotion of individual and social well-being by (1) strengthening individual competencies and resources and (2) creating a healthy environment. In these concepts, behavior-related measures target the improvement of social and emotional competence in the young and their ability to deal with conflict. They also support healthy attitudes and the ability to develop an active involvement in a healthy lifestyle. Furthermore, this approach is based on the assumption that an optimal design of the social and natural environments of human beings can contribute significantly to individual well-being.

All measures to increase individual self-esteem and competence in students, as well as to improve working, learning, and living conditions, are of fundamental importance here (Hurrelmann, 1990; Tones, et al., 1990). In recent years, emphasis has been placed on family, youth work, school, nonschool education, and vocational training, not only to promote individual competence, but also to highlight the relevance of the social world and environment for health-related behaviors in children and adolescents. Among the range of measures, the school is assigned a dominant role because nowadays the school can unwillingly contribute to the incidence of health impairments in both teachers and students (Cole and Walker, 1989; Nordlohne and Hurrelmann, 1990).

The role of the school in comprehensive health promotion

What role can realistically be assigned today to the social institution of the school within the spectrum of measures to promote health? The potential of schools is easily overestimated in the public discussion. As most members of an age cohort attend school up to their teens, it guarantees relatively good access to the young generation. However, the task of teaching knowledge and awarding certificates sets structural constraints. In order to promote health, measures should be directed toward all areas of the daily life of children and adolescents. The school is only one area among many others. It cannot counteract all stresses and tensions originating in other life areas such as the family, leisure time, and housing. In addition, the school itself has become a serious stress factor, a potential risk factor for the healthy development of the young through increasingly higher qualification demands.

The official introduction of health education into the schools in recent years has been an encouraging step toward the general adoption of health-related topics in the school domain. However, the role of the school regarding comprehensive measures to promote health is increasingly less evident in cognitive, curricular, educational components. As in the program formulated by David and William (1987), health promotion in schools refers not only to the provision of knowledge and information on health-related topics but also to the following:

1. Supporting healthy lifestyles and presenting realistic possibilities and alternatives for leading a healthy life by providing children and adolescents with competencies that enable them to participate without restrictions in all social processes.
2. Promoting the ability to shape and exploit physical, mental, and social potentials that help to stabilize the self-concept.
3. Furnishing and developing abilities and social life skills such as the ability to make one's own decisions and stand by them, to cope with stress, and to deal with conflictual situations in a healthy way.
4. Encouraging a sense of responsibility for individual, family, and community health.

Health promotion addresses the entire ecological, social, and emotional school life and experience of children and adolescents. Therefore, a purely cognitive orientation toward health education would overlook the fact that the school itself represents an essential criterion on the health of students (Kolbe, 1987). As research on school climate, school efficacy, organizational development, and school ecology has shown, each school provides a specific (quality) profile that is relevant not only to students' academic achievement, but also to their emotional, affective, and social development (Allensworth and Wolford, 1988; Anderson, 1982; Epstein and Jackson, 1981; Hoy, Tarter, and Kottkamp, 1991; Lange, Kuffner, and Schwarzer, 1983; Moos, 1979; Rutter, Manghan, Mortimore, and Ouston, 1979).

Although not all of these studies focused explicitly on relationships to health and health behaviors in students (as well as teachers), their findings provide important information on how far specific school conditions promote those areas of personality development that are essential prerequisites for a healthy lifestyle (self-esteem, strategies for coping with problems and conflict, perception of anxiety, etc.). There is an urgent need for further studies in this field, addressing the relationship between school-specific effects and health-related aspects of student behavior. With a few exceptions, insufficient attention has also been paid to the ecological (physical) environment of the school (Drach, 1985; Dreesmann, 1983; Weinstein, 1979). It also should not be overlooked that their specific openness to and connection with nonschool organizations (e.g., counseling centers, health departments) enables schools to become a major resource in promoting healthy behavior (Green, 1984; Kolbe, 1987).

Possibilities of promoting health in schools

The following section analyzes the potential for and limitations in promoting health in schools. As shown previously, the capacities and channels through which the school can promote student health and health-related behaviors do not lie in specific measures alone, but also in the social and ecological conditions of the school and school life in general. Therefore, we shall consider in more detail (1) the curricular dimension, (2) the social dimension, (3) the ecological dimension, and (4) the community dimension of health promotion in schools (see Figure 5.1).

These dimensions are dealt with separately only for the sake of presentation. Naturally, they are very closely interwoven in real life. All four dimensions are of equal significance. Accordingly, they should receive equal consideration when evaluating schools that are participating in a health promotion network.

The curricular dimension of promoting health

For a long time, there were great hopes that school education would be able to deal with all issues comprehensively through a curriculum-related, informative health education strategy. Reported outcomes are not bad, but they clearly show the limitations of this strategy. It is only under specific circumstances that knowledge and information are factors that can modify socially embedded health behavior because it is not at-

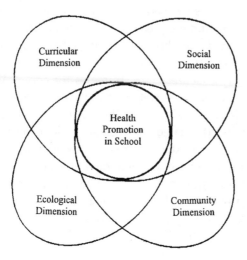

Figure 5.1. Health promotion in school.

tractive and meaningful, in the world of the young, to behave in an objectively healthy way in every situation. Particularly in childhood and adolescence, health-threatening behavior is closely linked to daily routines and included in a typical lifestyle. Therefore, mere knowledge about the health risk of a behavior does not play a controlling role in the arrangement of personal activity. As available outcome evaluations of curricular health education confirm, teaching cannot be assumed to have a direct effect on the behavior of children and adolescents (Botvin, 1986; Connell, et al., 1985; Rundall and Bruvold, 1988; Zins, Wagner, and Maher, 1986).

However, well-designed teaching programs attain a clear improvement in knowledge and also influence health-related attitudes. Here, it is very important to connect up with children's and adolescents' subjective ideas about health and illness, as well as their self-image and lifestyle. Health in schools has to take into account the specific lifestyle of children and adolescents and has to be supported by a life-affirmative concept. Moral admonishments and threats do not help in this domain; they may even be counterproductive. Health education has to try to go beyond influencing attitudes; it has to reach behavioral dispositions by imparting specific professional and social skills and abilities that are relevant to everyday situations. This brings us close to the topic of the social dimension, which will be discussed in the next section.

At the moment, a substantial anchoring of health-promoting measures in the school lesson is difficult. Should they – as in the dominant practice up to now – be presented outside of school subjects? This might create the risk that the measures will fall between individual school subjects. Would it not be a good idea to select one or, at most, two subjects – for example, biology and social studies – and anchor the majority of health teaching in their curricula? A further question arises from the diversity of topics in health-promoting measures. The presently still separated programs of health education in nutrition, hygiene, exercise, coping with illness, drug prevention, strengthening self-esteem, and so forth, need to be combined into a cohesive concept. There is an urgent need for model projects to test possible ways of improving the intermeshing and networking of these programs.

Modern programs in this field – for example, programs of addiction prevention – start from the premise that preventive measures for adolescents must regard drug use as a functional component of daily life and as an attempt to cope with the demands of this particular life phase. Correspondingly, the focus of all measures is on the psychosocial functions of drug use as a method of coping within the cultural and social conditions relevant to adolescence. The school, as an institution of education and an important area of social experiences, plays a decisive role here. Programs attempt to include concepts in which the active acquisition of information and knowledge and the productive processing of information and knowledge are placed in the foreground.

The German "Life Skills Program" (Landesinstitut für Schule und Weiterbildung, 1988/1993) involves a combination of strategies for influencing information and attitudes. Measures that convey knowledge concerning legal, physiological, and psychological aspects and consequences of drug use and abuse are referred to as *information strategies*. Measures for promoting communication and decision-making abilities, self-assertion, and the ability to define value systems, as well as attempts to convey positive emotional experiences, are referred to as *affective strategies*. Materials and media for this program have been developed as practical aids for work in schools. The program's idea is to support a curriculum, which has a prophylactic effect on addiction.

Its central aim is to encourage social, affective, and cognitive learning; to promote coping in regard to life tasks; and to aid in the acquisition of social and personal competencies. A concept of addiction and drug prevention in school is presented, which is oriented toward theory and practice and which at the same time offers a model of further education for teachers dealing with addiction prevention and drug use in general.

The material is categorized according to focal areas related to lessons, to curricula, and to their application in the classroom:

1. Cognitive contents and relevant information
   a. Information concerning addiction and addictive substances (nicotine, alcohol, medication, illegal substances) and their effects.
   b. Possibilities of therapy and counseling.
   c. Drugs and society.
2. Exercises for developing psychosocial identity
   a. Becoming aware of group pressure.
   b. Developing resistance and learning to say "no."
   c. Becoming aware of group interactions.
   d. Being able to cope with insecurity, anxiety, frustration, failure, and rejection.
   e. Developing decision-making abilities, improving communication, and solving problems.
   f. Improving ego strength.
3. Exercises for improving self-perception
   a. Techniques for increasing and decreasing muscle tension.
   b. Perceiving, verbalizing, and accepting feelings and moods.
   c. Training sensory perception.
4 Becoming aware of values and norms
   a. Becoming familiar with different norms and their consequences for behavior.
   b. Development and change in norms and values.
   c. Becoming aware of personal value scales.
5. Exercises and games for increasing bodily experiences
   a. Experiences with one's own body, reactions, and feelings.
   b. Experiencing emotional reactions to physical symptoms.
   c. Perceiving and overcoming fear of physical contact.

Addiction prophylaxis in school is not only the domain of individual school subjects. The material referred to previously should assist teachers in incorporating the elements into their curricula so that they can utilize their competence as experts and educators. Great importance is placed on the areas of school life that extend beyond the classroom lessons. Within the framework of required subjects, study groups, and common-interest groups, methodical forms of work and social forms can be accentuated to supplement and enrich classroom lessons in an organizational way. School life can emerge only when there is cooperation between curricular and extracurricular activities. Such a school life can then be the platform on which the various appropriate measures against addiction may be implemented in school, coordinated, and brought to fruition.

The central goals of the German Life-Skills Program in school are as follows:

1. To promote adolescents' ability to cope with personal and social problems, conflicts, and the demands of reality in an appropriate and responsible manner.
2. To promote adolescents' ability to deal with drugs in a manner that is conducive to good health, responsible, and in accordance with the law; that means, in particular:
   a. Complete abstinence from illegal substances.
   b. A responsible, self-controlled approach to alcohol, with total abstinence as the ultimate goal.
   c. A responsible, self-controlled approach to tobacco products, with total abstinence as the ultimate goal.
   d. Use of medication in the proper dosage.

With respect to these goals, prevention of addiction in school is not an individual, isolated, drug-specific measure. On the contrary, it is a comprehensive task for all those involved in school: It is a part of the school's task to educate.

The German Life-Skills Program emphasizes that the school cannot be responsible for, nor can it tackle, the wide variety of stimuli and incentives that encourage attitudes to addiction and addictive behavior. At the same time, the program demands that the school define its attitude to the possible causes of and incentives supporting addiction, to be aware of these factors; and, in terms of preventive action, to have a self-critical attitude toward its own role in this respect. In addition, the program refers to experiences with conflicts and problems, which are related to school attendance and consequently must be addressed by preventive measures in school. For many students, the importance of school-leaving certificates for the employment sector, conflict management, and disciplinary measures may lead to experiences of anxiety, failure, insecurity, and helplessness. An active and constructive ability to cope with such experiences and their causes is regarded as an important task in addiction prevention. Teachers as well as students must also view their place of work critically, and accept that they are both participants and target persons.

To enable students to develop such abilities, they should be given ample opportunities to be active, responsible, and autonomous. In this way, numerous forms of dependency that can result in motivational problems, anxiety, and feelings of failure and helplessness can be avoided. The school should in no way be put into a space void of problems and conflicts. Rather, it must provide a positive climate, oriented toward trust and learning, so that the adolescent can develop a confident, appropriate and responsible approach to meeting scholastic demands and dealing with personal difficulties.

The German Life-Skills Program relies on abilities of specially trained contact teachers for health promotion. They are trained for specific tasks of counseling and providing information:

- Problem-oriented and situation-oriented information and counseling from teachers, parents, and students concerning addiction, addictive substances and related attitudes, causes of drug abuse, and alternative behaviors for all concerned.
- Counseling for teacher conferences, common-interest teacher groups, and individual teachers in regard to problems concerning drugs and addiction as a curriculum within various school subjects.
- Counseling for teachers, parents, and students in regard to information, attitudes, and behavior when dealing with students at risk of becoming addicted to drugs.

The social dimension

As the previous analysis has shown, it is important for effective measures to include the entire social environment of children and adolescents in health-promoting measures. Addressing adolescents' relationships to family, school, work, and friends is an appropriate way. As we know, most young persons typically view the school as a kind of workplace for not-yet adults. Characteristic and dominant is the opinion that one has to attend school, because this is the only way to obtain the necessary qualifications and privileges for the time after school, which is practically equated with adulthood (Hurrelmann, 1990). Most students base their school experiences on an instrumental idea: The young view the main task of the school as preparing them for and awarding school-leaving certificates that represent proof of the right to enter certain types of further education and vocational training. This creates major problems for the achievement motivation of children and adolescents.

Today many teachers sense the irritation, the uncertainties, the anticipation, and the pressure to achieve with which students enter school. Many teachers face up to these demands and do their best to respond to the changed needs of their students in an educationally appropriate manner. However, more and more educators are also feeling that they have reached their own limits. Anxiety and restlessness, as well as the increasing susceptibility to psychosomatic and health impairments among students, call for a higher level of educational competence among teachers as well. Probably teachers are objectively facing stronger challenges than before because they are confronted with changed and educationally more difficult demands. The proportion of teachers who themselves suffer from mental, nervous, and health stress has increased greatly in recent years. The term *burnout* describes the final stage of a process in which persons tackle a vocational task with great enthusiasm and idealism and, after a phase of disappointed expectations, unanticipated difficulties, and mounting problems, fall into irritability, indifference, cynicism, and depression. This state of mental exhaustion is found frequently among teachers and other professional groups with a strong focus on working with other people, giving, and helping (Cole and Walker, 1989).

For these reasons, both students and teachers require health education measures that strengthen not only achievement but also personal and – in teachers – professional identity. The potentials available in the school should be exploited fully through educational measures. The literature on the quality of schools provides interesting suggestions here. In recent years, modern pedagogues have repeatedly attempted to determine the social criteria that a school has to meet in order to provide a good social climate and a range of identification possibilities for all persons working in the school domain.

The culture of a school, its specific climate, seems to be the decisive factor in the success or failure of a school as a location of shared learning and living. Corresponding studies have mostly measured quality according to (1) the students' academic achievements and (2) the social qualifications they exhibit (e.g., social responsibility, moral development, cooperativeness [Hoy et al., 1991; Moos, 1979; Rutter et al., 1979]). Some of the criteria found to be decisive in the studies are the following:

1. A good school is characterized by intensive cooperation between teachers on subject matter. Educators do not view themselves as "fighting alone" and doing their best with great mental and nervous

effort, but as cooperating, corresponding, and mutually benefiting professionals.

2. A good school is characterized by continuous shared discussions, explanations, and, as far as possible, commitments to general educational rules of behavior (maintenance and minimum standards of discipline and order, rules for dealing with each other in everyday school life, and rules on homework requirements). This also requires a minimal consensus because it is the only way in which students can perceive the school as a consistent system of rules and as a social system constructed according to recognizable patterns.

3. The effective participation of students and parents in major school and educational concerns is a characteristic of a good school. When students and parents have an opportunity to be involved in planning certain areas of teaching and school policies, they also identify with the school itself. This is of inestimable value for the social climate and the quality of the relationships inside school, and thus for the healthy personality development of the students.

These findings have direct relevance for health promotion. They demonstrate that it is favorable for a school to aim for consensus on important educational program issues that will lead to the development of a characteristic school profile. Clearly structured rules and expectations, opportunities to participate, and cooperation between teachers and students are probably the prerequisites for giving students the feeling of belonging to the community of the school. Students' identification with their school is better in good schools than in others, because good schools take more account of the needs of their students, both in the personal domain and in the design of everyday school life.

The ecological dimension

The school has now become one of the most important places where children and adolescents stay until the end of their teens. If it wants to fulfill its task as an educational institution, it must provide pleasant social and ecological life spaces that are rich in experience. It must offer children and adolescents chances to grow, not only intellectually but also physically, emotionally, and in all the sensory modalities.

For this reason, the ecological setting takes its own place in promoting health in schools. As research on environmental psychology has shown, spatial properties have a direct impact on the well-being of students and teachers and also seem to influence behavior (Weinstein, 1979). The following areas could be components of a healthy school from an ecological perspective:

1. A pleasant and safe building, hallways, and classrooms; outside facilities and sports fields; break rooms and sports facilities, good sanitary facilities.
2. Good working conditions in group activity rooms and classrooms; adequate provision of chairs and tables; sufficient lighting and ventilation; a reliable source of energy; and economic energy usage.
3. Stimulating and safe conditions during breaks and during journeys to and from school; safety measures regarding possible injuries and accidents; architectural blending of the school into its surroundings; improving the paths and links to the community surrounding the school.
4. Good planning of the entire daily program, including the length of work phases, the rhythm of arousal and relaxation, spatial and social niches for individual and group activities, and engaging breaks.
5. Nutritionally well-balanced food and drink on the school premises; gradual introduction of whole foods.
6. Environmentally sound cleaning of school premises; avoiding waste in teaching; and using recyclable materials.

This list should clarify the importance of spatial design, construction, and architecture, as well as the importance of working and environmental conditions for a healthy school. This spectrum of measures has been neglected in recent years because criteria have concentrated too strongly on the curricular and, to some extent, the social dimension. Only slowly is the ecological dimension of health promotion now being discovered.

The community dimension

Finally, we will consider the school in the context of the surrounding community. Many schools have already addressed measures in this area under headings such as "community education" and "opening up the school." This involves opening up the school not only to the world of work (through practical courses, visiting companies, permanent contacts, etc.) but also opening it up to as many organizations in the community as possible (Masey, Gimarc, and Kronenfeld, 1988).

The idea is to integrate the young and their teachers into the life of the community by viewing the possibilities and situations available there as a learning experience. Conversely, the school should be used as a community resource by presenting the role of the school to the public. The idea is to make the school externally conspicuous as an institution in which something is created or produced – in which exhibitions, entertainment, and discussions are held. In addition, clubs and associations, particularly sport associations, should be encouraged to hold activities in their local school.

Opening up the school should include the entire area of psychosocial as well as medical care. An easily accessible and informal counseling system is more important than ever before for children and adolescents. Experience has shown how skeptical particularly the young are toward "health experts" (Engel and Hurrelmann, 1989). Compared to persons in other age groups, 10- to 20-year-olds have little contact with social, psychological, and medical counseling and treatment centers. In this respect, the young, above all those between 10 and 20, are an inadequately serviced population. Although major and far-reaching social, psychological, physiological, and physical changes typically occur in this life phase, fewer members of this group visit physicians and counseling centers compared to members of other age groups.

Visits to general practitioners and internists are not as frequent as they objectively should be. For example, 22% of the young have reported that they suffer from circulatory disorders, but only one-half of this group visited a physician for this reason. It is a similar story for allergies; 18% of the respondents reported that they frequently suffer from such symptoms, but only 12% went to a physician. Many of the young have had no contact with medical or psychological centers for several years (Engel and Hurrelmann, 1989). It is estimated that up to 15% of adolescents do not receive urgently needed medical care. These rates increase dramatically in groups such as ethnic minorities, who live under less favorable economic conditions.

The main reason for insufficient medical care of the young is probably their own behavior. Young people have social and psychological barriers to visiting a physician or other professional counselors. This insecurity among the young is frequently reflected in an insecurity among professionals. Physicians, receptionists, and psychological counselors who have not been specially trained are not prepared for the specific health problems that the young bring to them. This applies particularly to problems that are not discussed openly in our society, such as sexual problems, sexually transmitted diseases, venereal diseases, contraception, and the like. Professionals consider the young to be difficult clients to whom a strong commitment is neither socially nor financially rewarding.

Uncertainty and a lack of commitment by professionals are transmitted, in turn, to the already reticent young, so that these two effects are mutually reinforcing. Therefore, there is an urgent need for new approaches in this area – for example, counseling centers that are less specialized, have low social barriers, are as close to the community as possible, or are even set up close to schools, in order to serve as a first port of call for adolescents with mental, social, and health problems. This could include counseling teachers at schools, counseling services in schools, cooperation with psychosocial and medical services in the community, "school clinics," or other forms of intensive cooperation with the medical service.

Young people need to feel that someone will care about them without reservation or moral criticism when they are faced with mental, sexual, financial, achievement-related, or relationship problems. They will not come if they are anxious about entering into a complicated organization with unclear functions. Therefore, support should be given to all health-promoting schemes that help the young to control and organize their needs themselves. This also urgently requires model projects in the area of health education in the strictest sense. Here as well, the school can be an important provider or partner in providing measures, despite its structural limitations mentioned earlier.

Evaluation and monitoring approaches

Previous evaluation research on measures to promote health in schools has shown how meaningful but also how restricted those measures are that refer to the teaching (curricular) area. It is highly apparent that this area should be conceived as only one of several input variables. Other, important input variables are found in the structural work conditions of schools, their organizational features, their staff facilities, their architecture, and their ecological design, as well as in the framing conditions that contribute to the quality of the social and educational process in the school. These factors together determine the outcome of the school promotion process (Cook, Anson, and Walchli, 1993).

This outcome, in turn, has to be measured on various levels: on pure attitudes, on emotional development and behavioral impulses, as well as on the important variable of social competence. Further development of concepts to promote health in schools involves the methodologically and theoretically difficult task of using this complex model of variables as a background for interpretation. In other words, it is necessary to find out which input variables are most responsible for the quality of school work and at the same time have the most direct impact on the output variables. As soon as this complex network of interactions is understood, it can also be anticipated that specific intervention measures will be applied at precisely those locations in the network that promise a successful outcome.

One important intervention should be to access and address the interaction between teachers and students and between male and female students in the class. The success of input variables is dependent upon their interaction within the educational relationship. For this reason it is, for example, very important that measures to promote health are designed in such a manner that they address individual students in their interactions. Tracing the effects of intervention measures initially requires very broad observations and research approaches. With reference to other fields of the health care system, we could also consider the construction of a monitoring system here.

The goal of such a monitoring system would be to set up sensitive measurement stations at the largest possible number of relevant areas of the school system that could provide reliable and continuous reports on input and output variables. Then it could be possible to introduce changes and connections between the variables on the basis of permanent observation. In concrete terms, this means that a permanent "health report" should be implemented in a school in which precise data could be collected on the following aspects: the social background of the students; the situation in the parental homes, neighborhood, and community influences; baseline conditions in the school; structural and organizational framing conditions of the school and teaching; and so forth.

These data could then be contrasted with the output variables, that is, data on students' academic achievement, their social behavior, and their psychosocial and emotional life situation. Data should be collected carefully over a long period of time. In this way, the work situation of schools could be analyzed by an accompanying research team. If input or output variables change, the school could then respond with appropriate measures. This would equip schools with a feedback system that would not only keep them continuously and precisely informed about their developmental status, but would also enable them to learn gradually how to modify this developmental status. Strictly speaking, specific intervention measures should be applied only when such a precise monitoring system has been established. Only then could those sensitive intervention points be addressed with any empirical certainty.

References

Allensworth, D. B., and Wolford, C. A. (1988). Schools as agents for achieving the 1990 health objectives for the nation. *Health Education Quarterly, 1,* 3–15.

Anderson, C. S. (1982). The search for school climate: A review of the research. *Review of Educational Research, 52,* 368–420.

Anderson, R., Davies, J. K., Kickbusch, I., McQueen, D. V., and Turner, J. (Eds.). (1988). *Health behavior research and health promotion.* New York: Oxford University Press.

Botvin, G. J. (1986). Substance abuse prevention research: Recent developments and future directions. *Journal of School Health, 56,* 369–386.

Coates, T. J., Petersen, A. C., and Perry, C. (Eds.). (1982). *Promoting adolescent health: A dialogue on research and practice.* London: Academic Press.

Cole, M., and Walker, S. (Eds.). (1989). *Teaching and stress.* Oxford: Alden Press.

Connell, D. B., Turner, R. R., and Mason, E. F. (1985). Summary of findings of the school health education: Health promotion effectiveness, implementation, and costs. *Journal of School Health, 55,* 316–322.

Cook, T. B., Anson, A. R., and Walchli, S. B. (1993). From causal description to causal explanation: Improving three already good evaluations of adolescent health programs. In S. G. Millstein, A. C. Petersen, and E. O. Nightingale (Eds.), *Promoting the health of adolescents: New directions for the twenty-first century* (pp. 339–374). New York: Oxford University Press.

David, K., and William, T. (Eds.). (1987). *Health education in schools.* London: Harper & Row.

Drach, W. (1985). Psychologie der Schule. In W. Twellmann (Ed.), *Handbuch Schule und Unterricht* (pp. 1140–1166). Düsseldorf: Schwann.

Dreesmann, H. (1983). Bauliche und physikalische Faktoren der Schulpsychologie und ihre Beziehung zum Verhalten. *Unterrichtswissenschaft, 11,* 149–165.

Engel, U., and Hurrelmann, K. (1989). *Psychosoziale Belastungen im Jugendalter. Empirische Befunde zum Einfluss a von Familie, Schule und Gleichaltrigengruppe.* Berlin: De Gruyter.

Engel, U., and Hurrelmann, K. (1993). *Was Jugendliche wagen. Eine Längsschnittudie über Drogenkonsum, Stressreaktionen und Deliquenz im Jugendalter.* Weinheim: Juventa.

Epstein, J. L., and Jackson, P. W. (Eds.). (1981). *The quality of school life.* Toronto: Lexington.

Franzkowiak, P. (1986). *Risikoverhalten und Gesundheitsbewasstsein bei Jugendlichen.* Berlin: Springer.

Franzkowiak, P. (1993). Gesundheit und Gesundheitsförderung – Ein Ueberblick. In G. Graeaner, C. Mauntel, and E. Püttbach (Eds.), *Gefährdungen von Kindern* (pp. 132–146). Opladen: Leske and Budrich.

Green, L. W. (1984). Modifying and developing health behavior. *Annual Review of Public Health, 5,* 215–236.

Hesse, S., and Hurrelmann, K. (1991). Gesundheitserziehung in der Schule. Ein Ueberblick über inländische und ausländische Konzepte und Programme. *Prävention, 2,* 50–57.

Hoy, W. K., Tarter, J., and Kottkamp, B. (1991). *Open schools – healthy schools: Measuring organizational climate.* Newbury Park, CA: Sage.

Hurrelmann, K. (1989). *Human development and health.* New York: Springer.

Hurrelmann, K. (1990). Health promotion for adolescents. *Journal of Adolescence, 13,* 231–250.

Hurrelmann, K., and Lösel, F. (Eds.). (1990). *Health hazards in adolescence.* New York: De Gruyter.

Jessor, R. (1984). Adolescent development and behavioral health. In J. D. Matarazzo, A. Herd, N. E. Miller, and S. M. Weiss (Eds.), *Behavioral health: A handbook of health enhancement and disease prevention* (pp. 69–90). New York: Wiley.

Kleiber, D. (1992). Gesundheitsförderung: Hintergründe, Grundauffassungen, Konzepte und Probleme. *Psychomed, 4,* 220–230.

Kolbe, C. J. (1985). Why school health education? An empirical point of view. *Health Education, 16,* 116–120.

Kolbe, L. L. (1987). Appropriate function of health education in schools: Improving health and cognitive performance. In N. Krasegnor, I. Araseth, and M. Cataldo (Eds.), *Child health behavior* (pp. 171–216). New York: Wiley.

Landesinstitut für Schule und Weiterbildung (1988/1993). (Ed.). *Sucht- und Drogenvorbeugung in der Schule. Materialien und Medien* (2 volumes). Soest: LSW.

Lange, B., Kuffner, H., and Schwarzer, R. (1983). *Schulangst und Schulverdrossenheit.* Opladen: Westdeutscher Verlag.

Lösel, F., and Bender, D. (1991). Jugend und Gesundheit. In J. Haisch and H. P. Zeitler (Eds.), *Gesundheitspsychologie* (pp. 65–86). Heidelberg: Assanger.

Masey, D., Gimarc, J., and Kronenfeld, J. (1988). School worksite wellness programs: A strategy of achieving the 1990 goals for a healthier America. *Health Education Quarterly, 15,* 53–63.

Millstein, S. G. (1989). Adolescent health: Challenges for behavioral scientists. *American Psychologist, 5,* 837–842.

Millstein, S. G., Petersen, A. C., and Nightingale, E. O. (Eds.). (1993). *Promoting the health of adolescents: New directions for the twenty-first century.* New York: Oxford University Press.

Moos, R. H. (1979). Educational climates. In H. J. Walberg (Ed.), *Educational environments and effects. Evaluation, policy and productivity* (pp. 79–100). Berkeley: Ica McCutchan.

Nordlohne, E. (1992). *Die Kosten jugendlicher Problembewältigung, Alkohol-, Zigaretten- und Arzneimittelkonsum im Jugendalter.* Weinheim: Juventa.

Nordlohne, E., and Hurrelmann, K. (1990). Health impairment, failure in school and the abuse of drugs. In K. Hurrelmann and F. Lösel (Eds.), *Health hazards in adolescence* (pp. 149–166). Berlin: De Gruyter.

Remschmidt, H. (1987). *Kinder und Jugendpsychiatrie: Eine praktische Einführung.* Thieme: Stuttgart.

Rundall, T. G., and Bruvold, W. H. (1988). A meta-analysis of school-based smoking and alcohol use prevention programs. *Health Education Quarterly, 15,* 317–334.

Rutter, M., Manghan, B., Mortimore, P., and Ouston, I. (1979). *Fifteen thousand hours: Secondary schools and their effects on children.* London: Open Books.

Tones, K., Tilford, S., and Robinson, J. K. (1990). *Health education, effectiveness and efficiency.* London: Chapman and Hall.

Weber, I. (1990). *Dringliche Gesundheitsprobleme der Bevölkerung in der Bundesrepublik Deutschland. Zahlen-Fakten-Perspektiven.* Baden-Baden: Nomas.

Weinstein, C. F. (1979). The physical environment of the school: A review of the research. *Review of Educational Research, 4,* 577–610.

World Health Organization. (1986). *Charta health promotion.* Ottawa: Author.

World Health Organization. (1994). *Health behaviour in school aged children: A WHO Cross-National Survey.* Copenhagen: Author.

Zins, J. E., Wagner, D. I., and Maher, C. A. (1986). *Health promotion in the schools. Innovative approaches to facilitating physical and emotional well-being.* New York: Haworth Press.

6. Education for healthy futures: Health promotion and life skills training

BEATRIX A. HAMBURG

Guiding concepts and a coherent strategy for the health education of children and youth are just beginning to emerge. The inclusion of health education as a serious and integral part of the school curriculum is a relatively new idea in the United States. Until recently, health education classes for adolescents were delegated to physical education staff and were viewed narrowly as add-ons that, although they had no academic merit, could serve to satisfy mandates in response to alarms and fears such as those created to address problems of alcohol or drug use or teenage pregnancy, or to satisfy parental wishes for options such as driver education. Fortunately, a new awareness of the centrality of health education for adolescents is coinciding with serious efforts at school reform. This chapter discusses the content and implementation of the new approaches to health education and life skills training programs for adolescents and draws on the current state of knowledge from the behavioral sciences, social sciences, health sciences, and pedagogy.

Adolescent health status

In part, the narrow view of adolescent health education reflected a widespread misconception that adolescence is the healthiest period of the life span; as a result, there were no educational needs to be served. Several factors contributed to this erroneous view. First, adolescents appear to be healthier than they are in reality because they have avoided using health care services for reasons of access, cost, consent, and privacy. Second, many of their medical disorders, including scoliosis, hypertension, diabetes, or human immunodeficiency virus (HIV) infection, are not associated with visible symptoms or evident mortality. Finally, the rise of adolescent problem behaviors was not universally seen as a health problem. Gradually there began to be an appreciation of the relevance of the new morbidity (Haggerty, Roghmann, and Pless, 1975) to those conditions, as well as to adolescent health conditions more generally. In fact, it is now established that the preponderance of health problems during adolescence is related to psychosocial factors and health behaviors. By age 15, about 25% of American youth are engaged in such preventable health-damaging behaviors as smoking, drug use, inappropriate sexuality, and injury-prone activities.

The true issue for adolescent health is unrecognized and unmet health needs rather than an absence of health concerns. In addition, there is the equally important fact of the critical significance of behaviors and lifestyles adopted in adolescence as determinants of adult illness and mortality.

Adolescent behaviors that have serious health-damaging adult outcomes include the following:

• Use of tobacco – increases the risk of cancers, lung diseases, and cardiac and vascular disorders.
• Use of alcohol and certain other drugs – increases the risk of injury due to automobile and other accidents, as well as intentional injury such as assault, homicide, or suicide.
• Use of alcohol and other drugs – increases the likelihood of impulsive or inappropriate sexual behaviors, with possible outcomes of unplanned pregnancy, sexually transmitted diseases, or HIV infection.
• Dietary habit of overeating rich foods – predisposes to diabetes and a range of cardiovascular conditions.
• Fad diets, bulimic behavior, or excessive dieting – leads to significant nutritional deficiencies; any of these factors can also be linked to a behavioral disorder.
• Alcoholism – causes liver disease and/or neurological disorders.

These are concerns for *all* adolescents. However, the risks are much higher for minority and disadvantaged adolescents. Clearly, there are compelling reasons to mount health education programs that will encompass teaching about both the immediate and the long-term health concerns that have such high salience for all adolescents.

Adolescent socialization and life skills

In contemporary America, adolescents are confronted with crucial personal, health, and school decisions that affect life options at increasingly younger ages, often as early as 10 or 11 years old. There are new and heavy demands for appropriate education and socialization to prepare children and youth to play constructive, productive, and satisfying roles in our modern multiethnic, postindustrial society. The requirements now and in the future for jobs or careers in high-technology or service industries are challenging, diverse, and not easily achieved. There are many choices and much uncertainty in the modern world. Responsible citizenship in our society requires not only a broad fund of knowledge, but also a range of social competencies that include such life skills as social problem solving, conflict resolution, decision making, and evaluating powerful media messages and other persuasive messages. However, contemporary families and community institutions are contributing far less to the teaching of these vital life skills than they did in earlier periods.

The structures and functioning of American families have undergone substantial change over the past 50 years. The nuclear family, a stable unit of two biological parents and their offspring, is far less prevalent today than in the first half of this century. This notable change is due to the high rate of divorce, the number of remarriages with blended families, and the increasing number of unmarried mothers and single-parent households. Another striking difference in contemporary families is the very large number of working mothers, both married and single. Women's employment rates have escalated sharply and are still rising because it takes at least two incomes to maintain an acceptable standard of living. Many modern households are experiencing great strain, with the result that traditional family socialization, educational, and supportive functions are performed less dependably.

In addition, parents of adolescents mistakenly believe that it is developmentally appropriate to accord substantial independence to adolescents and to withdraw much of their guidance and monitoring at this life period. In this vacuum, the socialization of young adolescents can be disproportionately influenced by television and other media messages, as well as by the norms, risks, and opportunities of the neighborhood. When stressed families also reside in urban areas of concentrated poverty, positive role models and compensatory positive socialization opportunities are also likely to be missing. In the past, it was possible to overlook the social learning and life skill deficiencies of these highly disadvantaged children and youth because very little was expected of them. Far too many of them have been accorded marginal status, with low expectations and constrained opportunities in school, the community, and the general economy.

For historical reasons, a disproportionate number of children and families who live under marginal conditions and who experience undesirable life outcomes are black, Hispanic, or other minorities. Their contributions to the nation can no longer be considered marginal; they will be needed as an important component of a modern, productive workforce. As a result of differential birthrates and immigration patterns, minorities are becoming an increasingly large percentage of the total population.

Regardless of societal conditions, all adolescents have basic human developmental needs that are crucial to their growth to healthy adulthood. These include the need to be a valued member of a group that provides mutual support and caring relationships; the need to become a cognitively and socially competent individual who has the skills to cope successfully with everyday life; and the need to believe in a promising future with real opportunities.

Preventive approaches, including health education, life skills training, and the creation of social networks, can provide the foundation for promoting successful outcomes for all adolescents. In this way, the adverse impact of multiple risk factors concentrated in lower socioeconomic groups can be offset, and the likelihood of successful outcomes for mainstream youth can be enhanced. It is feasible to teach these life skills to all adolescents as an integral part of the school curriculum. It is logical to target health education and life skills training efforts at young adolescents in middle or junior high school. Developmental and sociocultural transactions of early adolescence also dictate this choice.

Early adolescent development and life skills

Early adolescence is a time of life unparalleled in the number and importance of decisions that will be made over a very short period of time. Furthermore, these crucial decisions that will determine future life options, adult health status, career, and family life are largely being made under conditions of inexperience, ignorance, strong emotion, and great uncertainty. Young adolescents urgently need dependable adult guidance and help in gaining valid information, decision-making and problem-solving skills, and skills in negotiating interpersonal transactions, especially with peers.

Failure to appreciate that there are three distinct stages of adolescent development has imposed heavy burdens on young adolescents because the role expectations for them and popular stereotypes about them derive from late adolescence. As a result, for young adolescents, now defined as youngsters aged 10–14, there has been far too much emphasis on the "adolescent need" for independence and a related withdrawal of parental and other adult guidance and support. On the contrary: As they experience puberty, with its intense internal and external pressures for "grown-up" behaviors, including smoking, drinking, or sexuality, young adolescents have a developmental need for adults who can be positive role models, mentors, and providers of useful information.

Young adolescents who live in single-parent, mother-headed homes are the most likely to lack firm parental guidance. Without a parent who serves as a model and gives structure or provides coping resources, many young adolescents seek peer support and adopt the badges of group conformity.

Many young adolescents are exceedingly lonely in the absence of parent and community support and in the context of schooling that has become large and impersonal. This drives many to seek peer support and, in the extreme, a sense of family among peers through gang membership. Uncritical allegiance to the peer group may be useful in allaying immediate anxieties, but it has serious limitations. At best, the peer group at this stage is usually too shallow and rigid to afford the necessary resources for growth and development. If the peer group is organized around drugs or acting-out behaviors, there is potential for considerable damage.

Developmentally, therefore, young adolescents are immature and inexperienced at a time of multiple, novel, and stressful challenges. For youngsters who enter the early adolescent period with deprivation or adverse prior experiences, the negotiation of this critical period is much more problematic. Failure to cope with the challenges of early adolescence has immediate consequences. It has become painfully clear that severe problems such as school dropout, drug abuse, alcoholism, early pregnancy, and suicide begin and show rising rates in these youngest adolescents. In the long term, the success of the young adolescent in handling basic life tasks sets a developmental trajectory. Adult functioning is crucially linked to the success with which the young person copes with the earliest stage of adolescent development.

Developmental tasks, coping challenges, and life skills

In early adolescence, there are three sets of new, preemptive demands in major spheres of functioning (Hamburg, 1974a). First are the *challenges posed by the biological changes of puberty.* Adolescents must learn to cope with the undeniable impact of major changes in body configuration. These changes are not only the most far-reaching of a lifetime, but may be unpredictable in timing of onset or in rate of physical change. The adolescent may perceive that his or her bodily changes are too early or too late, or that the emerging physique, with its awkwardness or perceived imperfections, will be characteristic throughout adult life. Concerns about body image are pervasive. Young adolescents have deep concerns about their physical attractiveness and often feel vulnerable to real or imagined assaults on bodily integrity.

They also experience baffling changes in mood and temperament. These may result in part from direct effects of the gonadal hormones, but they also may have amplifying effects on interpersonal transactions and contribute to much of the frustration and stress that are frequently reported for this age period. In the current climate of high aggression and violence, minor disputes can escalate impulsively to physical assault or gunfire. At other times, there may be responses of withdrawal or depression.

Young adolescents have relatively little valid information about pubertal processes, the wide range of normalcy, or the varying timetables or patterns of hormonal and physical changes. Despite the prevalence of provocative sexual imagery often directed at teenagers, and the explicitness of television and movie programs, young adolescents are both ignorant of and have misinformation about the effects of changes in gonadal hormones, broader issues of sexuality, and sexually transmitted diseases including, but not limited to, the acquired immunodeficiency syndrome (AIDS). They are unprepared for peer pressures regarding sex.

Troubling issues can be raised for youngsters who mature either very early or very late. Although the issues are quite different for boys and girls, all young adolescents need to understand puberty, to learn about human biology including relevant psychosocial issues, and to be educated about important health issues and health-related behaviors that will be significant for them. Chapter 7 of this volume discusses a life sciences curriculum for young adolescents that addresses these issues.

Second, there are the *challenges posed by the entry into a new social system – middle or junior high school.* With this transition, the student relinquishes the former security of membership in the single, stable classroom of elementary school and is faced with the task of negotiating six or seven changes of teachers and classes each day, often with no dependable social support. Junior high school is a replication of high school. It is another example of the inappropriate imposition of older adolescent standards on young adolescents. The context of junior high school is particularly ill suited to the developmental needs of the young adolescent (Hamburg, 1974b). There are greater academic demands, but these occur in adverse learning contexts of rotating classes and teaching approaches that reduce achievement motivation. Typically there is a drop in academic performance in junior high school, shown to be related to motivation rather than to intelligence.

Young adolescents have a realistic uncertainty about their ability to make new friendships in this rather intimidating new school context of heightened social demands. Developmentally, they lack many of the behavioral skills, social competence, or supports needed to handle the academic and social tasks of junior high school. In response to the coldness and complexity of the junior high school climate, Felner and Adan (1988) developed the School Transition Environment Project (STEP) to reorganize and humanize the school environment. The goals were to ease and simplify the social and physical setting of the school and to provide a warm social support system by restructuring the roles of homeroom teachers and guidance personnel to provide more personal contact and caring. The program was found to enhance school achievement, to raise self-esteem, and to decrease school dropout.

The third set of *challenges derives from the sudden entry into a new role status.* The admission into junior high school has become a convenient marker for the conferring of adolescent status and is the badge of entry into the teen culture. The young adolescent urgently feels in need of a new set of behaviors, values, and reference persons. Parents also view the junior high school student as entering a new world. They expect to treat their child differently and try to think of him or her now as an adolescent rather than as a child. They generally believe that they should withdraw, and accord more independence and greater personal responsibility to the young adolescent.

Developmentally, early adolescence is a time of heightened exploratory and, at times, risk-taking behaviors. These days, more than ever before, young adolescents feel pressures to experiment, to adopt new behaviors that are seen as exciting, grown up, or a passport to friendship. These pressures are partly internal.

Pressures also come from such external sources as peers, the influence of adult models, or provocative messages from movies, music, television, and advertising. Because there are no clear guidelines for young adolescent behaviors, the ambiguity of the new social role causes even the

soundest adolescents to lack self-confidence. They are unusually suscep-
tible to outside influences and insecure about their personal values and
judgments. In response to this uncertainty, they vacillate and experiment
with many roles and styles of behavior. In the face of these anxieties,
there is a constant scanning for models and mentors from whom they
can learn. Today, unfortunately, some of the most significant of these are
popular athletes or entertainment figures from pop or rock music, television, radio, and movies. Typically, there are few opportunities for
meaningful contact with nonparental adult figures who can serve as real-
world positive role models, advocates, and informants, and who can
provide social support and teach life skills.

However, under the right conditions, there is also the potential for
much social growth. With guidance and support, there is a renewed
opportunity for all young adolescents to realize their unfulfilled potential. Where there has been deprivation or adverse prior experience, this
period offers a special opportunity for reorientation. Health education
and life skills training have much to contribute to finding a new way.

School as a context for health education and life skills

With the growing awareness of the inadequacies and mismatch of the
junior high school format as a context for young adolescents, there have
been experiments with middle (and intermediate) schools. Unfortunately, most of these experiments have not created new or more nurturing environments. Very few truly restructured junior high schools and
middle schools succeed in creating a learning environment and a positive
social experience tailored for young adolescents. However, imperfect as
they are, public schools remain as the locus of choice for the implementation of health education and life skills training for the simple reason
that the vast majority of all children are in those schools. The need for
health education and life skills training, both now and in the foreseeable
future, is so compelling that it should be as universal as possible.

The interventions discussed in this chapter are those directed specifically to the young adolescent in junior high school. It should be noted
that, ideally, health education and life skills training should encompass
the full K–12 school experience. This is based on findings to date that
show maximal efficacy for programs that are developmentally appropriate and comprehensive and that have continuity over a number of
years. Although schools should be the primary vehicle for health education and life skills programs, there are roles for other institutions

as well, including the family and programs in youth-serving clubs, churches, and other community agencies. Whenever possible, family and community efforts should be coordinated with in-school programs.

Cognitive development and learning

Research has shown that the teaching of junior high school students has not been responsive to their developmental status (Eccles and Midgley, 1989). At a time when young adolescents are developmentally ready for more demanding intellectual challenges, there is, paradoxically, often a decrease in the more stimulating methods of teaching upper elementary grades and a rise in rote learning. Further, the schedule of rotating classes presents disconnected learning experiences that can discourage integrative or higher-order thinking.

Employers today complain that schools do not produce young people who can move easily into the more complex kinds of work now demanded. What employers seem to be seeking are persons who can work effectively in teams with diverse membership and who have a high level of general skills, such as competent verbal and writing skills, the ability to learn easily on the job, the quantitative skills to master modern technology, the ability to read and understand complex material, and the ability to construct and critique arguments. These are all competencies that are not taught or acquired in the low-level literacy curricula typically designed for students in urban poverty areas and for other non-college-bound students.

Resnick (1986) has said, "It is a new and extremely challenging notion to assume that everyone, not just an elite, can become a competent thinker" (p. 7). The groundwork for higher-order thinking skills can and should be laid in the middle school/junior high school years. This can be accomplished in academic learning, but it can also be an integral part of life skills training and other nonacademic learning experiences. A life skills curriculum can be presented using active learning strategies rather than rote learning. In such a curriculum, higher-order thinking skills are continuously developed over the course of the program. A preventive program with urban minority youth, the Violence Prevention Project (Wilson-Brewer, Cohen, O'Donnell, and Goodman, 1991), places strong emphasis on this aspect of their intervention. Program staff feel that this component is very important for youngsters who otherwise would have had virtually no experience with training in higher-order thinking skills in their regular schooling.

Cognitive development through nonacademic channels needs to be highlighted. There is firm evidence that active learning strategies that are project based or that link concepts to real-world experience are highly effective in raising motivation and enhancing all types of learning. Health education and life skills training offer many such learning opportunities.

Social competence

In the new social world of early adolescence, there is a heightened awareness of social interactions, particularly peer relationships. A developmental task of this period is to move from the superficial, egocentric bases and processes of childhood friendships to more reflective, mature, and mutually collaborative relationships of adolescence. As they enter early adolescence, youngsters differ in their experiences and innate skills in negotiating social relationships. Normatively, they are inept in initiating, broadening, sustaining, and deepening relationships. They are hesitant; many suffer acute embarrassment and experience severe disappointments as they gain experience and mastery. Most young adolescents wish to acquire communication and interpersonal skills.

Junior high school does not help young adolescents who are trying to negotiate their social tasks because its social environment is that of a very large, impersonal institution with many changing sets of brief contacts with teachers and classmates. Structured after-school clubs or activities are sharply limited, if they exist at all. The cliques that typify this age tend to be rigid. They exclude aspiring new members and tend to restrict the social scope of their in-group. One of the most commonly expressed concerns of youngsters about to enter junior high school or middle school is the fear that they will not be able to make friends.

It is perhaps not surprising that such prominence is given to teaching social competence in life skills training programs. This training, as will be shown, has focused on awareness and labeling of feelings in self and others, as well as the learning of strategies and practice in interpersonal encounters. Asher and Gottman (1981) call attention to attributional biases in youngsters as a neglected aspect of social incompetence in children. Unpopular children attribute their lack of success to internal, stable personal deficiencies. These perceptions of unchangeable personal inadequacy lead to feelings of low self-efficacy and low self-worth. Asher and Gottman further point to the fact that a prior reputation can be a barrier. When unpopular children try to gain social entry, they are rejected by peers even when using the same strategies that are effective with popular children. The implications of this line of research for interventions to enhance the social competence of young adolescents need further study.

Another aspect of social competence that deserves further attention in early adolescence is the degree to which social competence is domain specific, that is, linked to a particular social context. Many minority youngsters who come from disadvantaged backgrounds have a number of social competencies that are highly adaptive for their particular sociocultural circumstances. However, some of these same competencies may be maladaptive for important mainstream situations, notably schooling or the world of work.

For example, for many minority, disadvantaged adolescents, it is important to ethnic identity and pride to avoid being seen as trying to "act white" (Ogbu, 1978). Often there are strong peer pressures to enforce this norm. Use of ethnic language (black English or Spanish) in preference to standard English is an important ethnic marker. The motivation to learn and to get good grades may be seen as "acting white." While in its own context, adherence to the peer norms maintains group approval and personal friendships, and is therefore socially competent, in the mainstream there are adverse long-term effects on overall adaptation and life options. It is a challenge to help minority disadvantaged youngsters to negotiate adolescence while preserving the best of their unique sociocultural heritage and competencies and, at the same time, to acquire the competencies needed for success in the mainstream.

Decision making

The importance and scope of decisions to be made in early adolescence are greater than at any other developmental period. As was previously emphasized, these decisions have major effects in the immediate situation and consequences for future adult options and functioning. Although decision making and problem solving are significant components of most adolescent life skills training curricula, they have been relatively neglected in the field of adolescent developmental research. Early adolescence is an important transition period in cognitive development. There is a shift from the concrete thinking of childhood to the capability for formal operations and abstract thinking. With training, young adolescents are capable of making complex and contingent decisions using sophisticated information processing.

Comprehensive life skills programs generally include decision-making and/or problem-solving training. The forms of decision making generally taught are based on a model that implicitly assumes that a rational procedure for appraisal of situations, with review of options and their likely consequences, will result in prudent choices. This methodology is best exemplified in the curriculum of Weissberg, Caplan, and Bennetto (1988), in which the students are taught to identify situations in their own lives that are conflicted. They are then taught the following six-step decision-making strategy:

1. Stop, calm down, and think before you act.
2. State the problem and describe how you feel.
3. Set a positive goal.
4. Think of many solutions.
5. Think ahead to the consequences.
6. Go ahead and try the best plan.

In research on adult cognition, this assumption of the prudent person has been shown to be untrue under conditions of uncertainty or strong emotion (Tversky and Kahneman, 1986). Under those conditions, even for adults who have mature cognitive abilities and skills and substantial life experiences, decision making has been shown to be far less rational than was once believed and to have predictable, systematic biases. Many adolescent decisions are highly charged emotionally, such as whether to yield to peer pressure to smoke, drink, or have sex. For young adolescents whose reasoning skills are not yet mature, and who are just beginning the process of trial-and-error learning in important situations, bias effects are probably even greater.

Research strongly indicates that in early adolescence, situations are egocentrically appraised, and decisions and strategies are predominantly emotion focused rather than rational (Compas, 1993; Selman, Beardslee, Schultz, Krupa, and Podorefsky, 1986). Evidence suggests that for most young adolescents, their potential for competent decision making in real-world situations is far greater than their actual performance. These considerations will help deepen our understanding of how and why specific types of situations are appraised as stressful or not by young adolescents, and how these appraisals differ systematically for differing subgroups of adolescents.

Appropriate studies, including research based on well-designed life skills interventions, will tell us the degree to which and in what ways developmental processes interact with personal experiences to influence the range of strategies or options that will actually be used by young adolescents in stressful situations or in making fateful decisions. The Weissberg, Caplan, and Siva (1989) decision-making model has proved useful. It may be particularly valuable because, when taught properly, it provides anticipatory coping through a review of options and rehearsal of responses. As a result of these overlearned, practiced responses, the young adolescent is protected from having to improvise under stress. This prior preparation decreases the likelihood of impulsive or unwise decisions.

Social support

There is a body of evidence showing that social support is effective in preventing or reducing the impact of high stress and mediating a number of positive health outcomes. In general, these studies rely on adult data and have not been carried out with children or adolescents. Research by Beardslee (1990) shows that when support systems are weak or absent, stressful life events are strongly correlated with depression in adolescents.

For children, families have been appropriately viewed as the major support system, and most studies have focused on the supportiveness of the parent–child relationship. This exclusive focus on the nuclear family as social support no longer seems appropriate in light of the changed nature of the American family and its impaired ability to provide dependable support. Most modern families are in need of support. Some studies, particularly among black families, have found a broad, informal network of social support that serves to promote favorable personal adjustment and positive health outcomes. This deserves further study as a potential contributor to resilience.

New models of multiservice schools offer needed support to parents (Dryfoos, 1994). These schools collaborate with health and social service agencies to provide "one-stop shopping" for a comprehensive array of social and medical services at the school site. They also offer literacy training and make job training referrals for the parents. Full-service schools have extended hours, are often open on evenings and weekends, and serve breakfast and lunch to the children. After-school recreational, homework, and remedial programs are provided on the premises. The school personnel have no direct responsibility for these programs, even though they are situated on school grounds. When full-service schools are found, teachers report increased parent participation and involvement.

School–community linkage

There are school–community linkages involving service roles for young adolescents that can provide life skills training and/or augment the health education curriculum. In such programs, higher-order reasoning and analytic skills can be developed when adolescents are mentored by adults who provide guidance in planning and carrying out assigned tasks, and who promote critical examination by the youngsters of their work. Young adolescents have been found to develop a sense of self-worth and efficacy through participation in meaningful, needed community activities, such as tutoring, helping the elderly, working in hospitals, assisting in day-care centers, or cleaning up a neighborhood to make a play area.

The potential for encouraging constructive participation by young adolescents has been sadly neglected. Properly carried out, it can enhance learning motivation and could link academic exercises to meaningful demands of the community and the world of work. It offers girls the chance to explore jobs and roles previously believed to be restricted to boys, and vice versa, thus helping to transcend gender-role stereotypes.

Youth service programs can also enlarge the scope of a young adolescent's experience with adults of all ages as sources of information, friendship, and support. Youth participation may be the only way to lay a foundation of positive achievement motivation for youngsters who have had consistent academic failure and negative reinforcement for learning throughout their school years, or who may have specific learning disabilities but are quite capable of higher-order thinking. The kind of participation described also maximizes the likelihood that young adolescents will begin to learn work habits and the work ethic as well as develop positive expectations of future work and career choices.

The Early Adolescent Helper Program is a youth service program for young adolescents (Schine, 1989). It enables them to make meaningful contributions to the community through structured job experiences. In the process, students are connected with supportive nonparental adults who act as role models and mentors. They learn by doing, and most often there is a linkage with the school such that academic and life skills taught in school can be practiced in the real world. Conversely, job experiences can be examined, understood, and refined at school in supervised discussion and review.

Students performing youth service experience the gratification and respect engendered by prosocial activities; for some, this is the only opportunity for such activities. They make substantial gains in self-esteem and self-efficacy. Rigorous program evaluation is now under way, but preliminary findings suggest that there are gains in school achievement, communication, and interpersonal skills and a decrease in the likelihood of involvement in delinquent activities. The youth service programs also help to forge stronger links between school and community.

Although the integration of health education and life skills training into regular school curricula is highly desirable and reasonably well accepted, it cannot be assumed that universal or even widespread adoption by public schools will be assured in the near future. Given the pervasive need for health education and life skills, it is important to explore the availability of other resources for this purpose. Community-based programs have the added advantage of reaching youth after school and on weekends. They are the only resource for school dropouts, who are a very high-risk population that is perhaps in the most urgent need of the services. The core elements of school-based and non-school-based programs are very similar. Newer programs have made fruitful linkages between school and community programs.

Health education and life skills training – core elements

Health education

A brief overview of the evolution of health education programs is instructive. The integration of life skills and social competence into health education is of crucial importance, inasmuch as the leading causes of illness and death in adolescents are due to the "new morbidities" and are linked to psychosocial factors and lifestyles (Haggerty et al., 1975). The newest generation of health education programs has made such syntheses.

The initial large-scale health education programs directed at young adolescents were introduced in the 1960s in a climate of great public concern about the rapidly rising use of illegal drugs, particularly marijuana, among broad sectors of American youth. From a historical baseline of negligible use prior to 1960, there was a rapid rise in experimentation and regular use of marijuana that involved over 50% of youth by the end of the decade.

The major initial response was a series of movies, each depicting the perils of a specific drug. The best known of these films was the exaggerated, dramatic film *Reefer Madness*. These movies were shown after school in the auditorium to the assembled student body, often accompanied by a stern commentary, in a public health campaign that was notably unsuccessful and perhaps counterproductive. These movies were generally dismissed by the students with laughter and derision. The rates of adolescent drug use continued to climb in the 1970s.

A number of lessons were learned. The first was that forceful scare tactics alone are not likely to work. This was confirmed definitively in a study of changes in attitudes toward smoking following exposure to varying levels of threats of lung cancer that included vivid, frightening medical pictures and x-rays (Janis and Mann, 1977). The most positive response was found when the level of anxiety caused by the propaganda was in the mid-range, where sufficient concern was required to gain and maintain attention to the message. However, when fear was raised to the highest levels, denial and rejection occurred. Other research has shown that messages are also more likely to be accepted when they are coupled with a feasible action plan. The second lesson was the lack of efficacy of passive presentations to large groups. The third lesson was the importance of providing more than one exposure to educational material.

The second generation of theory-based adolescent health education programs was introduced in the 1970s. These programs were designed to deter smoking in young adolescents by using more persuasive presentations of the adverse consequences of smoking and providing a plan to develop refusal skills. The researchers responded to the salience of peers as determinants of adolescent attitudes and behaviors. They coupled this with a social learning approach (Bandura, 1995). Social learning theory highlights the power in childhood and adolescence of learning by observation, imitation, and practice of behaviors that are modeled by key persons in the social environment. For the young adolescent, the family and peers can be most significant, but there is also high attentiveness to popular figures in sports, the media, and advertising.

The program content focused on two areas. The first was the presentation of developmentally appropriate, factual messages about the health risks of smoking. Films using slightly older peers, rather than adult authority figures, presented factual information about social and health risks pertinent to adolescents. In the film, through role play, the adolescent actors modeled strategies for resisting the pressure to smoke (Evans, Hansen, and Mittelmark, 1977).

The second area involved the use of social learning principles. Appropriate high schoolers were recruited and trained to serve as peer leaders of small groups of seventh graders in active learning sessions. The curriculum included facts about the physiological effects of smoking, correct normative information ("most everybody is *not* doing it"), discussion of social pressures to smoke, assertiveness training, and role playing by the seventh graders to resist peer pressures to smoke. Evaluation of this approach showed that a year later, only 7% of the treatment group had started smoking compared to 19% of the control group (Perry, Killen, Slinkard, and McAlister, 1980). Clearly, these types of programs represented a major advance in health education and demonstrated that health attitudes and behaviors can be changed.

On longer-term follow-up, it was found that the effects were not sustained. However, it should be noted that for young adolescents there is a benefit to any delay in initiating health-damaging behaviors. Early onset is associated with the likelihood of more extensive and intensive involvement (Kandel, 1978). Also, young adolescents are more likely to adopt multiple problem behaviors once they have initiated the first one. Nonetheless, there is a consensus about the desirability of mounting programs that will have sustained effects throughout adolescence, not simply at one point in time. Starting in the 1980s, new types of programs were designed, with the goals of enhancing the power and impact of health education programs, as well as ensuring that there will be long-term effects. These third generation interventions have relied heavily on the addition of life skills training.

Life skills training

Life skills training (LST) was explicitly introduced by Botvin (Botvin and Eng, 1982) as a new model of a multicomponent approach to the prevention of smoking in young adolescents. He theorized that the earlier programs were too narrow, limiting their focus to factual information. The antecedents of smoking are multifactorial and require a comprehensive program of knowledge, motivation, perceptions, life skills, and social competencies to enable youth to become informed, motivated, and active agents for change in their health behaviors.

Moreover, Botvin's group compared LST across several modes of pres-

entation: regular classroom teachers, peer leaders, and outside professionals. All modes demonstrated effectiveness, with the combined peer–
adult leadership having somewhat better results. In later studies by this
group, their broader multicomponent LST program was designed to reduce alcohol and drug abuse and prevent unprotected sexual activity
that could lead to AIDS. Recent data also show that it is as effective with
minority populations as among whites.

LST draws heavily on the social competence curricula of Weissberg
and his colleagues (1989) and Elias (1985) for generic social skills training
components that are adapted and targeted as preventive measures for
substance abuse. Therefore, LST is a psychoeducational program that
combines generic elements of social competence with domain-specific
materials for a targeted adolescent health issue.

Botvin paid considerable attention to implementation. Recognizing
that the pressures to engage in risky behaviors increase over the course
of junior high school, LST is administered as a 15–session program in
seventh grade, a 10–session booster in eighth grade, and a 5–session
booster in ninth grade. Throughout, the consistency and quality of the
presentation of the program are carefully monitored.

Core elements of the program

Motivation determines whether or not youngsters will pay attention and
make a persistent effort to acquire knowledge, to attempt to master skills
that are well within their abilities, or to work hard to attain goals that
they value. Bandura's theory and research (1995) give clues to ways of
enhancing motivation. He has shown the centrality of perceptions of self-
efficacy in motivation and related behaviors. Self-efficacy is a personal
judgment of the likelihood of success in accomplishing a given task. Bandura's recent research has focused on methods for increasing self-
efficacy. There is an emphasis on frequent rewards for desired behaviors,
negotiable tasks presented in successive approximations, and directed
practice. Bandura has given useful information about the nature of feedback that individuals use in making the self-efficacy judgments that, in
turn, affect motivation.

Knowledge base requirements for social competence training have been
influenced by a developmental perspective. As issues become developmentally relevant, there is heightened interest in and receptiveness to
learning in those areas. For example, with the drastic body changes of
puberty that focus adolescent interest on the body image and body in-

tegrity, knowledge of human biology and health issues becomes salient. In addition, developmental considerations underlying adolescent needs for peer approval and peer affiliation enhance receptiveness to learning about communication skills and interpersonal negotiations, especially with peers but with others as well.

The *socioenvironmental context* also sets an agenda for adolescents. Adolescents are very responsive to the pressures, fads, and media influences around them. Currently, their milieu is disproportionately weighted with information of varying quality and much myth about violence, substance use, sexuality, AIDS, and sexually transmitted diseases. Young adolescents need valid, credible information on these topics, as well as teaching about legal rights and responsibilities and knowledge of community resources. At the same time, it must be recognized that basic information must be reviewed and updated to include new and important issues. For example, the widespread availability and use of guns is a new, highly important issue for American youth. Adolescents need to receive clear, credible, and useful information on the salient aspects of firearms.

Social skills of individuals vary predictably with developmental level, but they also vary widely within age groups as well. These skills in communication, ability to listen, to "read" the body language and intentions of others, to self-regulate, and to empathize greatly affect the capacity to build and maintain stable, rewarding relationships. Beyond social skills, the social environment also influences social behavior and acceptance. A source of high social status in one context may be an impediment in another. For example, school achievement is usually highly valued in middle-class schools but often disparaged in ghetto schools. An extremely aggressive response may be expected in one context but not tolerated in another. Young adolescents are particularly lacking in social skills and social competence across many domains.

Assertiveness training has become a prominent aspect of LST. It is probably not well named because it may imply a level of aggressiveness that is not intended. It generally refers to modulation of responses to an appropriate level for effectiveness in the active pursuit of one's needs while recognizing the needs and feelings of others. At times, this requires reducing an overly aggressive response. At other times, it may refer to increasing a very weak, passive reaction that may be maladaptive, causing vulnerability to exploitation or extreme compliance. Another aspect of assertiveness training refers to taking the initiative and energetically seeking resources and opportunities. Role playing is a prominent technique in this training. Assertiveness training techniques have a prominent role in teaching resistance to peer pressure regarding smoking, substance use, and precocious sexuality.

Cognitive skills

An emerging trend in the teaching of social skills is the focus on using the methods and techniques of teaching to develop higher-order reasoning and critical thinking skills. Spivack and Shure (1974a, 1974b, 1982) introduced a question-and-answer interaction technique called *dialoguing*, in which the reasoning skills are developed by eliciting active discovery from the child. The youngster is always encouraged to think of several possible options and to recognize that there never will be only one answer. This emphasis on higher-order thinking is coming to pervade all aspects of the social competence programs. Newer teaching methods focus on the use of a spectrum of active learning strategies that enhance reasoning skills.

Decision making

Most current life skills programs have a decision-making component. In many current versions, the decision-making skills are seen as a number of subtasks that need to be memorized and performed in sequence. The basic cognitive properties of adolescent decision making are not well understood. This cognitive area may benefit from drawing on some new conceptual bases. It is an aspect of life skills that has crucial importance and deserves urgent attention on the research agenda.

There are good models of adult decision making under conditions of uncertainty (Beyth-Marom, Fischhoff, Jacobs, and Furby, 1989). Adults have been found to be risk averse under uncertainty. It is not known whether, for developmental reasons, adolescents will have differing perceptions of risk from adults. Although not proven, there are reasons to suspect that for many adolescents risks are attractive and are sought out, not avoided. This area of adolescent decision making deserves further study. Much more needs to be learned about the full range of factors and circumstances that may systematically influence risk taking and risk avoidance among adolescents in general and in specific subgroups.

The Midwestern Prevention Project (MPP) is the most recent version of health education and life skills training. It has tried to address the shortcomings of prior programs, most notably the short duration of effects. It is a comprehensive intervention mounted in 15 communities and aimed at the prevention of smoking and drug abuse (Pentz et al., 1989). This model incorporates all the features of the Botvin LST Program and moves beyond it to include a strong emphasis on changing community norms as an integral component. The researchers were influenced by the studies of successful community-based programs for the prevention of cardiovascular disease (Farquhar et al., 1985) in which community norms were changed by a focused multimedia campaign. This expanded program was designed with the goal of achieving maximal efficacy of the intervention, as well as sustaining the effects over a period of years.

MPP is a comprehensive school- and community-based program that includes a formal in-school life skills and health education curriculum, extensive television and newspaper coverage, health policy programming, community organization, and parent involvement. The entire adolescent population of the 15 experimental communities participated in the project. There was a "booster" design with components added on a yearly basis from 6th to 12th grade. Evaluation found that among program students the rate of initiation of drug use was 50% lower than that of controls, with the good results maintained over the long term. The cost effectiveness of the program is being evaluated.

This program demonstrates the feasibility and promise of extending health promotion beyond the exclusive emphasis on training individuals to take personal responsibility for their health. It has shown the feasibility of modifying socioenvironmental and social policy factors in ways that contribute to positive adolescent health outcomes.

High-risk adolescents

Programs in life skills training were originally developed using mainstream white youth but are increasingly being directed to urban minority youngsters who are seen as being at high risk for adverse outcomes. Many disadvantaged youth have experienced difficulties in taking full advantage of educational, job training, and employment opportunities because they lack the social strategies and life skills for mastering the interrelated psychological and social skills that are necessary for success in these tasks. They also are disproportionately afflicted with the problems of the "new morbidity," such as early pregnancy, sexually transmitted diseases, drug abuse, learning problems, and violence. Many of these adolescents come from social environments that over the course of their lifetimes have been disorganized, lacking in dependable family, school, and community resources. Therefore, unlike most mainstream adolescents, they lack familiarity with the most basic skills, strategies, and knowledge of resources that are required preparation for living and succeeding in the mainstream.

These lacks frequently become the basis for highly emotional responses to the frustrations of finding themselves unequal to a life task. As this frustration mounts over time, it may lead to shame, guilt, apathy, anger, aggressive acting out, or a feeling of alienation. There is evidence, however, that when appropriate knowledge and life skills are provided and the seemingly overwhelming tasks are disaggregated into negotiable subunits, those negative emotions are supplanted by positive attitudes and persistence in attacks on new problems (Adkins, 1970). There are clear advantages to providing appropriate life skills training to young adolescents before self-defeating attitudes and behaviors are solidly entrenched.

Key elements identified for life skills programs for disadvantaged youth include the following:

A need for structured, problem-focused sessions: Utilize prepared materials and exercises. In initial encounters, the young people may lack basic skills for engaging in focused, goal-directed discussion. When they are presented with a topic, free discussion quickly becomes disorganized and attention of the group is not sustained.

A common basis for interaction: When sociocultural differences exist between the teacher and group members, words and concepts very often have no common meaning. There is literally a need to learn to talk each other's language.

A strong need to be treated with respect and dignity: Teachers must be aware of students' high vigilance for perceived slights and disrespect.

High peer influence: This peer power can at times be a barrier but could be readily mobilized for peer teaching and cooperative learning.

Preservation and constructive enhancement of ethnic pride and ethnic identity. There is a need for explicit attention to the positive effects of ethnic and cultural values. The task is to preserve these effects while teaching skills to function effectively in the mainstream and enhance life options.

Two programs specifically designed for disadvantaged minority adolescents should be highlighted:

1. *"Bridging the Gap"*: This Salvation Army program is specifically designed for high-risk urban youth who live in areas of concentrated

poverty. In addition to providing a basic curriculum encompassing social competency, issues of behavior and health, and use of community resources, this program focuses on acquiring familiarity with institutions that affect rights and responsibilities as citizens, such as voting, taxes, legal rights and responsibilities, the justice system, and personal involvement in community affairs (Hamburg, 1990, pp. 63–72).

2. *The "Violence Prevention Project"*: Using many of the same principles described by Adkins (1970), this school-based violence prevention curriculum taught conflict resolution and control of anger. The program had a heavy emphasis on positive peer pressure and highlighted the responsibility that friends have for helping friends to avoid assault and injury through use of conflict resolution skills. This primary prevention project also represents an early and strenuous effort to change community norms as part of a health education program. There was broad outreach and an effort to engage the widest possible range of community settings – retail stores and restaurants, community agencies, churches, the health system, television and newspapers – in a vigorous anti-violence campaign. So far, the results of this comprehensive effort are ambiguous and further evaluation is needed (Hamburg, 1990, pp. 86–97).

A promising direction, exemplified by Botvin and Eng (1982), is to modify existing mainstream programs of proven efficacy for implementation with high-risk and minority groups by inclusion of culturally sensitive content and strategies.

Implementation and assessment

Attention to the quality of implementation and the rigorous evaluation of programs is critically important. Without credible evidence of benefit, we cannot be sure that the adolescents are receiving the help they need. Careful evaluation will not only provide information about the level of success, but will also indicate which program elements are the "active ingredients." As interventions become more comprehensive, their expense also increases. More than ever, policymakers are requiring evidence that the money will be spent on programs of proven efficacy because these are the only programs that can be cost effective.

In the final analysis, it is the implementation of the program that will determine its success or failure. Regardless of the soundness of the conceptual base, clarity of purpose, appropriateness of design, and curricular content, a program cannot succeed unless it is carried out as intended, in all of its aspects. One of the critical tasks of evaluation is to examine the fidelity of implementation.

Knowledge of implementation is also crucial for dissemination. Replication of the program in a way likely to maximize effectiveness depends on detailed understanding of all relevant components. In the implementation of an intervention there are six key dimensions:

1. Assessment of the specific needs of the target population.
2. Selection of program site – accessibility, acceptance by the community, adequacy of space and structure for the program's needs.
3. Entry into the system (school, community setting) – collaborative, accepting attitudes of the indigenous persons and mutual respect.
4. Training of the trainers/teachers – structured curricula, manuals, adequate time to master the materials, monitoring of ongoing performance.
5. Procedures for data collection and an adequate information management system.
6. Evaluation – matching outcomes to goals, quantitative measures for key variables, multiple methods and measures.

Evaluation

A definitive evaluation of the effectiveness of a model program and its dissemination was initiated in 1979 by the U.S. Department of Health, Education, and Welfare in a research project entitled the School Health Education Evaluation (SHEE). It stands as a model of excellence in demonstrating the concept, study design, and methodology that are crucial to valid and reliable evaluation of health education and life skills training (Connell and Turner, 1985; Connell, Turner, and Mason, 1985). A brief, rigorous evaluation of this project showed that implementation factors determine the effectiveness of the program. Evaluators found that health behavior change was best achieved with a heavy commitment of classroom hours, with diminishing impact as class time decreased. Effectiveness of the program was also highly dependent on substantial teacher training and program support resources. Overall, this exemplary study unequivocally demonstrated the effectiveness of school-based health promotion.

Concluding remarks

There is a clear need for health and life skills training for young adolescents. They are in a formative period of the life span that poses an array of preventable health risks at a time when, developmentally, they are immature, ignorant, and inexperienced. Beyond the immediate risks that are prominent, early adolescence presents a major preventive opportunity because it is the time when attitudes, values, and behaviors are adopted that will characterize the health-related behaviors most crucial to adult health status and longevity.

The knowledge base for health education and life skills training has advanced considerably over the past two decades and currently rests on firm conceptual and empirical foundations. Current knowledge can be translated into programs of health education and life skills of proven value to young adolescents. It is also clear that there are continuing opportunities for further productive research. The field is now poised for ongoing growth and development.

Life skills training in other countries

Considerable progress has been made in placing adolescent health education on the agenda in many countries. The World Health Organization (WHO) has played a prominent role. In particular, the Division of Mental Health of WHO has actively supported life skills education in the schools. In 1993, a monograph was published to provide a framework for life skills program development. *Part I: Introduction to Life Skills for Psychosocial Competence* presents the conceptual base and rationale for the program. *Part 2: Guidelines: The Development and Implementation of Life Skills Programmes* presents curricular material and classroom activities. It is designed to give encouragement, knowledge, and practical advice to teachers who may wish to introduce this training into their classrooms.

In a related activity, WHO also publishes a networking newsletter, *Skills for Life*. It is directed to a broadly representative group that includes national departments of health and education, universities, teacher training colleges, and nongovernmental organizations. This approach will be further pursued as a joint effort with the United Nations International Children's Education Fund (UNICEF). The Pan American Health Organization (PAHO) has supported this program. So far, life skills training has been more widely adopted in Latin America and the Caribbean than it has in Europe.

The book *Schooling in Modern European Society* (Husen, Tuijnman, and Halls, 1992) summarizes the challenges and opportunities for school education. Concerns are expressed about the psychosocial impacts on young people of societal change, especially those due to changes in the structure and role of the family, rapid modernization, and immigration. Youth in Europe are now manifesting attitudes and problem behaviors that are very similar to those in the United States: alienation, violence, and alcohol and drug abuse. In the discussion of opportunities for school reform there is no mention of life skills or social competence training; however, based on accumulated experience in the United States, it would appear that this approach has much to offer.

References

Adkins, W. R. (1970). Life skills: Structured counseling for the disadvantaged. *Personal and Guidance Journal, 49,* 108–116.

Asher, S. R., and Gottman, J. M. (Eds). (1981). *The development of children's friendships.* New York: Cambridge University Press.

Bandura, A. (Ed.). (1995). *Self-efficacy in changing societies.* New York: Cambridge University Press.

Beardslee, W. R. (1990). Development of a clinician-based preventive intervention for families with affective disorders. *Journal of Preventive Psychiatry and Allied Disciplines, 4,* 39–61.

Beyth-Marom, R., Fischhoff, B., Jacobs, M., and Furby, L. (1989). *Teaching decision making to adolescents: A critical review* (working paper). Washington, DC: Carnegie Council on Adolescent Development.

Botvin, G. J., and Eng, A. (1982). The efficacy of a multicomponent approach to the prevention of cigarette smoking. *Preventive Medicine, 11,* 199–211.

Compas, B. E. (1993). Promoting positive mental health during adolescence. In S. G. Millstein, A. C. Petersen, and E. O. Nightingale (Eds.), *Promoting the health of adolescents: New directions for the twenty-first century* (pp. 159–179). New York: Oxford University Press.

Connell, D. B., and Turner, R. R. (1985). The impact of instructional experience and the effects of cumulative instruction. *Journal of School Health, 55,* 324–331.

Connell, D. B., Turner, R. R., and Mason, E. F. (1985). Summary of findings of the school health education evaluation: Implementation and costs. *Journal of School Health, 55,* 316–321.

Dryfoos, J. G. (1994). *Full-service schools: A revolution in health and social services for children, youth, and families.* San Francisco: Jossey-Bass.

Eccles, J. S., and Midgley, C. (1989). Stage/environment fit: Developmentally appropriate classrooms for early adolescents. In R. E. Ames and C. Ames (Eds.), *Research on motivation in education: Volume 3. Goals and cognition* (p. 140–186). New York: Academic Press.

Elias, M. J. (1985). *Formative and summative evaluation of the improved social awareness–social problem-solving primary prevention curriculum program.* New Brunswick, NJ: Rutgers University Press.

Evans, R. I., Hansen, W. B., and Mittelmark, M. B. (1977). Increasing the validity of self-reports of behavior in a smoking in children investigation. *Journal of Applied Psychology, 62,* 521–523.

Farquhar, J. W., Fortmann, S. P., Maccoby, N., Haskell, W. L., Williams, P. T., Flora, J. A., Taylor, C. B., Brown, B. W., Jr., Solomon, D. S., and Hulley, S. B. (1985). The Stanford five city project: Design and methods. *American Journal of Epidemiology, 122,* 323–334.

Felner, R. D., and Adan, A. M. (1988). The school transitional environment project: An ecological intervention and evaluation. In R. H. Price, E. L. Cowen, R. P. Lorion, and J. Ramos-McKay (Eds.), *Fourteen ounces of prevention: A casebook for practitioners* (pp. 111–122). Washington, DC: American Psychological Association.

Haggerty, R. J., Roghmann, K. J., and Pless, I. B. (1975). *Child health and the community.* New York: Wiley Interscience.

Hamburg, B. A. (1974a). Early adolescence: A specific and stressful stage of the life cycle. In G. Coelho, D. Hamburg, and J. Adams (Eds.), *Coping and adaptation* (pp. 102–124). New York: Basic Books.

Hamburg, B. A. (1974b). Coping in early adolescence: The special challenges of the junior high school period. In S. Arieti (Ed.), *American handbook of psychiatry* (Vol. II, pp. 385–397). New York: Basic Books.

Hamburg, B.A. (1990). *Life skills training: Preventive interventions for young adolescents* (working paper). Washington, DC: Carnegie Council on Adolescent Development.

Husen, T., Tuijnman, A., and Halls, W. D. (Eds.). (1992). *Schooling in modern European society.* Oxford: Pergamon Press.

Janis, I., and Mann, L. (1977). *Decision making: A psychological analysis of conflict, choice, and commitment.* New York: Free Press.

Kandel, D. B. (1978). *Longitudinal research in drug use.* New York: Halstead Press.

Ogbu, J. U. (1978). *Minority education and caste.* New York: Academic Press.

Pentz, M. A., Dwyer, J. H., MacKinnon, D. P., Flay, B. R., Hansen, W. B., Wang, E. Y. I., and Johnson, A. (1989). A multi-community trial for primary prevention of adolescent drug abuse: Effects on drug use prevalence. *Journal of the American Medical Association, 261,* 3259–3266.

Perry, C., Killen, J., Slinkard, L. A., and McAlister, A. (1980). Peer teaching and smoking prevention among junior high students. *Adolescence, 9,* 277–281.

Resnick, L. (1986). *Education and learning to think. Special report to the Commission on Behavioral and Social Sciences.* Washington, DC: National Academy of Sciences.

Schine, J. (1989). *Young adolescents and community service* (working paper). Washington, DC: Carnegie Council on Adolescent Development.

Selman, R. L., Beardslee, W., Schultz, L. H., Krupa, M., and Podorefsky, D. (1986). Assessing adolescent interpersonal negotiation strategies: Toward the integration of structural and functional models. *Developmental Psychology, 22,* 450–459.

Spivack, G., and Shure, M. B. (1974a). Evaluation measures. *Social adjustment of young children* (pp. 192–202). San Francisco: Jossey-Bass.

Spivack, G., and Shure, M. B. (1974b). From theory to training program. In *Social adjustment of young children* (pp. 22–34). San Francisco: Jossey-Bass.

Spivack, G., and Shure, M. B. (1982). The cognition of social adjustment: Interpersonal cognitive problem-solving thinking. In B. B. Lahey and A. E. Kazdin (Eds.), *Advances in clinical child psychology* (Vol. 5, pp. 323–372). New York: Plenum Press.

Tversky, A., and Kahneman, D. (1986). Rational choice and the framing of decisions. *Journal of Business, 59,* 252–278.

Weissberg, R. P., Caplan, M. Z., and Bennetto, L. (1988). *The Yale–New Haven social problem-solving (SPS) program for young adolescents.* New Haven, CT: Yale University Press.

Weissberg, R. P., Caplan, M. Z., and Siva, P. J. (1989). A conceptual framework for establishing school-based social competence promotion programs. In L. A. Bond and B. E. Compas (Eds.), *Primary prevention and promotion in the schools* (pp. 255–296). Newbury Park, CA: Sage.

Wilson-Brewer, R., Cohen, S., O'Donnell, L., and Goodman, I. F. (1991). *Violence prevention for young adolescents: A survey of the state of the art* (working paper). Washington, DC: Carnegie Council on Adolescent Development.

World Health Organization, Division of Mental Health. (1993). *Life skills education for children and adolescents in schools.* Geneva: World Health Organization.

7. HUMBIO: Stanford University's human biology curriculum for the middle grades

H. CRAIG HELLER AND MARY L. KIELY

"School is boring. It doesn't have anything to do with me." That is a familiar statement to many parents of adolescents, and it was one of the most common responses received by Paul Hurd in his many surveys of junior high school and middle grades students in the United States (personal communication, January 19, 1989). Moreover, it is a statement of fact resulting from a serious mismatch between the developmental stage of students and the structure and content of the educational system to which they are subjected.

Young people come out of their elementary schooling generally excited about learning, full of questions about the world around them, and eager to receive affirmation and praise from their teachers and parents. Only a few years later, however, many of these students are uninterested in their studies, alienated from school, in conflict with their parents, and engaging in high-risk behaviors. The dimensions of this problem are enormous and well documented in reports and books (Carnegie Council on Adolescent Development, 1989; Children's Defense Fund, 1991; Hamburg, 1992; Hechinger, 1992; Scales, 1991; Takanishi, 1993).

It is hardly necessary to repeat the litany of deeply troubling statistics. We would like to make two simple points, however: First, in our current world, it is virtually impossible to be a maximally healthy, productive, participating citizen without some basic understanding of science. Yet, students alienated from school as adolescents rarely achieve a higher level of science education. Second, science literacy is crucial for health promotion. We can develop program after program aimed at decreasing teen pregnancy, decreasing drug, alcohol, and tobacco use, decreasing violence, and promoting healthy behavior. The effectiveness of such programs will be severely limited if youth do not have the knowledge base to understand the relationships between their behaviors and the consequences. The most valuable and durable investment we can make in young people is an educational foundation that will serve them well in making their own decisions.

There are attempts to blame the failures of youth on families, on the media, on society, and on the youth themselves. Increasingly, however, concern has been directed at the content of the school curriculum and the structure of the educational process as possible contributors to the problem, and therefore as possible opportunities to find solutions. This issue is stated succinctly in *Turning Points: Preparing American Youth for the 21st Century*, the seminal report from the Carnegie Council on Adolescent Development. "Middle grade schools – junior high, intermediate, or middle schools – are potentially society's most powerful force to recapture millions of youth adrift. Yet all too often they exacerbate the problems youth face" (Carnegie Council on Adolescent Development, 1989, p. 32). With respect to school structure, the report points out that adolescence is the wrong time for the stress of shifting from a school organization characterized by the stability of a primary classroom, a primary teacher, and a stable class membership to one characterized by changes in all of those factors every 50 minutes. With respect to curriculum, *Turning Points* criticizes the lack of intellectually challenging materials aimed at being relevant to adolescents as well as sensitive to their social, physical, and emotional development. Materials are needed that foster interest in school and hone decision-making as well as academic skills.

One organization in the United States that is active in promoting school reform is the National Middle School Association (NMSA). It has recognized that adolescents should have more, not less, contact with adults who deal with them as complete individuals. This argues against making the transition to a discipline-based educational structure (the high school model) in the middle grades. The NMSA has recognized the importance of curricula that help adolescents make sense of themselves and the world around them, and that are responsive to the adolescent's stage of intellectual, physical, social, and emotional development. Paul Hurd has characterized the typical discipline-oriented, watered-down high school texts in the sciences as being "beautifully illustrated vocabulary lists" that have little relevance to the concerns of the adolescents (personal communication, January 19, 1989).

What is needed instead is the development of integrated core curricula that show the interconnectedness of life and deal with issues of interest and concern to youth. Furthermore, the NMSA recommends involving students in problem solving, experiential learning, and public service and in developing communication skills. The Association's recommendations have major implications for the design, structure, and nature of the curriculum and pedagogy in middle grades schools. They call for a phasing out of many standard practices that currently characterize the schooling of a large proportion of adolescents in the United States.

The Stanford University Human Biology Middle Grades Project is in agreement with the philosophy and recommendations set forth by the NMSA and the Carnegie Council on Adolescent Development. We believe that we have produced a curriculum, known as HUMBIO, that embodies those ideals. The HUMBIO curriculum focuses on the human and specifically on the adolescent. It teaches modern biology in greater breadth and depth than do existing middle grades life science textbooks, and it extends the study of science through applications to health, the environment, and social issues. Relevance to the interests, concerns, and experiences of adolescents is used to capture the students' attention and motivate them to learn. The HUMBIO curriculum easily constitutes the equivalent of a middle grades life science course and a health course, and can potentially serve as the basis for a middle school core curriculum. For that reason, the curriculum units also incorporate information from the behavioral and social sciences, and they encourage the use of quantitative skills and language arts. Extensions to physical science and earth science can also be made. Before explaining the HUMBIO curriculum and its development in more detail, some background on its origins may be of interest.

The program in human biology at Stanford University

Human biology, one of the largest undergraduate majors at Stanford, is an interdisciplinary program in which students can earn a bachelor of arts degree. Initiated by a group of campus leaders, most of whom were chairpersons of their departments in the late 1960s, it was designed to integrate the biological and the behavioral and social sciences as they relate to the study of humans. The rationale of the program was that the problems and the opportunities that humans face now and in the future have deep roots in science and technology, but they also have dimensions related to human behavior. You may understand the scientific aspects of a problem, but to arrive at a solution, you frequently must also understand human behavior and how to change it. The ultimate goal of the program is to produce effective leaders. Such individuals must be able to view an issue from many perspectives and extract ideas and solutions from the diversity of those perspectives. It is difficult to work toward consensus if you cannot fully appreciate the bases for the opinions and conclusions of others.

Undergraduates begin the program with a year-long sequence of concurrent courses in biology and in the behavioral and social sciences. The sequence is punctuated by modules that require integration of both sides of the sequence. Usually these modules focus on controversial issues and on the analysis of public policy. Occasionally faculty from different disciplines debate, providing the students with widely divergent views. In this way, students see the importance of their broad education, deal with real-world issues, and develop the skills of evaluating evidence and analyzing arguments.

From this broad interdisciplinary beginning, students go on to take several courses, each of which examines an interdisciplinary issue or public policy area in detail. They also design an area of concentration that involves advanced coursework in a specific subject area, so that they can appreciate the importance of depth of expertise in addition to the value of interdisciplinary breadth. Various foundation courses such as statistics, economics, and physical sciences are another requirement, and all students must gain practical experience through an internship.

It is frequently asked, "What do you do with a degree in human biology?" The answer is: "Anything you want." Judging from the enormous diversity of professional activities of the graduates of the program over the past 23 years, ranging from astronautics to zoology, this is a statement of fact. The largest single profession of human biology graduates is medicine, but even here there is a high proportion involved in Third World health, health policy, and teaching. The key point is that graduates report that in comparison to their peers, they find themselves different in terms of how they approach problems and deal with difficult issues; they credit their human biology background for this difference. By any measure, Human Biology has been enormously successful as an undergraduate program, but how does that success translate into an effort to reform middle grades life science and health education?

Beginnings of the Humbio Middle Grades Project

The faculty of the Stanford undergraduate Program in Human Biology was encouraged by Carnegie Corporation of New York to think about how the excitement of an interdisciplinary education focusing on the human might be adapted for use at the middle grades: 6 through 8. At first, we were skeptical about whether we could offer anything of value, but we were convinced that the middle grades was the appropriate level to address problems of alienation from science, equity in access to science education, and the onset of high-risk behavior. Because middle grades students and college undergraduates are interested in different issues, it was clear from the outset that the content of the university curriculum could not simply be watered down to the middle grades level. Nevertheless, we came to believe that a focus on the human body and on adolescence itself would capture the interest of middle grades students while creating the opportunity to give them the knowledge necessary for making wise personal decisions about healthy lifestyles and high-risk behaviors.

An activity-based approach would also serve to keep their interest and be a means of imparting useful problem-solving skills. We were confident that by departing from the traditional tiptoeing through the phyla and naming all the parts of grasshopper legs, we would be able to get the students more interested in science education, and therefore would be able ultimately to achieve a much broader education in life science than the focus on human biology would imply. We strongly believed that our approach would make possible a more advanced education in the life sciences than is currently the norm. In addition, by directly addressing issues such as human sexuality and reproduction, effects of drugs on the nervous system, peer pressure, and family conflict, we believed a middle grades curriculum could contribute greatly to improving the health and well-being of youth.

With continued support from Carnegie Corporation and new support from the U.S. National Science Foundation, we launched our effort. We established collaborations with colleagues in the School of Education and with a group of local middle and high school teachers. One of our School of Education colleagues, Paul DeHart Hurd, performed extensive background research on adolescents, the middle-level science curriculum, and education reform, which together shaped the development of the HUM-BIO curriculum. We developed a detailed curriculum outline, and then several faculty undertook the task of drafting units. Our teacher collaborators served as reality checks and worked hard to produce meaningful and innovative activities. Graduate students and undergraduates served as assistants and brought to the process considerable skills in such areas as computer art and desktop publishing.

We gradually acquired the skills of curriculum development and exposed the fruits of our early labors to critical evaluation by 13 interdisciplinary teams of teachers from middle schools test sites across the country. These superb teacher teams have become partners in the development of the HUMBIO curriculum. Their critical but constructive input during annual summer institutes at Stanford and their hard work and innovation during field testing have been invaluable in the editing of the print materials for publication. It was their initial input that led us to develop individual curriculum modules rather than a textbook. We have learned that if you give teachers good materials, they can generate great education.

HUMBIO curriculum for the middle grades

The HUMBIO curriculum is comprised of 22 modules that can be used in any combination or order at the teacher's discretion (Figure 7.1). Each unit is designed to be used, on average, for 3 weeks, although many modules have been extended through the activities and projects for up to 6 weeks. The units have been written by Stanford faculty in collaboration with our local middle and high school teacher consultants, and other project staff, including graduates of the Program in Human Biology and science education doctoral students in the School of Education. The modules provide a solid foundation in the life and behavioral sciences, and then extend this knowledge through applications to health, social, and environmental issues.

Student interest in this curriculum is driven by the rich variety of hands-on, minds-on activities. Students do not merely read about human biology. They are more likely to perform an experiment, become engaged in a group activity, make a calculation, answer a challenging question, investigate a topic of thematic interest as a project, or prepare and debate an issue with classmates. For example, in the unit on the circulatory system, one of the suggested projects is *How to Be Heart Smart*. What does it mean to be heart smart? What kinds of behaviors are healthy? How can young people lead healthier lives? Why should they want to? In this project, students examine these questions and devise strategies to improve their own health.

Teachers at East Lyme Middle School in Niantic, Connecticut, report that the HUMBIO materials have allowed their students to talk and think more about themselves. When presenting the units on Changing Body, Reproduction, and Sexuality, the teachers spend the first day discussing their involvement with the Stanford project, how they and the curriculum developers are trying to address sensitive issues in a direct and

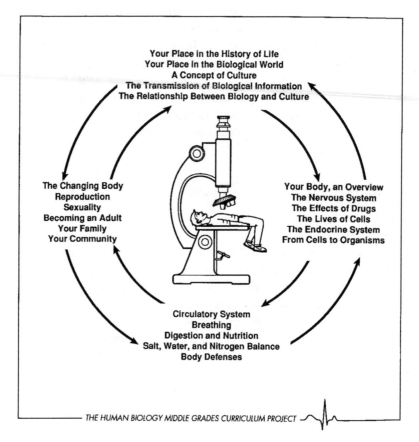

Figure 7.1. Guide to the curriculum units.

respectful way. The teachers use *respect, responsibility, cooperation*, and *communication* as key words in discussing the biological and behavioral aspects of adolescent development in the classroom and with parents. As a result, parents' requests for their children to be assigned to the HUMBIO project teacher team are double the number that can be accommodated.

Student involvement with the HUMBIO materials is not limited to the science classroom. The teacher teams extend the core science materials to mathematics, social studies, language arts, and often physical education and health. This interdisciplinary approach to the materials presents greater opportunities for students to develop the critical thinking and problem-solving skills that are essential as they prepare for careers and citizenship in the twenty-first century. It also allows them to apply their science knowledge to issues confronting them at this time in their lives, as well as to other issues that will confront them in the future.

The teachers at Anson-Jones Middle School in San Antonio, Texas, found that their students had an increased sense of ownership of and investment in the curriculum and in their community. In conjunction with the HUMBIO unit on Ecology, students at Anson-Jones started a program called "Graffiti Grapplers." Beginning with a group of 9 students and science teacher Linda Pruski, the program now involves over 125 student workers who are actively involved in community outreach and cleanup efforts to help reclaim their inner-city neighborhood. This student initiative has resulted in cooperative efforts among the students, police personnel, and other groups in the community. As a result, they are finalists for a national award for community service.

The HUMBIO materials also aim to make the ideals of equity, and the inclusion and encouragement of women and minorities in science, a reality in the classroom. To that end, the HUMBIO curriculum presents instructional strategies that include group work for diverse classrooms where students have limited English proficiency and/or a wide range of previous academic achievement. These carefully designed activities have been developed by members of Elizabeth Cohen's complex instruction research team at Stanford's School of Education, noted experts on group work in diverse classrooms. In the HUMBIO group activities, students use different intellectual and practical abilities as they rotate through different tasks. Positive interdependence is created in the group, so that each student has the opportunity to make a substantial contribution and to be recognized for that contribution. Each student also is held accountable for contributing to the group's success and for mastering the essential concepts of the curriculum unit.

In this carefully designed group work, students have the opportunity to discuss ideas, ask questions, offer solutions, and negotiate conflicting interpretations of data (Cohen, 1994). For example, in the unit on Genetics, groups of students design and present a genetic engineering project. They focus not only on the technological aspects of the project, but also on ethical considerations. Should genetic engineering be used to cure genetic diseases? Should money and effort be spent on developing a human youth hormone to keep people looking and feeling young? Should a gene for being slender or being tall be inserted into a person's genetic makeup? By combining aspects of science and technology with social and ethical considerations, many different points of view are expressed and students come to realize that science is not detached from everyday life (Lotan, Bianchini, and Holthuis, 1996).

Work with test site middle schools

The project's test site middle schools were chosen to represent both geographic and student diversity. We have schools serving predominantly low-income African Americans or Hispanics in inner-city New York; Norfolk, Virginia; San Antonio and Dallas, Texas; and San Diego, California, as well as in the more rural environment of Las Cruces, New Mexico. Other test sites serve suburban populations with mixtures of Anglos and Asian Americans in Kentucky, Connecticut, Kansas, Virginia, and California. The remaining school, in the rural panhandle of Florida, has a mix of low-income Anglo and African American students.

Interdisciplinary teams of teachers from our test site middle schools attended annual 2-week summer institutes at Stanford between 1991 and 1994 to work on the units they field tested during the academic year. A typical team of four was comprised of science, mathematics, social studies, and language arts teachers. Some teams included teachers in special education, physical education, and health. All teams worked and planned together during the school year. The most successful teams have the support of their principals and other district administrators, many of whom have attended part of the summer institutes at Stanford with their teams. In interviews conducted with the teacher teams in 1994, we found that support of the administrators was critical for the successful implementation of the curriculum at the school site.

The summer institutes at Stanford provided an opportunity for the teacher teams to discuss the content of the units with the Stanford faculty authors and the local middle and high school teacher consultants, who have developed many of the curriculum activities with the authors. The teams made suggestions to the authors and teacher consultants on revisions of the topics and organization of the materials, and in turn the Stanford faculty provided more in-depth information on the science content. The project's teacher consultants served as staff for the team working sessions during the summer institutes.

We know from reports of the participants that this arrangement provided rich, meaningful professional experiences. "The Stanford Institute is a source of creativity, networking and energy," said lead science teacher Ann Marie McDonnell from St. Elizabeth Catholic School in Dallas, Texas. Teachers from Egan Middle School in Los Altos, California, commented that the summer institutes facilitated collaboration among their team members and with teachers from the other test site middle schools. The Egan team reported that the summer institutes and those collaborations "changed their philosophy of teaching to a more interdisciplinary approach." The importance of the summer institutes to their professional development was mentioned by each of the teams as an essential ingredient in the successful implementation of the HUMBIO curriculum in the schools.

We organized the summer institutes at Stanford to model the underlying philosophies of the professional development of teachers and middle grades science education reform that are supported by middle-level and science education professional associations and noted scholars in the field of education. We viewed and treated our test site teams as our collaborators in this curriculum development effort. Giving teachers the opportunity to work with the curriculum as they adapt it to their school settings and student population reinforces the concept that teachers are not simply faithful implementors of completed materials, but rather decision makers and fellow developers.

The test site teams began their work on each of the HUMBIO curriculum units through their active engagement in the activities rather than by merely reading the material. Intensive, lively activity sessions were a significant part of the institutes. The teachers rotated through activities in groups, sometimes with their team members and at other times mixing members of different teams together. Each approach facilitated wonderful exchanges of ideas and built strong professional collaborations.

The teams used these experiences with the hands-on activities during the summer institutes as a springboard to their work on the curriculum units. They created lesson plans for the units they field tested with their students during the academic year. Most of the teams created extensions of the HUMBIO materials across the middle school curriculum, from science to mathematics, social studies, and language arts.

As one example of these extensions, the team from Kansas developed an interdisciplinary unit on smoking from the HUMBIO modules on the Circulatory System and Breathing. In science class, students learned about the physiology of the heart and lungs and performed research on diseases of these systems. When the students went to math class, they worked on several connected activities calculating the amount of smoke inhaled by a cigarette smoker, as well as the amount of secondhand smoke inhaled by nonsmokers sharing work space with smokers. The students also derived estimates of the monetary cost to an individual of smoking one pack of cigarettes per day from age 17 to 70.

In social studies, the students became involved in public policy debates on smoking. The class was divided to have students represent the tobacco industry, antismoking citizen groups, prosmoking groups, and public health officials in the community. Students performed research on their positions using data collected in their science and math classes, as well as from the library or other sources in the community.

In their language arts class, students were asked to write persuasive essays on smoking. Some addressed the advisability of smoking advertisements in magazines aimed at young people, and others wrote letters to older siblings who had begun to smoke as teenagers. Each student's work from these classes was kept in a special folder on smoking. The student's collected work comprised a portfolio of products that could be assessed by the teacher team for the student's understanding of the content and the interconnections of the material presented across the curriculum.

The test site teams have found that the links among the subject areas and the enrichment of the science through applications to actual social and public policy issues are strong factors motivating these students to learn this material. We plan to incorporate examples of the extensions created by the test site teams into the published version of the HUMBIO curriculum modules to show other teachers how science may be extended across the middle school curriculum. The penetration of science into the other disciplines provides rich contextual experiences for middle school students that more closely reflect the way science is performed, its applications to real-world situations, and its role in society. Indeed, a language arts teacher from the team at Wakulla Middle School in Crawfordville, Florida, says that "although science is not my thing, I am absolutely convinced that a science-driven curriculum is the way to go – everything is interrelated. Science is everywhere. I can't walk down the street without noticing it."

Stanford project staff visited the test site schools during each academic year to observe teams teaching with the HUMBIO materials. The visits helped to sustain the strong professional relationships between the Stanford staff and the test site teams, and gave us greater insights into the diversity of middle school students and their schools. To help strengthen the collaboration among the teacher teams across the country, we linked the test sites middle schools electronically in 1993. The electronic network enables the teachers to communicate with each other and with the Stanford project team as they continue to field test the curriculum units, and allows project staff to study the effects of the network on the implementation process at the individual school sites.

Several test site schools developed their own projects on the network. One is comparing road kill along local highways as an indicator of the geographic diversity of animals. Another involves schools along the Eastern seaboard who exchange information on migratory birds. There is also a pen-pal board for students to exchange points of view and a very popular "Ask Dr. Jim" column, with faculty author and physician James Lawry answering student questions on health.

To help us improve the curriculum materials during the development process, we collected extensive formative evaluation data each year through surveys completed by the teachers and students on the content, format, and effectiveness of the HUMBIO units. The data were analyzed and then used to guide the final revisions of the materials. Results of the formative evaluation between 1992 and 1994 showed a high level of satisfaction with the curriculum units. The categories of responses included comparisons to other science materials, level of student interest in HUMBIO, sensitivity to diverse populations, effectiveness of the activities in understanding the content, changes in student behavior, community involvement, and the extent to which the materials lend themselves to interdisciplinary extensions.

Professional development for middle grades life science educational reform

As the HUMBIO project moves toward publication of the middle grades life science curriculum, our attention has turned to issues of dissemination, implementation, and teacher professional development. Quite simply, we have found that to reach the students, you must first reach the teachers. The development of new, innovative materials is but the first step toward educational reform. The implementation of these materials by skilled practitioners in classrooms is the key to sustained change.

Stanford project staff and test site teacher teams have gained extensive experience with implementation of the HUMBIO materials and have been involved in many professional development activities. Over the past 3 years, project staff and test site teams have jointly presented teacher workshops at the annual and selected regional meetings of the National Middle School Association and the National Science Teachers Association in cities across the United States. Project staff also have presented workshops for middle schools in California and Illinois that are involved in the Middle Grades School State Policy Education Reform Initiative supported by Carnegie Corporation of New York. Participants in these workshops report being very excited by the HUMBIO materials presented and eager to try them out in their classrooms. The Illinois State Board of Education has invited project staff to present a second summer institute in 1996.

At Stanford we have a unique collaboration between the Program in Human Biology and the School of Education that has enabled us to link curriculum content to instructional practice. HUMBIO is a rich, comprehensive set of materials that represents a philosophy underlying middle level education. The materials have great potential for teaching young people science in the context of the biological, behavioral, and social transformations they are undergoing during adolescence.

To realize the potential in these materials, teachers need to learn how to use more effectively their curricular insights, their pedagogical knowledge, and their professional creativity. The realization of curriculum potential depends on strengthening teachers' knowledge of subject matter, further developing their interpretive skills, and supporting their awareness of new ideas (Ben-Peretz, 1990). Good professional development experiences offer meaningful intellectual, social, and emotional engagement with ideas, with materials, and with colleagues, both in and out of teaching (Lieberman and McLaughlin, 1992; Little, 1993). Talbert and McLaughlin (1994) found that communities of teachers, based in collegial networks, districts, whole schools, or departments, constitute a meaningful unit for professional development. Their research showed that teachers who participate in strong professional development communities within subject area departments or in other teacher networks have higher levels of professionalism than teachers in less collegial settings. They also report higher levels of shared standards for curriculum and instruction, evidence of a stronger service ethic in their relations with students, and a stronger commitment to the teaching profession.

Our initial implementation goal is to create and sustain a model national network of regional professional development communities dedicated to improving the content of the middle grades science curriculum and the pedagogical practices of middle grades teachers. These groups could be organized through the creation of regional councils comprised of experienced HUMBIO project middle school test site teams; school, district, and state education administrators; representatives of the established professional development organization or network in each region; education policymakers; and university or college education faculty.

Recent research points to the necessity for collaborative efforts among experienced middle-level practitioners, administrators, education policymakers, and university or college education faculty for the successful implementation of new curriculum materials and for building and sustaining a broad-based professional development community.

Stanford could provide the professional development experiences for the regional councils through summer leadership institutes at the university. In turn, the lead teams would conduct a series of professional development workshops for middle grades teachers and future lead teacher teams in their regions that focus on middle grades life science educational reform, using the HUMBIO materials.

Building healthy lifestyles

The HUMBIO curriculum materials are designed to support the changes in the education of young adolescents called for in respected national reports from the Carnegie Council on Adolescent Development (1989), the National Middle School Association (1993), and the Federal Coordinating Council for the Review of Education Programs in Science, Mathematics, Engineering, and Technology (1993). By engaging students in issues and curricular content they view as relevant and interesting, it is possible to reach a much higher level of intellectual challenge and accomplishment than is currently the norm in the middle grades. Also, by being activity oriented, the curriculum fosters habits of inquiry-based learning that extend beyond the classroom.

The integration of science with health in the curriculum and the emphasis on decision-making skills give students a solid foundation on which to build healthy lifestyles and avoid high-risk behaviors. The modular format of the curriculum and the abundant support given to the teachers offer teachers professional development opportunities to expand their pedagogical skills, their curricular creativity, and their insights into the lives and concerns of their students.

The HUMBIO curriculum materials are especially appropriate for use in schools that are committed to achieving the structural changes recommended by *Turning Points* (Carnegie Council on Adolescent Development, 1989) and by the National Middle Schools Association (1993). They also offer the means of attaining the knowledge standards set by *Project 2061 – Science for All Americans* (American Association for the Advancement of Science, 1989) and by the U.S. National Research Council in their *National Science Education Standards* (1996).

Although the HUMBIO curriculum was developed for the U.S. educational system, the interests and problems of adolescents are more similar than different in developed nations. With not too much effort, HUMBIO could be translated, revised, and repackaged to fit into the educational systems of most European countries. Wherever the curriculum materials are to be used, programs for professional development of teachers will be essential for successful implementation.

References

American Association for the Advancement of Science. (1989). *Science for all Americans: A Project 2061 report on literacy goals in science, mathematics, and technology.* Washington, DC: Author.

Ben-Peretz, M. (1990). *The teacher–curriculum encounter, freeing teachers from the tyranny of texts.* Albany: State University of New York Press.

Carnegie Council on Adolescent Development, Task Force on Education of Young Adolescents. (1989). *Turning points: Preparing American youth for the 21st century.* Washington, DC: Author.

Children's Defense Fund. (1991). *The state of America's children 1991.* Washington, DC: Author.

Cohen, E. G. (1994). *Designing groupwork: Strategies for heterogeneous classrooms* (2nd ed.). New York: Teachers College Press.

Federal Coordinating Council for the Review of Education Programs in Science, Mathematics, Engineering, and Technology. (1993). *The federal investment in science, mathematics, engineering and technology education: Where now? What now?* Arlington, VA: National Science Foundation.

Hamburg, D. A. (1992). *Today's children: Creating a future for a generation in crisis.* New York: Times Books.

Hechinger, F. M. (1992). *Fateful choices: Healthy youth for the 21st century.* New York: Hill and Wang.

Lieberman, A., and McLaughlin, M. W. (1992). Networks for educational change: Powerful and problematic. *Phi Delta Kappan, 73,* 673–677.

Little, J. W. (1993). Teachers' professional development in a climate of educational reform. *Educational Evaluation and Policy Analysis, 15,* 129–151.

Lotan, R. A., Bianchini, J. A., and Holthuis, N. C. (1996). Complex instruction in the science classroom: The human biology curriculum in action. In R. Stahl (Ed.), *Cooperative learning in science: A handbook for teachers* (pp. 331–354). Menlo Park, CA: Addison-Wesley.

National Middle School Association, Curriculum Task Force. (1993). *Middle level curriculum: A work in progress.* Columbus, OH: Author.

National Research Council. (1996). *National science education standards.* Washington, DC: National Academy Press.

Scales, P. C. (1991). *A portrait of young adolescents in the 1990s.* Carrboro, NC: Center for Early Adolescence.

Takanishi, R. (Ed.). (1993). *Adolescence in the 1990s: Risk and opportunity.* New York: Teachers College Press.

Talbert, J. E., and McLaughlin, M. W. (1994). Teacher professionalism in local school contexts. *American Journal of Education, 102,* 123–152.

8. Education for living in pluriethnic societies

EUGEEN ROOSENS

Perspective

Living in a multicultural and multiethnic society like the United States or the European Union (EU) requires dealing with multinomy, the co-existence of many, possibly divergent norms. Moreover, every culture in our contemporary complex societies is subdivided into so many subcultures and lifestyles that quite a few social scientists wonder if such a thing as a culture – a system of meaning shared by people of a given population – really does exist. The term *postmodern condition* is sometimes used to indicate this multinomy.

Nevertheless, Hannerz (1992) rightly states that culture remains a reality. This type of reality, however, is far removed from the uniform, monolithic systems we are accustomed to meet in the descriptions of the so-called primitive tribes by the anthropologists of generations gone by. At closer sight, every single culture appears to be internally pluralistic and unevenly distributed over social categories and groups. In the contemporary world, mass media and power relations play an important role in the dissemination and distribution of culture.

Subcultures and lifestyles are in permanent flux. A culture is not a monolithic thing, a package inherited from one's ancestors, as is often suggested in popular political discourse.

In the context of this continuous cultural flow and instability, a considerable number of political leaders and groups are struggling to maintain or create a multitude of ethnic, ethnonational, national, hypernational, and cultural identities, and are trying to express and organize these forms of auto- and hetero-identification (Hobsbawm, 1993; Moynihan, 1993; Schlesinger, 1991; Smith, 1986). Ethnicity is fashionable. This type of identity implies a feeling of continuity, of staying the same through time, of being linked to a self-ascribed and heteroascribed cultural and genealogical filiation (Barth, 1969; Horowitz, 1985; Hutnik, 1991; Roosens, 1989). It requires forms of shared meaning and their externalizations (culture) that are said to contain genuine elements of a tradition. In this sense, culture is not simply about meaning and its externalizations but is inextricably interwoven with ethnic, ethnonational, and national identities and groups.

To feel menaced in one's shared identity can lead to ethnicism or nationalism. Ethnicity, however, can also be used as an aggressive weapon by groups who in power and initiate battles of their own making. Ethnicism and nationalism unavoidably lead to old or new racist ideologies (Taguieff, 1988), cutting up humanity into discontinuous blocs, which are distinguished by genealogy and culture and represented as unequal by nature. In this perspective, cultural differences appear as unbridgeable, which makes genuine communication between antagonistic ethnic groups impossible. Similarities between cultures, humanity as a unity, the universal in humans, and the human being as an individual entitled to maximum freedom are portrayed as unreal abstractions.

The picture is quite complicated. Formal education can supply some powerful skills for coping with the complexities of contemporary society even though it may not provide everything one needs.

In the first part of this chapter, I outline my interpretation of the phenomena and challenges we face in contemporary multiethnic and multicultural society, using developments in Brussels, the capital (or one of the capitals) of Europe, as a case in point. I draw on field research conducted by the Leuven Department of Anthropology over the last 20 years (Cammaert, 1985; Hermans, 1992; Leman, 1987; Roosens, 1989, 1992; Stallaert, 1993). At the end of each major section, I formulate what, in my opinion, must be dealt with throughout the school curriculum. Being only an anthropologist, however, I feel incompetent with regard to the educational and pedagogical aspects of this transfer to the younger generations.

In the second part of the chapter, I discuss two models of education, already operational, that seem able to perform the task I sketch in the first part: the "European School" model and the "bicultural and trilingual education" system of Foyer, a local nonprofit organization. The European School reflects what people do for themselves and for their own children in a multicultural and multiethnic society when they have ample education, power, and human and financial resources at their disposal. The Foyer model, on the other hand, embodies the efforts of European, mostly autochthonous intellectuals, who are trying to develop a system of education for the children of ethnic minority immigrant workers. The initiators of this project come close to achieving with very limited means what the European School is effectuating with vastly greater amounts of money. I highlight the similarities in the two projects: what people of various backgrounds under very dissimilar material conditions do spontaneously to cope with a similar problem, that is, the education of children who constitute a numerical ethnic or national minority and have to deal with at least two subsystems of meaning. I sketch the context of the two systems but give more attention to the immigrant laborers because their situation is more complex.[1]

The third part of this chapter contains some tentative recommendations about the expansion of the systems discussed in the second part.

The complexity of culture in a multiethnic society

The rational in culture

Transcultural values. In each culture, be it from the North, the West, the East, or the South, there is a domain or an area that is rational in a double sense:[2] First, people use reason to create this domain of culture; second, the outsider or the researcher is capable of formulating critical evaluations in the cultural domain that have, at least to a degree, an authoritative character. Alongside this rational domain, one finds in all cultures an irrational and a nonrational domain (Shweder and Levine, 1984). In the irrational domain, one goes *against* reason, generally for affective and emotional motives of which one is not fully aware. The nonrational or the arational domain, by contrast, is constituted by conceptions, plans, or values that reason has no immediate hold on but that are not contradictory to the *ratio*. In other words, one can talk about and discuss certain elements of a culture (the rational and irrational fields), and the one will be right and the other wrong. For discussions or exchanges of opinion about other kinds of cultural elements (the nonrational field), however, this does not apply.

The rational domain concerns primarily the zone of science, technology, and their products. On this level a broad consensus is attainable, not only between experts but also between the populations at large of many nations. Thus, for example, it is undeniable that large groups of people are interested in the products of the industrialized countries. Radio, TV, film, modern means of transportation like cars and airplanes, and the entire paraphernalia of objects and institutions that are related to the comforts of life create a demonstration effect that is at the foundation of the problem of development in many regions of the world.

It would seem shortsighted to attribute this state of affairs simply to a purely socioeconomic conditioning process, as though the dominating classes are spitefully enticing the less powerful and the less well off with a kind of fool's gold, the primary purpose of which is to continue to exploit them. There is much more involved in many products that are desired by the masses: Not only are many of the goods from the industrialized countries more interesting ergologically in practical life than those one finds in preindustrial cultures, but they also symbolize the hold humanity has over its world and thus reflect superior insight and more adequate knowledge.

Indisputably, there is a great deal of fool's gold in circulation, and exploitation is widespread. But this is only one side of the reality. If my position is correct, it implies directly that it is difficult to maintain absolute cultural relativity, for indisputably there are common insights and values found in humanity that are just as real as the cultural and value differences.

Northwest Europe: An attraction pole. There is no doubt that Northwest Europe has developed cultures with achievements that are attractive to many people, notwithstanding their many negative aspects. The millions of immigrants and economic refugees from the South, from Turkey, and from many countries of Africa who have settled in the North are attracted by these cultural aspects. Higher wages, an abundance of material products, a greater degree of social security than in their own country, better medical care, better education, and so on are valued very highly. As a result, the cultures of these immigrants, in the eyes of many, are *unequal*.

First-generation immigrants express this appreciation. Many among them hope eventually to return to their home countries, but they want to do so with significantly improved resources in order to enjoy a higher socioeconomic status in their home region. The prosperity they have acquired in the North is intended to make this possible. That most of the children of these immigrants, who came with their parents at a young age or who are born in the host countries, want to construct a material situation for themselves after the model of the host countries is simply a fact. Many consider the home country of their parents as backward and underdeveloped.

It seems to me to be totally unproductive to gloss over these aspects of reality. If one substitutes total cultural relativity for them, one not only reasons erroneously on the theoretical level but also loses sight of the fact that both the allochthon and autochthon children on this same territory strive spontaneously for the same products and advantages. Competition and rivalry are thus unavoidable. To disregard this is to distort both policy and practical social intercourse.

This directly implies that immigrants who have come to live in the North, as well as their children, have a number of cognitive and evaluative traits in common with the local population groups. There are indeed similar perceptions and values, notwithstanding the very different ethnic and cultural backgrounds of the minorities and majorities.

Common values: A source of conflict. Paradoxically enough, it is generally similarities in the value orientation of the majority and the minority groups that give rise to tensions and conflicts, much more than objectively demonstrable differences in cultures. Everyone wants to obtain the same thing, and this leads to conflicts of interest, to tensions, and to oppositions. In turn, these stresses generate diverse reactions in the different socioeconomic and ideological groups and categories.

Some autochthons want and even demand that the allochthons of the guest worker type who are not from an EU country leave the country because they have become useless in a time of unemployment. These autochthons obviously see competitors in this category of immigrants or "public charges" who are after the scarce good that everyone desires. Others find it irresponsible to expel these immigrants in less prosperous times because these people or their parents contributed to the general prosperity when employment was not a problem.

Still others, both autochthons and allochthons, are of the opinion that the children and grandchildren of allochthons must be given equal opportunities, which implies that education and training must be adapted to the needs and the multicultural situation of these children more than is the case at present. In this line lie a number of experiments with intercultural, multicultural, and bicultural education.

Still others argue that the immigrants and their descendants may stay in the host country but that they must integrate totally, by which they actually mean assimilate. It is intended that the foreigners disappear as much as possible and become like the others.

In these four trends, there is an identical point of departure: One attributes – rightly so – to the autochthons and the allochthons a number of similar, if not identical, insights and desires. But there is also a tendency *not* to count this common core as the culture of the groups involved. And this is wrong. In this way, the cultural oppositions are maximized, and the common terrain on which the competition occurs is left out of consideration. It is precisely in this terrain that one must first come to a viable understanding.

But then, of course, it also remains true that there are a series of demonstrable cultural differences that complicate and impede the living together of diverse ethnic groups. And in this sense, the differences as well as the similarities can be considered a source of conflict. This problem of diversity is incorrectly omitted from consideration by those who only see the conflict element and depict the entire immigration event as a simple variant of the historical class struggle.

Those who contend that the ethnic minorities must be able to maintain their own culture thus must realize what they are saying. For as regards political ideology development and the working out of educational and training programs, one can make dramatic errors if one does not take account of the living and dynamic reality of differences and similarities. For example, if one, with the best intentions, thrusts the children of immigrant parents into the corner of their *own* culture with too much emphasis, one gives the appearance of fostering subtle forms of discrimination. Thus, the so-called Africanization of education as it was implemented some 30 years ago in a number of former colonies, generally by outsiders with no or only very limited familiarity with the local cultures, gave rise to many picturesque scenes in which the Africanizing teacher was mocked as backward and primitive by his students, even though he wanted to give them back their cultural tradition.

Consequences for socialization and education. What I have called the *rational in the culture* is a point of convergence: People come together, but this coming together can just as easily lead to conflicts as to the growth of mutual understanding.

It seems to me to be of capital importance that both the autochthon and the allochthon children and youth be made aware of what they all have in common, without distinction of nationality or ethnicity. The discussion of conflicts that have arisen from interethnic competition and that will probably occur again in the future may also not be neglected.

In this context, it is necessary that quite a number of lessons be devoted to the economic dimensions of interethnic and interracial relations. Indeed, tense interethnic relations almost always involve socioeconomic relations, which, in turn, revolve around the possession of goods, resources, and advantages. Everyone wants as many of these things as possible for themselves, so others are inevitably seen as competitors and as threats. In times of stable and favorable economic conditions, tensions can arise here and there with regard to language and cultural differences, and the physical appearance of other categories of people may cause friction, but rarely does tension rise to a significant level.

In the Brussels EU and diplomatic circles, for example, many people who belong to very different cultural and ethnic groups come in contact with each other daily without giving rise to openly racist or xenophobic reflexes. And wealthy Turks, North Africans, and Arabs are welcomed in many places. Apart from this, the skin color, or phenotype, of the Japanese has taken on a much nobler cast now that Japan has become rich and dominant with respect to Europe and the United States.

Unskilled immigrant workers are also quite well accepted if, during good economic times, they indisputably provide services to the host country by, for example, doing jobs refused by the autochthons. Only when the immigrants become economically less profitable do groups of the majority begin to point to the "fact" that they endanger the cultural purity of the majority or threaten to bastardize the "race." The religious irreconcilability between the minorities and the majority is also stressed. In other words, arguments are sought for rejection, expulsion, or other kinds of discriminatory action in the biological and physical, the ethnic, or the cultural uniqueness of these people.

Throughout the years of the educational program, one must offer a view of the concrete way in which the relations between various ethnic groups in a particular country have developed historically. Thus, for example, it is relevant for all those involved to know that immigration in Belgium is already an old phenomenon; that immigration received a substantial stimulus after the Second World War when no native workers could be found for vital sectors like mining, even though at the time there were more than 100,000 unemployed Belgians; that it was the Belgian employers and the Belgian government who took the initiative to recruit massive numbers of workers, partially with the intention of populating Wallonia. Such facts can serve to correct the notion that most of the foreigners are black-market workers who sneaked in or professional welfare bums.

Further, immigration can be placed in the context of the international power relations and the so-called development problem, a problem that is critical for several regions, also in a unifying Europe.

The phenomenon of racism also deserves attention. The term *racism* has several meanings and, not rarely, generates emotional reactions: some find the depreciative and derogatory attitude that is adopted with respect to immigrant ethnic minorities not at all out of line and therefore judge it erroneous to speak of *racism,* with all the odium attached to this term. Others are of the opinion that these negative mind sets can hardly be understood except as an expression of racism. Experience shows that it is difficult in these matters, which concern values, emotions, and commitments, to convince others to change their position by formulating accusations and moral reprimands.

The only thing one can do in education and training is to engender insights as objectively as possible that will enable people to make responsible judgments for themselves. However, there is nothing to guarantee that the public at large will acquire uniform opinions because the values a person will hold later do not depend only on insight and reasonability. One can only hope, however, that a thorough analysis of interethnic relations will give young people a firmer basis on which to act constructively than when the whole affair is left to the rhetoric of contending groups.

It seems to me to be especially important that this entire problem field be skillfully explained over the years of education of both the allochthon and autochthon children so that the nuances of this complex matter can be clarified. It is also of great importance that this problem be cast sufficiently in the world context and so clarified. The often heard opinion that "all those Turks and Moroccans should be sent home" can be a solution only for those who have no notion of what international consequences such a measure would have for the country that takes this step.

First, it is forgotten that the political decolonization, which occurred some 20 to 30 years ago, was accompanied by a growing ethnic consciousness in most population groups and that the dominance of Western Europe and the United States has faded. Nations like Japan, South Korea, and China are clearly working their way to the fore. Moreover, the international power relations between, for example, Belgium and the countries from which the immigrants have come are of such a nature that Belgium cannot permit itself simply to send the immigrants en masse back home. For such measures would be official acts of government and thus highly visible internationally. And international reactions to such measures are sufficiently well known.

Paradoxically enough, it is precisely what groups of human beings have the most in common – namely, the desire to possess and dispose of advanced material resources – that brings them to emphasize the cultural differences between them. However, the cultural noncomparability, which is indeed present on the level of the nonrational in culture, is often applied as a form of "equality" that, in turn, must serve to support the demand for equal economic and political rights. Young people must have the opportunity to understand how this kind of logic works.

The nonrational in culture

Characteristics of the nonrational. As noted earlier, social and cultural anthropology has sufficiently demonstrated that there is an enormous number of nonrational meaning and value systems. Each of these subsystems has turned out, at least in certain conditions, to be viable, and no sensible person can contend that he or she is capable of establishing a hierarchy that could place all of them on a universally applicable value scale. In any case, nobody has yet succeeded in having such a hierarchy accepted by most, let alone all, of the population groups concerned.

This issue can be easily demonstrated on the basis of the diversity of languages. Language is, for all groups of human beings, a cultural element par excellence. Children acquire a world view via language: Elements, and relations between elements, are given names. Now it has long been obvious to everyone that each language gives "reality" a particular cast in its own way. Some scholars have gone so far as to state that a specific *world*, in the literal sense of the term, corresponds to each language and thus that there are as many worlds as there are languages. Each culture is virtually completely determined by the corresponding language. This extreme position could not be maintained, but it has been accepted that, in many areas of linguistic usage and the corresponding presentation of things, one particular culture cannot be judged more correct than another, at least not on rational grounds.

From this perspective of cultural relativity, one may consider taste in clothing, house construction styles, home furnishings, the use of inner and outer spaces, the cultural structuring of the male and the female, religious symbolism, representation of life after death, and so on. One can believe on other grounds that one is right in any of these areas for one reason or another, but *through reason*, one will not arrive at a compelling conclusion.

It is understandable, however, that many people, also in these areas, think they are right. For once someone has grown up in a particular system and has developed along the lines of force of this system, it is difficult to go back. I am not capable of simply casting off a whole series of dimensions of the reality that I have learned to see and partially to construct in a specific way, even if I want to do so. Many aspects of my culture I do not even perceive as cultural data, but rather as natural, as self-evident. One has to live intensively for years in another cultural community and continuously speak another language before one grasps what elements of what is called *nature* are actually culturally determined. In other words, they could have been different for me if I had been born into another cultural community.

The affective and religious dimensions of the nonrational. What makes this issue complicated is that most people become attached to their own sub-cultural system and its nonrational elements and, as I work out in more detail subsequently, identify with a number of cultural values and em-blems. Whoever criticizes the cultural expressions of a particular group or person in one way or another at the same time oppresses this group or person.

The entire matter becomes even more delicate if religious forms of expression suffer, for many take no account of the degree to which re-ligious expression forms are culturally determined. Indeed, it is often postulated that some prescriptions and representations of reality origi-nate in the supernatural world and therefore cannot be questioned. When the religious dimension touches virtually all aspects of reality, the relations between groups of people, with their differing religious or cos-mological representations and value systems, become very complicated. The case of Islam in Belgium could well become an example of this (Dassetto and Bastenier, 1988; *Islamitisch Dialoog Forum F. V.*, 1993).

Since 1974, Belgium has officially recognized Islam as a religion. It is probable that the authorities who made this decision meant by the term *religion* what most Belgians mean by it: a subsystem that does not coin-cide with the political or the economic domain, a sector that has its own character to a degree but that may not be primarily concerned with sec-ular matters. Things are completely different with Islam: Islam is very comprehensive. In addition, laicization notwithstanding, the Catholic re-ligion in Belgium is also built into a "pillar," a complex of social, eco-nomic, and political institutions. All of this leads to situations that are often difficult to disentangle.

Thus, it is a fact that many Muslim children attend Catholic schools.

They come to Catholic education because their parents are of the opinion that Catholic education is, all in all, less pagan than other educational systems and also because Catholic education is perceived as better than the others. In some Catholic schools, more than 80% and even 90% of the children are from Islamic families.

This immediately raises a number of questions. The first thorny question is, of course, whether these schools are still Catholic schools and, as such, eligible for subsidies because the Catholic children, or at least the non-Islamic children, form a small minority in them. That such a question can become a source of tensions is obvious when one realizes that the official educational system – a rival authority – is empowered and even obliged to set up Islamic instruction if a minimum number of parents request it. Some authorities in the Catholic camp are of the opinion that it would be better if the Islamic authorities themselves established schools for Islamic children so that the Catholic schools could maintain their explicitly Catholic character. But this, again, is unacceptable for the staff of the Catholic schools, who fear that many jobs for Catholic employees would be lost. The situation is aggravated by the fact that about one child out of two born in the Brussels area is of immigrant parents.

Non-rational culture as emblem. Everyone can understand that such a situation becomes even more complicated when part of the population, in particular many immigrants from Morocco – more so than the Turks – use Islam as a cultural marker to set themselves off from the others and, more particularly, from the surrounding "unbelieving" majority. That religious symbolism and religious institutions often go back to arbitrary meaning constructions does not yet mean, therefore, that one can bring the parties involved more easily to "reason. " Rather, this is precisely what one cannot do in these matters. The non-rational in the respective cultures, not rarely, turns out to be the obstacle that is the most difficult to overcome in the establishment of intercultural communication.

Ethnic identity. A special subdomain within the objectively observable and accessible culture is constituted by the cultural traits with which members of a particular ethnic group or a particular nation distinguish themselves from other ethnic categories or nations. The nature of these traits is generally unpredictable or cannot be derived a priori from anything. They can be religious, geographic, linguistic, and so on. But what is certain is the following: The cultural traits by which a particular group or category of people distinguishes itself from the others are always a limited number of diacritical elements from a wider range of available cultural distinguishing criteria. In other words, each ethnic entity creates a social boundary by means of a specific number of cultural traits that are stressed. This action works together with the minimalization of other cultural differences, which are just as real, or with ignoring or brushing aside cultural similarities with other groups.

Generally, the traits used to distinguish an ethnic group come from the domain of the nonrational culture, so all rational discussion can be excluded if this is one's intention. Indeed, one can always stress that one is different from the others, not reducible, original, etc. These diacritical traits can, moreover, differ in time and space: The same code is not always used in every company and in all circumstances. Individuals also display great differences among themselves. Nevertheless, there is a certain coherence in the whole span of cultural traits that is applied by a particular category or group of people as a social ethnic boundary.

Very often in the present historical context, the content of this boundary is called by those invol ed "our cultural uniqueness" or "our cultural heritage." Thus elements of the culture are used to give oneself a character with respect to the others. If one then asks for understanding of one's cultural uniqueness, one is asking for more than mere tolerance with respect to other ways of life: One wants primarily to be recognized. One wants to be accepted with one's own kind of dignity. Thus, deep-lying aspects of the person are brought into play: origin, source, "blood," "people"; parents and ancestors; loyalty; continuity between the past, the present, and the future, and so on.

It is this part of the culture, in particular the expressive culture – which is not subject to rational discussion and thus permits no hierarchy of culture in terms of higher and lower, at least not on a rational basis – that serves as a means of identification. And because this means of identification is not rationally comparable with analogous means of identification of other analogous ethnic categories or groups, it is immediately suggested that the ethnic entity involved is also not comparable with others and is thus at least of equal value in its noncomparability.

Education and child raising. From this perspective, one very important element for the construction of harmonious interethnic relations seems to me to give the parents of immigrant children the opportunity to participate in the decision of what cultural baggage their children will be given in school. Of course, limits will have to be imposed on the choices one may wish to make. But in no case is one on the right track if the children are denied any reflection on their own culture and their own language, as has been done up to the present. This way of acting gives the impression that the school is separating the children from their parents by imposing a completely different ideology and lifestyle.

Of course, the position can be taken that "foreigners" just have to "adapt" if they want to stay in the host country and that the government should not invest financial resources to maintain "foreign" cultures. Such an attitude, however, is becoming more difficult by the day to defend in the present world context. In the EU, there is the realization that more political and economic unity has to be obtained if Europe is to survive and preserve its relatively high standard of living. This cooperation presupposes a climate of mutual respect and equality combined with a great deal of flexibility in regard to geographic mobility. And all of this implies that ethnic identity and culture are mutually respected and that they are given reasonable opportunities for survival throughout the entire territory of Europe.

It is not certain, then, that bicultural education for children of ethnic minorities will significantly enhance their chances and performances in the job market. In all probability, it will be useful for a certain number of these children. But even then it is, in any case, useful to create this kind of educational facility in order to strive for affective and expressive harmony in terms of both macro-political relations and the adaptation of immigrant children.

In this way, one would also reduce the chances of creating quasi-castes that will use their ethnic and cultural uniqueness as a weapon. Experience shows that ingredients such as ethnic revendication and the militant use of so-called cultural disputes can be even more explosive than socioeconomic factors because they touch directly on the very being of the people involved, or at least are felt as such. History and the present state of autochthon intercommunity relations serve to illustrate the point.

Two models of multiethnic and multicultural education

The European school model

Aim of the founders (Schola Europea 1953–1993, 1993). Immediately after World War II, with the disaster of the war fresh in their minds, a number of responsible politicians and statesmen set out to find ways to avoid the repetition of that catastrophe. They founded the Communauté européenne du Charbon et de l'Acier (European Coal and Steel Community) in Luxembourg, the first institution in which six European countries, including Germany and France, collaborated. The ideology professed by these founding fathers is important in understanding the orientation of the European Schools.

When the first well-paid European civil servants, hailing from different countries, moved to Luxembourg with their families, the problem of educating their children arose. The parents opted for a "European" solution. Rather than open a school for each nationality, they put their children together in one institution in the spirit of European unification. The first school started in 1953. The following year, the initiative received the blessing of the political authorities of the countries involved, and an entire school curriculum soon developed. While striving primarily to achieve academic excellence, the school intended to produce a feeling of European togetherness without sacrificing the culture or the national identity of the pupils.

The implementation. Today nine European Schools[3] are operating in six different European countries, three of them in Belgium. The 10th school, for 2,400 pupils, will be built in Brussels very soon, and other European schools will open their doors in the new member states (*Schola Europea 1953–1993*, 1993). The European Schools, educating more than 15,000 pupils and employing well over 1,000 teachers and a number of part-time teachers, celebrated their 40th anniversary in 1993. Potentially there is a tremendous amount of data on multicultural and multinational matters available in this European system that has never been thoroughly exploited. Insiders confirm this perception, and efforts are being made from within to inform the outside world about it.

Several factors were involved in bringing about this exceptional educational system. The vast majority of the parents were and are highly educated people with ample salaries. Marked socioeconomic and status differences were absent, and the general climate encouraged the rise of an international European atmosphere. Moreover, the well-paid positions and careers of the parents depended and depend on the formation of a European identity.

The high educational level of most of the parents itself produced an open-mindedness in the families that might not be expected in a school of the median type. The exceptionally high teacher salaries the system was and still is able to offer permitted a rigorous selection of the teaching staff.

As already noted, the sending families constituted a very homogeneous socioeconomic group. Only the languages, the cultures, and the nations of origin differed. In this sense, the pupils offered an ideal sample. It is almost as though they were selected for a multinational educational experiment, all other factors (social status, income category, attitudes toward their own cultures and nations and toward Europe) being equal. Moreover, the parents had direct input into the development and monitoring of the European Schools, so a strong relationship between the families and the institution was able to grow over the years.

The curriculum was fully in line with the aim of the founders, and combined continuity in culture and national belonging with a multi- and international spirit without sacrificing academic excellence. Although the allochthonous pupils attend school in a foreign country, they are able to use their own first language (L1) as their main school language. This way they are given the means of developing their own linguistic potential and can use their own language to learn and study the most difficult subjects of the core curriculum. Mathematics and sciences are taught in their own respective languages. The first language establishes continuity between the home and the school. Moreover, the daily, institutionalized use of the parents' language fosters a feeling of family belonging and, by extension, of ethnic or national identity.

In an urbanized and industrialized part of the world like Northwest Europe, where a tremendous number of cultural patterns are offered through the media and through intensive traveling, language may be one of the last pervasive, flexible, and enduring means of expressing ethnic or national identity. In particular, the institutionalized use of L1 in the context of a multinational school is bound to make language use a salient ethnic marker.

The compulsory acquisition of two other languages (L2 and L3) is instrumental in producing cultural open-mindedness and, at the same time, constitutes a major asset for entrance into a multilingual professional world. L2 instruction starts at the age of 6, and L3 instruction in the second year of secondary school. It is possible to take a third foreign language (L4) as an optional course in the fourth year of secondary school. Pupils from various nations sit together in the same foreign language classes (*Les Ecoles Européennes*, s.d.). The atmosphere of multilingualism is itself a very powerful component of the system contributing to the formation of a multinational or multiethnic spirit.

The use of "vehicular languages" is another interesting educational tool. As one of the founders of the system reports, this practice was not established on purpose but resulted from the fact that parents requested equal treatment for their children (*Schola Europea 1953–1993*, 1993). In order to create mixed classes and to guarantee, at the same time, an identical academic workload for all pupils, it was decided that every student must attend the classes of geography and history (and other optional subjects) in L 2, starting in the third year of secondary school. This automatically produces international classes in which the teacher is the only "native" speaker, so that all students are forced to learn geography and history, including their own, from an instructor with another national and cultural background. In doing so, pupils are confronted with perceptions and interpretations different from their own national views.

The living together of children from different backgrounds in a close, balanced fashion is another important dimension of the system: Young people are forced to meet each other in their daily routines, with all the positive and negative aspects of such encounters.

The structural harmony of the different ingredients of the curriculum is striking. Considered as a sociological ideal type, the European School is fully attuned to its social milieu and maintains its own subculture in the surrounding society. Academic excellence is guaranteed. The European Schools issue the European baccalaureate, which gives access to all universities of the member states as well as to a number of universities in Austria, Switzerland, and the United States.

Unavoidably, the system has its limitations. For instance, it does not deal on a daily basis with social and economic inequality. The "aliens" one becomes acquainted with belong to one's own privileged category. The socioeconomic homogeneity of the school may facilitate appreciation for other lifestyles and languages, but it is unclear how far it prepares youngsters to deal with inequality among human beings. I have no reliable information about this topic and would not like to jump to conclusions of any kind. It certainly is a worthwhile subject for empirical research.

The Foyer model as a remedy

The creation of an enlarged multicultural society in which non-EU immigrant workers and their families would be included is no longer on the public agenda. Political figures confess in private that they are not willing to lose votes by bringing up this topic. The unification of Europe seems complicated enough. Europe does not seem to be moving in the direction of the United States, where the so-called multicultural society is made up of immigrants, layer after layer, taking the place of the natives (Portes and Rumbaut, 1990). This pattern is strikingly different from that of Europe, where most ethnic groups and all nationalities and their respective lifestyles have their own geographical anchor place.

What happens in Moroccan families in Brussels is very similar to what Ogbu found among black Americans in Stockton, California (Ogbu and Gibson, 1991): There, too, parents tell their children that the school is important, but only a few take the steps to supervise them carefully. The same story recurs in all possible milieus with all possible subcultures and lifestyles.

Although no one has yet been able to show in a fully convincing way what factors make for success or failure at school, it is highly probable that parents' care and attention, and their instantiated support of their children, is an important element transculturally, although not the only relevant factor. It seems right, then, to accept that a number of lifestyle elements hamper good school results, such as giving priority to family visits over study in examination time, not providing a quiet place to study, not giving the child a chance to participate in examinations because holidays must be spent with the family in the home country, and not returning in time to give the child the chance to participate in the second examination session (Hermans, 1992).

But the other side of the coin, the school system, may be more important. Most Moroccan parents lack the resources needed to find out what the good schools for their sons are. And if they do find out, the chances are high that they will be turned away with the excuse that enrollment has already stopped due to the large number of candidates or that only youngsters with exceptionally strong primary school results are accepted. It is a fact that elite middle schools avoid enrolling Moroccan pupils.

In the present situation, it is no overstatement to say that the enrollment of Moroccan or other North African or Central African students can be a disaster for the school. Once a certain number of Moroccan pupils are enrolled, the chances are very high that Belgian parents and parents with other alien backgrounds will withdraw their children from the school. This same mechanism has been in operation for years at the primary school level. A large number of these schools have become so-called concentration schools, in which more than 50% of the children are from non-EU migrant backgrounds.

Once the migrants have taken over the school, projects or programs or even experiments with intercultural education become totally impractical. There are no partners from the other side left, and it would seem like a joke if the teacher demanded mutual respect for different cultures and lifestyles.

The teaching of the mother tongue (*langue maternelle*) and the culture of origin is left entirely in the hands of teachers sent by the respective countries of origin and controlled by the respective consulates or embassies. These courses, in which only 22% of the primary school children participate at present (there are no figures for secondary education), are not compulsory: They are not part of the regular curriculum, nor are they taken into account in the calculation of the school results. The only link to the school is the building in which they are taught. In an overwhelming number of cases, the teachers sent by the countries of origin are ill prepared, do not know the language of the receiving school, are not aware of what is going on in the local immigrant community, and do not function as members of the school team. There are clear indications that at least some of these teachers are selected by their government with political aims in mind (*Rapport communautaire*, 1992).

Thus, the maternal language, or L1, and the culture of origin (C1) are associated with low status and unimportant curriculum topics (not compulsory and not relevant for school results). In a number of schools, Belgian teachers flatly refuse to collaborate with the foreign teachers and oppose any expansion of the "matters of origin." Although the system is parallel in some aspects to the European School model – L1 and C1, taught by teachers sent by the home country – the system turns into a caricature and is rejected by a large number of the youngsters involved. Without providing figures, the official report states that "the young people themselves reject the courses" and ask for additional, "useful" English and Flemish language courses.

The most promising experiment trying to deal with this situation in the Brussels area is the Bicultural and Trilingual Education Project of Foyer (the Foyer model), which started in 1981 and has now been extended to nine schools in the Brussels area. This formula is presently applied only to kindergarten and primary education, but it is a striking way of preparing youngsters for secondary education and could be continued throughout secondary school if funding were available.

The Foyer project works with already established local schools of the Flemish community in Brussels. Flemish schools were selected because they were considered to be more open to the multilingualism than the French schools and more efficient in teaching other languages. The po-

Table 8.1. *Foyer model*

Period	How children spend their class time
Kindergarten (ages 3–5) Years 1–3	50% separate in an ethnic-cultural group. 50% together with native or other children.
Primary school Year 1	~60% separate in an ethnic-cultural group, with their own language and culture + mathematics. ~30% separate, with Dutch as a new language. ~10% in integration activities, together with native or other children.
Primary school Year 2	~50% separate in an ethnic-cultural group, with their own language and culture but no mathematics. ~20% separate, with Dutch as a new language. ~30% in integration activities + mathematics, together with native or other children. In the course of the year, this 30% increases, depending on the progress of the immigrant pupils, with the foreign teachers helping and supporting the children in this transition as much as possible.
Primary school Year 3 and on	90% together with native and other children; classes taught in Dutch. From 3 to 4 hours per week of instruction in the mother tongue. A few hours per week of instruction in French.

Source: Byram and Leman (1990).

litical situation – the Flemish (or Dutch) speakers are themselves a 20% numerical minority in the capital – may have played a role. Nine schools are operational at present: three Italian, one Spanish, one Moroccan, three Turkish, and one Aramaic, involving about 550 children, among whom are about 60 Moroccan and 200 Turkish pupils.

The Foyer model is presented in Table 8.1. According to Byram and Leman (1990, pp. 13–14):

Initially the children are organized in separate classes, both in kindergarten and in primary school. In these classes, the core curriculum is taught in their own language of origin, and gradually they are introduced to Dutch at a time that is considered the most "rewarding" for the child. How the prototype model will be adapted to each ethnic subgroup, and in particular to the Moroccan immigrant children among whom the language situation is rather complex, will be discussed separately. . . . Both in kindergarten and in the first two classes of primary school, the mother tongue is taught by full-time foreign teachers, who take care of the subject "mother tongue" (i.e. language as object and language as medium) and who are part of the team of teachers. From the third class on, the mother tongue is again taught by one and the same, i.e. a third foreign teacher.

International professional evaluations have taken place several times. The results were both positive and encouraging (Byram and Leman, 1990). As a matter of strategy, some elite schools at the highest level were asked to collaborate as loci of the experiment, which they accepted. The Foyer model takes L1 seriously, with all the psychological and educational advantages involved. It recognizes in a socially institutionalized fashion the importance of the family language (or the variant that comes closest to it), showing respect for the cultural background of the parents and their ethnonational group. By adding two other languages progressively, it is opening up two other ways of talking about the world and provides the youngsters with a precious practical asset: being multilingual in a multilingual city. It seems to me that bicultural education, like the European School system, has the advantage of working with a very concrete tool that is at the same time expressive and instrumental: language.

Moreover, allochthonous and autochthonous children are educated in the same alert educational context. No bicultural formula for secondary education has yet been developed. In recent years, the Turkish projects have been the most successful for a number of reasons. To start with, unlike the Moroccans, the Turks do not speak French, so they are not particularly inclined to send their children to the French-speaking schools. Moreover, Turkish can be clearly defined and the school version is close to the language parents speak, so that Turkish provides continuity between the family and the school. Parents of Turkish children feel ethnonationally respected by the use of their language in the school context. If more schools were willing to collaborate and more funds were available, the expansion of the Turkish variant would be very easy.

Organizing the Moroccan variant has turned out to be more difficult. Flemish schools are not willing to take in these youngsters, as they consider Moroccans to be French speakers who belong in schools of the French community. It is difficult to find out how much the negative image of the Moroccans plays a role, but it certainly is operative. Moreover, many Moroccans are Berbers who speak Berber languages and dialects and do not identify with Moroccan or literary Arabic. This internal multilingualism among the Moroccans is a serious problem. Furthermore, most Moroccan parents themselves opt for French-speaking schools.

In an interview with the director and the coordinator of the project (July 1994), we learned that the relationship between the project and the parents is excellent. Even unskilled or low-skilled immigrant parents are perfectly able to understand what the project is about and are very willing to collaborate. Although most of the project personnel are Catholics and almost all of the Turkish and Moroccan families are Muslims, religious topics have never been an issue. Religion is not considered to be a part of the project and is handled by the parents as a private matter.

The most recent professional and published evaluation of the project took place in the late 1980s and showed that the aims of the project were being achieved in a very satisfactory manner (Byram and Leman, 1990). According to the director and the coordinator of the project, nothing has changed since.

The main problems in extending the Foyer model to more schools come from the school directors and teachers. Most school directors avoid working with migrant children for the obvious reasons mentioned earlier. Moreover, most school staff are not attuned to multiculturalism or to the maintenance of a multiethnic society. In one school that agreed to collaborate with the Foyer project, about 50% of the dissenting teachers admitted having voted for the xenophobic Vlaams Blok.

Recruiting suitable teachers is another problem. And, as might be expected, adequate teacher training in living in a multiethnic and multicultural society is totally lacking. Most teachers of L1 are sent by the embassies. Some others are recruited among immigrants who are good native speakers and have received their educational training in the respective countries of origin.

Educators in the project repeatedly note that L1 is a very important educational tool, both as an object of study and a tool in the process of learning and as a means of emotional identification. There is empirical evidence that this even holds for Italians of the third generation, that is, the grandchildren of immigrants. Here again, it would be worthwhile to conduct more systematic and professional research.

About 120 alumni of the Foyer system have now moved on to secondary education. Theoretically, a Foyer model at the secondary school level is conceivable. However, there are major practical and technical problems. After primary school, due to a number of factors, the youngsters spread out over more than 20 secondary schools. Only one secondary school has enough Foyer alumni (of Italian origin) to initiate a curriculum at the secondary level.

Conclusions

Both the European School and the Foyer model take into account the rational dimensions of culture and the fact that some systems of meaning are better than others in dealing with nature – which entails competition – by (1) taking L1 seriously as the most efficient medium in the process of learning; (2) providing adequate training in L2 and L3, making students multilingual and, hence, more competitive on the labor market; and (3) closely monitoring the system in terms of overall academic proficiency.

Both systems acknowledge the importance of L1 as a means of expression of one's origin and identity, valuing the relationship with the parents, the kin, and the family and, by extension, with the ethnic, ethnonational, or national group. L1 is the most pervasive, flexible, and resilient tool of ethnocultural identification in today's world. By opening the mind to the other language(s) and the other culture(s) of the pupils' peers in the personalized setting of daily school life, both systems prepare one to deal, in theory and praxis, with the nonrational in culture and the ways culture and ethnic identity are interwoven.

Recommendations

There exists a real danger that in countries like Belgium, the issue of creating an harmonious multiethnic or multicultural society sounds like a euphemism for approving that all kinds of predatory foreigners live on the native welfare system. This image is supported by several factors.

In the sector of education, government circles, after years of ignoring the developments, eventually agreed that something must be done about the alarming rate of school failure among non-EU immigrants – mostly called *migrants* – leading to truancy, dropout, and chronic unemployment. These alarming signals prompted the Belgian government to appoint a royal commissioner for immigration policy for a term of 4 years in 1988. The tasks of the royal commissioner were recently transferred to the more permanent Center for Equal Opportunities and Opposition to Racism, which reports directly to the federal prime minister.

The commissioner, who started her career as a social worker, chose a highly competent staff and launched an incessant personal battle in favor of tolerance and a multicultural society, producing an extremely complete and very well documented program totaling hundreds of pages. This gave the charismatic commissioner immense moral prestige and put the authorities under pressure to act, but it also produced thousands of passionate enemies.

In order to limit the often heard criticism that more is done in favor of the profiteering foreigners than for the less well-off Belgian citizens, Parliament and the ruling political parties decided that the Center must monitor policy and make recommendations with respect not only to the migrants but also to the native underprivileged. Thus the link between being a migrant and being disadvantaged was officially confirmed. And as the terms *multiethnic society* and *multicultural society* had been used almost exclusively in discussing the migrant problem, they became associated with foreigners, welfare, and, at best, charity. Many well-intentioned activists crusaded for the migrants as for the weak and the poor. (Ironically, although non-EU immigrant workers are ascribed very low socioeconomic status in Belgian society, most of them see themselves as people who have succeeded in life. They compare themselves with those who stayed behind in their country of origin.)

Immigrants of European origin and the tens of thousands of Eurocrats, international businesspeople, expatriate managers, who also live in Brussels, almost never appear in the media. Multicultural status is seldom associated with them but has to do in the first place with marginals, Muslims, Turks, and North Africans. When discussing issues concerning European nations, the terms *Europe* and *European* are used. Belgians never talk about *Flemings* and *Walloons* as ethnic groups; rather, they refer to *linguistic communities.*

Without suggesting in the least that careful attention to and professional monitoring of disadvantaged immigrant categories should be diminished – quite to the contrary – we think it might be wise to take initiatives to highlight and encourage multiculturalism, the multinational, and the multiethnic among the middle classes and the upper middle classes of the native populations of the European states and to develop young, enthusiastic leaders who themselves are educated in what would be, properly speaking, a multicultural setting of institutions similar to the European School.

It might be worthwhile to recommend that EU authorities add to the linguistic sections of the European Schools that are already operational, for instance, a Turkish section in which talented migrant children could be enrolled. Turkey is already a member of NATO and a candidate for the EU. Besides, the Turkish language may offer a challenge, as L3 or L4, for some of the brightest students of other linguistic sections. A widely publicized opening up of the European Schools would do away with their reputation of being elite caste schools for the hyperprivileged at the expense of the ordinary taxpayer. There would also be an opportunity for their pupils to be confronted with what it means to be poor, without status, and without work in a Europe for which many of them will be responsible in their adult careers.

Moreover, collaboration could be envisaged with the Japanese School in Brussels, which provides full Japanese education from ages 6 through 15 along the lines of the Japanese curriculum as prescribed in Japan (Pang, 1995). Once finished with middle school, most Japanese youngsters enroll at the International School, where they attend the English-as-foreign-language baccalaureate program, as most of them are not able to understand fully the lessons in the regular English program, which keeps them isolated from the other students. As the parents, especially the mothers, fear that proficiency in Japanese and mathematics may be problematic at reentrance to the highly competitive "examination hell" in Japan, complementary courses in both of these subjects are organized and attended in addition to the normal school curriculum.

Like the youngsters of the European Schools, the Japanese pupils come from well-to-do expatriate families. Their teachers are sent by the Japanese Ministry of Education, and 50% of the high tuition fees are paid by the Japanese government, the other 50% by the Japanese company employing the parent or parents. As shown by the field research of Lin Pang (Pang, 1995), another member of our Center, and as is widely recognized in Japanese circles, the Brussels Japanese, including their children, are actually living on an island. Without affecting their knowledge of Japanese and their academic excellence, the Japanese youngsters could improve their fluency in other languages and their intercultural skills by joining the European School or another school of that type to which a Japanese linguistic section could be added. In this case, young Europeans might learn a great deal from their daily contacts with their Japanese counterparts, even if learning Japanese, like Turkish, might be too much of a challenge.

It might be useful and beneficial to establish a few new schools in the major cities of Europe based on the European School and the Foyer model and accessible to children of all interested citizens and immigrants. The idea is to take L1 and C1 seriously; to provide excellent teaching training in L2 and L3; and to open the minds of the young to other cultural realities and lifestyles, broadening their horizons with at least one and possibly more non-EU languages and cultures and bridging somewhat the gap between the wealthy and the other nations.

It is totally unrealistic to expect relatively untrained, low-paid teachers who, taken as a group, were not selected on the grounds of intellectual excellence to provide good intercultural education. Without drastic interventions from the subsidizing authorities, decent and thorough training in the teachers' colleges, and extended reschooling, this will remain an illusion for years to come.

Notes

1. A Leuven anthropological team in which I am a principal investigator has devoted considerable time and effort to the insertion of ethnic minorities in the Brussels area since 1974.
2. In this and the following subsections, I have expressed identical ideas in French in a contribution to a book, edited by J. Leman: *Intégrité, intégration. Innovation pédagogique et pluralité culturelle.* Brussels: De Boeck Wesmael, 1991.
3. Luxembourg (1957); Brussels I (1958), Brussels II (1974), and Mol/Geel (1960) (Belgium); Varese (Italy, 1960); Karlsruhe (1962) and Munich (Germany, (1977); Bergen (the Netherlands, 1963); Culham (U.K., 1978).

References

Barth, F. (Ed.). (1969). *Ethnic groups and boundaries: The social organization of cultural difference.* Boston: Little, Brown.

Byram, M., and Leman, J. (Eds.). (1990). *Bicultural and trilingual education: The Foyer model in Brussels.* Clevedon, England: Multilingual Matters.

Cammaert, M. F. (1985). Migranten en thuisblijvers: een confrontatie. De leefwereld van Marokkaanse Berbervrouwen. Leuven/Assen: Leuven University Press/Van Gorcum.

Dassetto, F., and Bastenier, A. (1988). *Europa, nuova frontiera dell'Islam.* Rome: Edizioni Lavoro.

Hannerz, U. (1992). *Cultural complexity: Studies in the social organization of meaning.* New York: Columbia University Press.

Hermans, P. (1992). De inpassing van Marokkaanse migrantenjongeren in België. Een vergelijkend antropologisch onderzoek bij geslaagde en niet-geslaagde Marokkaanse jongens. Doctoral dissertation, Leuven University Department of Anthropology, Leuven, Belgium.

Hobsbawm, E. (1993). *Nations and nationalism since 1780: Programme, myth, reality.* New York: Cambridge University Press.

Horowitz, D. (1985). *Ethnic groups in conflict.* Berkeley: University of California Press.

Hutnik, M. (1991). *Ethnic minority identity: A social psychological perspective.* Oxford: Clarendon Press.

Islamitisch Dialoog-Forum F. V. (1993). Open letter. Dilsen, Belgium.

Leman, J. (1987). *From challenging culture to challenged culture: The Sicilian cultural* code and the sociocultural praxis of Sicilian immigrants in Belgium (Studia Anthropologica). Leuven: Leuven University Press.

Les Ecoles Européennes. (s. d.). Brussels: Office Central du Représentant du Conseil Supérieur des Ecoles Européennes.

Moynihan, D. (1993). Pandaemonium: Ethnicity in international politics. Oxford: Oxford University Press.

Ogbu, J., and Gibson, M. (1991). Minority status and schooling: A comparative study of immigrant and involuntary minorities. New York: Garland.

Pang, L. (1995). Controlled internationalization: The case of kikokushijo from Belgium. The International Journal of Educational Research, 1, 45–56.

Portes, A., and Rumbaut, G. (1990). Immigrant America: A portrait. Berkeley: University of California Press.

Rapport communautaire sur l'éducation interculturelle en Communauté française de Belgique (1992). Brussels: Secrétariat du Ministère de l'Education de la Communauté Française.

Roosens, E. (1989). Creating ethnicity: The process of ethnogenesis. London: Sage.

Roosens, E. (Ed.). (1992). The insertion of allochthonous youngsters in Belgian society. (Special Issue of Migration) Berlin: Migration.

Schlesinger, A. (1991). The disuniting of America: Reflections on a multicultural society. New York: Norton.

Schola Europea 1953–1993. (1993). Brussels: European Schools.

Shweder, R., and Levine, R. (Eds.). (1984). Culture theory: Essays on mind, self and emotion. New York: Cambridge University Press.

Smith, A. (1986). The ethnic origins of nations. Oxford: Blackwell.

Stallaert, C. (1993). El casticismo y la frontera etnica entre moros y cristianos en Espana. Una aproximacion historico-antropologica. Doctoral dissertation, Leuven University Department of Anthropology, Leuven, Belgium.

Taguieff, P. A. (1988). La force du préjugé. Essai sur le racisme et ses doubles. Paris: La Découverte.

9. The economics of education and training in the face of changing production and employment structures

HENRI NADEL
Translated by Miriam Rosen

The conference that brings us together today at Marbach Castle has sought to make a reasonable place for economics. But what can economics reasonably add to the work of sociologists of education, psychologists, and, more broadly, the educational sciences? This is the question that has guided my investigation.

For some time now, economics has occupied a dominant position among the social sciences. This has certainly not always been justified, but it is true. Are we to explain it by the economists' claim to measure and theorize? By our increasingly market-oriented and liberal societies that are preoccupied with the values of material wealth? Economics is thus continuously solicited (or perhaps imposes itself) to measure everything that can efficiently contribute to the accumulation of wealth, notably individual wealth.

The success of economic science over the past 30 years can be explained by the impressive growth of production and mass consumption in the developed countries, followed by the crisis of this form of growth. In the remarks that follow, I shall attempt to examine what economics has to say about this crisis, and in particular about the role of education in the creation of a new system of production and growth.

I shall begin by summarizing the main features of Fordism and its crisis, as well as its consequences on the wage–skills nexus and the institutional forms that surround it, including the educational system. This will be followed by a quick survey of the way economics has sought to interpret education and training as factors of growth, as an investment in human capital, and as a mechanism of selection and standardization. The different post-Fordian production regimes, which offer various trajectories, and an international comparison of the corresponding educa-tion-training configurations illustrate the key points of the virtuous relations between the institutional forms linking training and the wage re-lation will also be discussed. Finally, we shall offer a guarded remark about future directions for research, given the vast diversity and complex-ity of relations between education and the economy, and the dangers of any rash changes in the educational system and employment agreements.

The crisis of Fordism and the crisis of the wage society

The crisis of the Fordian production system was accompanied by a pro-found crisis of the wage society and an extremely sharp segmentation of wage earners. Many studies have come up with the thesis that the ex-ceptional growth of the developed capitalist countries between the 1950s and the beginning of the 1970s resulted from the creation of a system of accumulation that was entirely new and particular: *Fordism*.

This idea indicates that production and mass consumption develop simultaneously through the creation of a coherent group of institutional forms. There is a codification of agreements that tie wage increases to the rate of productivity growth (Boyer, 1990). Such a system stabilizes oligopolistic competition and goes along with social protection guaran-teeing income security.

The hypothesis of Fordism as a particular form of development does not imply that all developed capitalist countries adopted the same insti-tutional forms or followed identical trajectories, which would be impos-sible to maintain. On the contrary, the national trajectories of Fordism were different depending on the forms of adoption and adaptation of each social and cultural structure – the "heritage" of each country in-volved.

If Fordism is not to be conceived solely as a form of production or-ganization, it implies a major institutional participation in all the pro-cesses of macroeconomic accumulation and division of income that would be otherwise inexplicable and impossible. Its crisis leads to a dis-connection between the institutional forms and the production regime. Thus, we can identify different phases of the deregulation of this pro-duction regime, and with them, the manifestations of its crisis in the wage society: the production regime's inability to generate productivity gains, the breakdown of the technical and social forms of work organi-zation, the declining profitability of investments, the acceleration of in-flation followed by the crisis of the monetary system, ever-increasing competition between national economies, the tremendous expansion of the foreign debt, and the arrival of Japan and the newly industrialized countries. The list of major structural disequilibria following the crisis of the 1970s can also be added.

The essential point is that in spite of the resumption of slow, uncertain, and badly distributed growth, the virtuous ties among labor, employment, and wages that existed before the crisis have now been broken. Likewise, the Keynesian agreements supporting welfare policies have been weakened.

The different forms of Fordism explain the various trajectories of post-Fordism (Boyer and Caroli, 1993; Nadel, 1994a). Although it is far from obvious that a new, unifying model is emerging (e.g., the lean production inspired by the Toyota system), one thing is certain: A return to full employment and the institutional arrangements that accompanied it is impossible.

Where the labor force is concerned, unskilled industrial jobs are still showing a sharp, rapid decline; massive unemployment is overtaking most of the European countries; and employment in the service sector is rising, but without compensating for the losses in industry. These new jobs are usually of lower quality with regard to both content and status (as is largely confirmed in the United States).

The virtual disappearance of nonskilled industrial jobs in Europe is striking and serves to reveal the crisis of the Taylorist basis of Fordism. Not only does post-Fordian growth show diminishing returns on employment, but it demands an increasingly qualified labor force with skills that are ever more adaptable and flexible.

This mismatch has led to the appearance of a "new poverty" on the margins of the wage-earning class and even within it, and this is true in the richest countries of the world. The brutal forms of this exclusion, of massive long-term unemployment and poverty, have been accompanied by rising problems of delinquency, drugs, xenophobia, racism, and fascism.

This crisis and its consequences have coincided with the emergence of a critique of the state and its welfare role. The intense development of liberal and even ultraliberal ideology and the rise of individualist values go hand in hand with the segmentation of society. This means that the crisis of the welfare state has coincided with the emergence of segmentation, and this is hardly an accident: Budgets have been tightened, public finances are limited, and public expenditures are increasingly criticized.

The school: Innocent and guilty

This economic crisis and the decline of the welfare state have had decisive repercussions throughout society, notably on the educational system. It is not customary to characterize the school as a specific apparatus of the welfare state: Education has little to do with either health insurance or public assistance. Its economy and means of financing cannot be justified by the same criteria. It is hard to imagine the laws of the market determining how the educational system is funded, given the role of the school as a complex institution where the very legitimacy of public power is at stake. The educational institution is not affected for the same reasons and in the same way as the institutions of the welfare state. Quite the contrary. Its existence is not challenged (except by a handful of libertarians), but it has to assume all the feelings of guilt and all the responsibilities.

It is asked to produce and transmit the most specialized knowledge, to socialize individuals, develop skills, adapt to changes in the surrounding world, create ethically positive changes in the world, raise productivity, promote competitiveness, encourage innovation, stimulate and intensify growth, eliminate unemployment, equalize opportunities and incomes, curb poverty, reduce mortality, lower fertility, fight against delinquency, compensate for familial deficiencies, promote and protect democracy, and so forth.

This conception makes the education system into a demiurge that at one and the same time produces the world, ruins it, and is then summoned to save it. The image is utopian but nonetheless recurrent. Like other public institutions, the school as an economic structure also faces challenges to its goals, its achievements, and its modes of operation.

Our ambition here is much more modest. We propose to examine what the economists can teach us about the relationships between education, on the one hand, and training, production, and employment, on the other.

Economy and education, subject and theory

It may seem trivial to attempt to establish the existence of relations between the economy and education and define their nature. Isn't education a precondition, a factor of economic progress? The response to this simple question is far from obvious for economic theory, and it is not easy to give an empirical demonstration of the *direction* of a cause-and-effect relationship between a country's educational level and its economic development.

However, the question is a legitimate one: The prince (the democratic society) asks his counselor (the economist) to tell him how much he should dip into his treasure (the budget of the state or the local government) in order to increase that same treasure tomorrow (and by how much). If the prince is free to allot these efforts as he sees fit (or if the democratic society has the means of a redistributive justice accepted by the citizens), he can still ask to whom these financial means should optimally be allotted. Here the specialists of educational selection could also come into play – unless one indisputable mechanism (the market?) can be found to satisfy all these imperatives simultaneously.

We have no intention of recapitulating here the vast ensemble of economic thought devoted to this search, but it may be useful to recall several of the essential steps.[1]

Classical theory distinguished three production factors: labor, land, and capital. We shall not concern ourselves with the problems of the appropriation of these factors, their remuneration, and the kinds of incomes that they procure. The classical tradition based on Adam Smith (1776), adopting a substantive notion of value, made labor the source of wealth. The social and technical division of labor (the famous pin factory) and education (and through it, the scientific and technical capacity for development and innovation) are presented as sources of increased value and the wealth of nations. Smith accorded special attention to skills (this is often neglected), which he distinguished from common unskilled labor. Thus he classed skilled labor as an element of fixed capital, unlike the simple labor that he included in *variable* capital. Oi (1962) borrows this figure of labor, perhaps unconsciously, as a *quasi-fixed factor*. Smith is the first to mention the idea of *human capital* to take into account the fact that the skills acquired by the worker bring greater value to production.

Two essential ideas are to be found in Smith's writings: On the one hand, education forms the overall framework for a nation's ability to increase its wealth. On the other, productive skills are associated with the individual worker.

Karl Marx developed a *theory of "complex" labor* that is presented as a multiple of "simple" labor, but his conception of capital accumulation leaves no room for the idea that a worker possesses any capital at all. For Marx, capital is an accumulation of merchandise and value, and the worker is the owner of a "labor power" that simply allows him to reproduce himself as the seller of that particular merchandise (Nadel, 1994a). In addition, Marx offers no measure of *individual productivity*: The productivity of labor is collective and results from a complex social process of capital accumulation (relative surplus value). Marx also presents the social and technical knowledge available to a country at a given moment as a "social heritage" and a factor of powerful accumulation. In production, technical knowledge possessed and delivered by the collective worker is appropriated by capital. From this point of view, the shop is also a site of conflict, and the qualification of workers is always threatened by the technological progress incorporated into the machine system.

At that point in the development of capitalism, none of these authors linked the educational system to the production system. The school was cut off from production, and technical skills were obtained through precapitalist practices: guilds, apprenticeship, and so forth.

Machinism and mass production were forms of productive organization set up to combat the skilled labor of the time. What was important was creating machines capable of mobilizing peasants without technical or occupational knowledge, as well as women and children.[2] In the same way, Taylorism was later to constitute a scientific method of organizing the most simple work possible, thus depriving the rare, costly skilled workers of their technical know-how.

Marshall (Marshall and Tucker, 1992) was later to stress the role of informal practices for acquiring productive knowledge, as well as that of the family and of the communities. These institutions were to find an echo in studies of the "third Italy" and flexible specialization (Beccatini, Pyke, and Sengenberger, 1990; Piore and Sabel, 1986).

Stock of knowledge and human capital

The period just after the Second World War saw the development of statistical data and national accounting systems, as well as applied macroeconomics. The development of the educational system thus became a tangible reality, and economists attempted to interpret economic development by integrating education as a factor of growth and attempting to measure its influence.

Dublin and Lotka (1930) formalized the first attempts to calculate the returns of education expenditures during the life cycle through the current value of human capital. Knight (1944) sought to measure a company's stock of productive knowledge and attempted to show how a sizable stock could limit declining profits.

Schultz (1961) and Denison (1962) worked to show that the portion of growth that does not result solely from the participation of capital and labor in the models tested can be explained by the long-term improvement of competences, skills, and education. For them, human capital was thus determined by educational expenditures but also encompassed factors such as health, life span, and so on.

The idea that the differences in human capital explain the distribution of incomes thus led to statistical studies aimed at correlating expenditures for education and individual incomes (Miller, 1960). This is quite likely to be the origin of the numerous studies carried out in different countries on individual data. This research was to be systematized by Becker (1964) and to give rise to the so-called human capital theory that dominated, and still dominates, the economics of education.

Human capital and individual competences

Becker's theory formalized what had long been incubating in numerous studies, and what has since the Second World War and the development of salaried workers become both popular wisdom and collective ideology (a good diploma equals a good wage). Insofar as this theory, which is at once simple and rich in implications, has come to prevail, it is useful to present its strengths and indicate its limitations.

The model is based on a standard neoclassical conception: The free market is able to fix a price for labor that corresponds to its marginal productivity. Beyond the traditional hypotheses, the human capital theory postulates that individuals have knowledge of all the training offered by the educational system and that there is free access to it. By comparing the sacrifice represented by the investment and the failure to earn during the training period to the higher income anticipated once the diploma or training is obtained, each person is able to make a rational choice. The individual productivity of labor is thus a function of the competences acquired (insofar as they result from the investment in human capital), and income is proportional to productivity.

We shall not dwell on the implausibility of the hypotheses (free access to training programs and the financing needed to pursue them, inherent homogeneity of individuals, etc.); suffice it to say that if the model had not been verified, it would have been abandoned.

The educational model of human capital

In fact, one of the best (and perhaps the only) forms of verification of the human capital model is its educational variant. What is verified? A high individual return on the investment in education. An educational model (Mincer, 1974) applied to a sampling of individuals shows a return on the investment: One extra year of study explains a difference in wage earnings. Similar results are confirmed, in various countries, with sample group data following cohorts of individuals.

Because the entire increase in earnings cannot be reduced to the number of years in school (or university) alone, several authors have sought to expand the components of the human capital stock to other factors (Eicher, 1979; Griliches, 1977; Hause, 1975; Levy-Garboua and Jarousse, 1988). There has also been an attempt to incorporate elements such as innate characteristics, IQ, social standing, ease of comprehension, and so forth. You are certainly more familiar than an economist with this non-educational dimension and its conceptual weakness. One can imagine that on such delicate terrain it is possible to multiply applied studies to infinity, and economists have hardly deprived themselves of the pleasure. The results are far from convincing, but this does not detract from the essential point: the quality of the educational dimension of the human capital theory.

Let us admit that these aptitudes dubbed *complementary* (although it is by no means clear that they are simply complementary) can be objectified and measured. And let us also admit, for the sake of speculation, that it is possible to select adolescents of a given age group according to their potential ability to benefit from the educational investment. What advice can the economist give the prince? If this were an investment in nonhuman capital, things would be simple: What is the use of investing in a company with doubtful prospects? Better to place the money in a company with promise.

Once again, we are faced with a problem of allocation that opposes *efficiency* and *equity*. Among the families needing financial aid in order to invest in human capital, should the stipends be distributed equally, regardless of the children's abilities (education for all and free access to all training programs)? Should the least promising children be financed (redistributive equity: the least advantaged must be aided)? Should the adolescents with the most abilities be financed (in the hope of optimal returns on the investments)? Which of these options will be the best, not only for the individual concerned but for the society itself? The human capital theory has no response to this problem.

Signaling abilities or transmitting competences?

This ability, which I assume is of great interest for the educational sciences, could be said to introduce a systematic bias. Indeed, returns on individual investments in human capital are measured by individual incomes; aren't the poor those who have made the rational individual choice not to invest? And aren't the rich those who have actually demonstrated their abilities?

These remarks indicate the limitations of the human capital approach. A positive link between the investment in education and its return in terms of wage income is measured for the *individual concerned*. This link assumes that the educational system is the *institution that transmits competences that can be directly appropriated by the individual* and confirmed in the company. The theory of human capital cannot, however, measure the return on the investment for the society as a whole.

Finally, it is implied, but not theorized, that a constellation of characteristics constituting ability improves the return on the investment. The educational system does not *produce* these abilities, but it can *signal* them.

The selective function of the educational system

Certain authors will defend the idea that the educational system *serves only as a signal*, a filter: It is an institution whose role is to select individuals for the production system (Spence, 1973). These theories have been widely explored. The school is said to give the production system signals that permit a filtering, a selection of individuals on the basis of its own needs. Ultimately, the *content* of the education would have little importance.

Such a radical position is not obligatory, however. There is also room for a reasoned selection and for the idea that diplomas and ranks constitute necessary signs that would permit the application of socially just and legitimate selection criteria, not only for the companies but also for the individuals who have competed for these titles and diplomas, and who are themselves legitimated by the educational system.

The hierarchy within the company respects the diplomas and ranks that, established on the outside, reinforce its own legitimacy (Blaug,

1987b). Many empirical confirmations support this position (Caroli, 1993).

Reproduction and coordination

In addition to selection, the effect of reproduction (Boltanski, 1982; Bourdieu, 1979) and transmission of norms and social functions must be taken into account. The reproduction of elites is a familiar phenomenon, and it depends on a filter that must be legitimate. The Grandes Ecoles in France play this role to perfection.

The theory of the filter must, in turn, be complemented by the theory that presents the educational system as an institution producing social norms (Tyack, James, and Benavot, 1987), and the theses characterizing the same system as an apparatus of social control, a means of reproducing the social structures of capitalist domination (Bowles and Gintis, 1976).

Such theories are familiar to the educational sciences, and they undoubtedly enrich the understanding of an educational institution's role in relation to social reproduction. Paradoxically, these filter theories also give the educational system an additional social role. The idea that this system's ability to select and establish legitimate standards authorizes economic and social coordination is very rich. It allows the conceptualization of a coordinated labor market for diploma holders, of hierarchical relations, and of the way information and power networks are created.

All of these approaches allow us to define the educational system as one that transmits knowledge; shapes competences that can be validated in productive work; selects individuals; and integrates them into the production and reproduction of the social norms in which the whole society recognizes and reproduces itself.

Production regimes and training systems

If in-company training should be understood as the upgrading of individual human capital within the company, what is the content of that process? Does it involve the acquisition of knowledge strictly applied to productive requirements that the wage earner should respect at his or her work station[3] or also general knowledge? And if it involves general knowledge, why has this not been transmitted by the educational system? Why should the company be more capable of supervising and thus financing such instruction (Stankiewicz, 1995; Verdier, 1990)?

Speaking of general knowledge as inevitably interwoven with knowledge only shifts the locus of the problem: It becomes nec transform both the company and the educational system. In reali two entities are both extremely heterogeneous; educational syste _, uke company models, differ greatly from one country to another, as is the case for the forms of linkage and coordination between education and training.

The limits of the human capital theory are patent here. Although this approach has allowed a multiplicity of partial studies and individual follow-ups, it is clear that we are faced with a comprehensive investigation that goes beyond the individualist paradigm of human capital. What is required is the interpretation of the complex relationships arising between the technical changes in production and the social forms of work and training organization, which can be understood only in their specific national and historical dimensions. This training, and especially technical training, unlike initial general education by itself, requires an organic coordination between certain elements of the educational system and the productive system.

It is the *quality* of this organic coordination that determines the virtuous link between education and growth that we are seeking. Let us admit at the outset that the logic (should it exist) of this complicated ensemble cannot be reduced to one or two simple formulas. The particular combination that we need to understand could be called the *national education/skilling configuration*. Such a term stresses that each national history (because the school is always a national institution) is specific and gives rise to a particular coordination between the school and the productive system. The functions of filtering/selection; integration/reproduction of classes and social categories and access to diplomas; classifications; and the company hierarchy must all be taken into account.

Within this configuration, the *creation and validation of technical competences* depends on rules, agreements, or institutions that are very different from one country to another. Each configuration is at once *stable*, because it is historically rooted and armed with powerful institutions, and *unstable*, because the production regime is threatened with changes. Certain countries have relatively weak educational systems, but coordination with the companies and their participation is of high quality. Others can boast of very high-level scientific and technical training programs, but these are essentially offered to an elite or, for specific reasons, the relations between education and production are conflictual.

Education/skilling configurations: An international comparison

In *Germany*, the essential structure is based on apprenticeship organized within what is known as the *dual system*. This system combines in-company training and school-based education, with the two providing a comprehensive body of practical and theoretical knowledge. But above all, the management of this system depends on the quality of the institutional dialogue between the authorities of the *Länder*, the unions and the employers, in order to define a program adapting competences in relation to the companies and their skills needs.

In addition, the system is open, and apprentices can enter technical schools and continue their studies all the way to an engineering degree. However, most of them will be able to enter the labor market; apprenticeship is thus the main path of technical training in Germany. The qualifications acquired in this system are recognized by the employers. In Germany, the latter attach the greatest importance to technical training and broad competences, which are thus validated in terms of wages and participation in employment (Mobus and Sevestre, 1991). In this instance, cooperation wins out over a uniquely hierarchical relationship. The companies are familiar with the content of the diplomas because these have been developed with their strong participation.

Even if certain observers today fear a weakening of the system and observe a relative flight from apprenticeship to general studies, the proportion of skilled workers in Germany is far greater than that of its European competitors (Lutz, 1992; Steedman, 1993).

Japan does not offer a training configuration comparable to that of Germany. Indeed, the Japanese school system does not generate quality technical competences recognized by the companies. But the companies, particularly the *Keiretsu*, where lifetime employment is guaranteed (Aoki, 1988; Nadel, 1994b), have to assume responsibility for this technical training. And there is no doubt that they are especially successful. On-the-job training constitutes the essence of such programs, but the large companies offer high-level theoretical training themselves or subcontract it. However, once Japanese employees acquire good technical training, it will only be recognized in the parent company that has provided it.

The microcorporatist Japanese wage system encourages strong internal mobility and training, unlike the situation in Germany, where there is cooperation between companies (and sometimes between small companies) and with the training system that directs the acquisition of competences.

France offers yet another configuration. School-based technical training programs are, for the most part, provided on a full-time basis. Recent reforms have sought to develop apprenticeship programs and more organic relations with the companies, but such measures remain in the minority. In addition, apprenticeship is traditionally limited to the crafts and typically does not occur in hi-tech industry.

France's academic tradition is that of general education; technical instruction is its poor relation. Worker and technician careers enjoy little social prestige and low wages; families that have the means to do so orient their children toward general education. The selective, elitist educational system channels the best students toward classic instruction, which means that they are largely discouraged from pursuing technical training.

The central role of the state in French history is well known; the Republican school is traditionally run, without any real participation from the social partners. As a result, it is not surprising to find that, in general, technical competences are badly matched to company needs. This mismatch is sufficiently grave and long-standing that technical diplomas granted by the educational system have little standing with the companies. Because this system basically reflects a very compartmentalized view of manual and mental labor, even the most technically skilled workers rarely contribute to innovation – which makes such careers even more stultifying.

The technical training system in *England* is again different. Provided by the companies in the form of on-the-job training, it neglects formal and theoretical aspects. Until the 1980s, the apprenticeship system was organized in an elitist fashion under the control of the trade unions. Under the circumstances, the recognition of qualifications, which was hardly institutionalized or codified, was weakened, and the evaluation of technical training needs was left to the companies (Garnier and Hage, 1993; Lefresne, 1992). More recently, complementary training provided by the City and Guilds courses and by institutions of secondary and higher technical education offered relatively transferable qualifications. The result was paradoxical: The number of training courses provided by the companies themselves declined, and the same companies found themselves competing for apprentices (Marsden, 1990).

With the deregulation and union crisis that accompanied the decline of British industry, recourse to apprenticeship was even less frequent (Dolton, 1993). The 1983 reform introducing the Youth Training Scheme has not yet yielded convincing results. Thus the United Kingdom still has a shortage of technically skilled labor.

The situation in the *United States* varies greatly from one state to another, with a wide range of technical training programs at the secondary and postsecondary levels: comprehensive high schools, partnership academies, community colleges, technical institutes, and so forth. Most of these programs combine practical and theoretical components but rarely include on-the-job training. Cooperation between companies and technical schools can be observed, but it is difficult to evaluate this on a national basis. According to certain researchers (Baily, Burtless, and Litan, 1993; Marshall and Tucker, 1992), the technical training system is characterized by the low quality of entering students and the low level of final qualifications. These authors insist that such students have a level of competence significantly lower than that of their European and Japanese counterparts.

In other words, the configuration can be characterized by a weak educational system and a relatively low training capacity among the companies. This situation can be explained by the volume of turnover in American companies, which leaves little opportunity for internal career advancement; the low level of cooperation; and the high level of conflict in relations among the social partners. Attempts are presently under way to formulate agreements linking job security and commitments to training, but these remain marginal (Brown, Reich, and Stern, 1992). Overall, the low level of technical training in the United States and the fact that the companies do not compensate for this training result in a low-skilled work force and mediocre wages.

This admittedly rapid survey shows that the educational system is only one factor in the puzzle. Rather, what is decisive is the linkage between the technical/skilling component with the basic elements of the wage–skills nexus and the production regime.

Conclusion

This chapter makes no claim to comprehensiveness, and its arguments are far from definitive. However, we have sought to emphasize the idea that the training–employment relationship cannot be encapsulated in a simple formula. It involves long-standing social and historical dynamics.

It is remarkable that countries in which the wage relation generally dominates the modes of individual social reproduction – countries that participate in international competition in increasingly homogeneous markets (Reich, 1991), and where lifestyles seem to be largely convergent as well – should manifest such varied configurations of education and training. This diversity itself merits systematic research, which is, in a certain way, the aim of this conference. Indeed, such variety creates at least two methodological problems. For one thing, it precludes the search for a simple, generalizable formula.[4] For another, the configurations known to us today are subject to their own contradictions and dynamics, and will undoubtedly reveal weaknesses in the future that are preferable to anticipate in the present.[5] All that we can do is touch on them and thus immobilize complex formations that are constantly in motion.

Imitation is impossible: Even if we can export an entire factory, we now know that the determinants linked to the quality of the labor force cannot be obtained by simply applying one organizational model to another. The same is true for what we have called the *education/training/ production system configuration*.

But the international comparison does not simply reveal diversity. It allows us to verify that the countries that have configured the production of technical competences and their recognition by the productive system in a cooperative, dynamic way are the ones that enjoy the greatest success. The quality of training organized in a complementary way between school and company; the involvement of the companies; the commitment to finance the cost of this skilling training; strong institutionalization and codification of the system, whether implicitly (Japan) or explicitly (Germany); acceptance, participation, and involvement of the labor force: These seem to be the main elements of the virtuous success of the relationship among education, training, and the production regime.

In the absence of a universal recipe, each national, historic social formation will have to find the forms that permit greater cooperation among the actors in the complex play of the education–employment relationship. I fear that economists can only be modest participants in such a project. It is rather for ordinary citizens to select institutional and social alternatives whose cost and consequences will never be magically delivered by the market and whose medium- and long-term effects cannot be reduced to market and monetary issues.

Notes

1. In this chapter, I have abstracted from models that have tried to measure education's returns on growth. The analysis in terms of educational level poses problems of measurement, and the returns indicated by the incomes

are hardly convincing (Hartog, 1993). In general, the parallel between education and growth, including the situation in the newly industrialized countries, is undeniable. What is practically impossible to establish, however, is the *direction* of the causality. Does wealth push education forward, including by freeing a surplus to be invested (and in what measure)? Does the educational effort lead to measurable growth? The debate in terms of threshold is already more fruitful (Blaug, 1987a). The comparative institutional analysis, which is open to approaches other than that of the market, is also very promising (Boyer and Caroli, 1993).

2. Ricardo was the first to intuit this.
3. This recalls the position of Thurow (1975) and his critique of the human capital theory. For Thurow, the productivity of the work goes back to the *job* involved (job qualification), not to the human capital.
4. It would thus be difficult to endorse the appeal of Womack, Jones, and Roos (1990) for the universalization of lean production by proposing the excellent German dual system for the entire world. There have been convergent trends within the European Union for a number of years. It is certain, for example, that the reforms of the French vocational training system are influenced by the German model, but this does not mean that the legislature has voted any law instituting the dual system.
5. Paradoxically, an international comparison involves learning about the failures of others as much as their successes. What are the threats to the apprenticeship system in Germany? What is not working in the policies aimed at limiting violence and exclusion in the American school system? Why can the French school system function only with an elitist model?

References

Aoki, M. (1988). *Information, incentives, and bargaining in the Japanese economy*. New York: Cambridge University Press.

Baily, M. N., Burtless, G., and Litan, R. (1993). *Growth with equity: Economic policymaking for the next century*. Washington, DC: The Brookings Institution.

Beccatini, G., Pyke, F., and Sengenberger, W. (1990). *Industrial district and interfirm cooperation in Italy*. Geneva: Industrial Institute for Labour Studies, International Labour Organisation.

Becker, G. (1964). *Human capital* (2nd ed.). New York: Columbia University Press.

Blaug, M. (1987a). Where are we now in the economics of education? In M. Blaug (Ed.), *The economics of education and the education of an economist* (pp. 129–140). New York: New York University Press.

Blaug, M. (1987b). The rate of return on investment in education in Great Britain. In M. Blaug (Ed.), *The economics of education and the education of an economist* (pp. 3–49). New York: New York University Press.

Boltanski, L. (1982). *Les cadres*. Paris: Editions de Minuit.

Bourdieu, P. (1979). *La reproduction* (2nd ed.). Paris: Editions de Minuit.

Bowles, S., and Gintis, H. (1976). *Schooling in capitalist America*. New York: Basic Books.

Boyer, R. (1990). *Regulation theory: A critical assessment*. New York: Columbia University Press.

Boyer, R., and Caroli, E. (1993, September). *Changement de paradigme productif et rapport éducatif: performances de croissance comparées France-Allemagne*. Paris: Ronéotypé CEPREMAP.

Brown, C., Reich, M., and Stern, D. (1992). Conflict and cooperation in labor management relations in Japan and the United States. *IRRA Proceedings, Session XVI* (pp. 425–436). Berkeley: University of California, Lator-Management Cooperation.

Caroli, E. (1993). Les fonctions du systeme educatif vues par les economistes: quelques conceptions fondratrices. *Education et Formation, 35*, 53–59.

Denison, E. (1962). *The sources of economic growth in the United States and the alternatives before us.* New York: Committee for Economic Development.

Dolton, P. J. (1993). The economics of youth training in Britain. *The Economic Journal, 103*, 261–1278.

Dublin, L., and Lotka, A. (1930). *The money value of a man.* New York: Ronald Press.

Eicher, J. C. (1979). Education et réussite professionnelle. In J. C. Eicher and L. Levy-Garboua (Eds.), *Economique de l'éducation.* Paris: Economica.

Garnier, M. A., and Hage, J. (1993). *The technical training advantages.* College Park: University of Maryland Center for Innovation.

Griliches, Z. (1977). Estimating the returns to schooling: Some economic problems. *Econometrica, 45*, 1–22.

Hartog, J. (1993, October 1–3). *On human capital and individual capabilities.* Lecture presented at the meeting of the European Association of Labor Economists, Maastricht, the Netherlands.

Hause, J. (1975). Ability and schooling as determinants of lifetime earnings, or if you're so smart, why aren't you rich? In F. T. Juster (Ed.), *Education, income, and human behavior.* New York: McGraw-Hill.

Knight, F. H. (1944). Diminishing returns from investment. *Journal of Political Economy, 52*, 26–47.

Lefresne, F. (1992). Systèmes de formation professionelle et insertion des jeunes: une comparaison France-Royaure-Uni. *Revue de l'IRES, 9*, 3–38.

Levy-Garboua, L., and Jarousse, J. P. (1988). *L'investissement humain: Théorie et mesure* (Issue No. 106). Paris: Centre de Prospective et d'Evaluation.

Lutz, B. (1992). *The contradiction of post-Tayloric rationalization and the uncertain future of industrial work.* London: Altman and Al.

Marsden, D. (1990). Institutions and labor mobility: Occupational and internal labor markets in Britain, France, Italy, and West Germany. In R. Brunetta and C. Dell'Aringa (Eds.), *Labor relations and economic performance* (pp. 414–438). London: Macmillan.

Marshall, R., and Tucker, M. (1992). *Thinking for a living: Education and the wealth of nations.* New York: Basic Books.

Miller, H. (1960). Annual and lifetime income in relation to education, 1929–1959. *American Economic Review, 50*, 962–986.

Mincer, J. (1974). *Schooling, experience, and earnings.* New York: Columbia University Press.

Mobus, M., and Sevestre, P. (1991). Formation professionelle et emploi: Un lien plus marqué en Allemagne. *Economie et Statistique, 246–247*, 77–90.

Nadel, H. (1994a). *Marx et le salariat* (2nd ed.). Paris: L'Harmattan.

Nadel, H. (Ed.). (1994b). *Emploi et relations industrielles au Japon.* Paris: L'Harmattan.

Oi, W. (1962). Labor as a quasi-fixed factor. *Journal of Political Economy, 70*, 538–555.

Piore, M., and Sabel, C. (1986). *The second industrial divide: Possibilities for prosperity.* New York: Basic Books.

Reich, R. (1991). *The work of nations.* London: Simon and Schuster.

Schultz, T. (1961). Investment in human capital. *American Economic Review, 51*, 1–17.

Smith, A. (1776). *The wealth of nations* (1975 ed.). New York: Dutton.

Spence, A. M. (1973). Job market signaling. *Quarterly Journal of Economics, 83*, 355–374.

Stankiewicz, F. (1995, September). Choix de formation et critères d'efficacité du travail. *Revue économique, 5*, 1311–1331.

Steedman, H. (1993). The economics of youth training in Germany. *Economic Journal, 103*, 1279–1291.

Thurow, L. (1975). *Generating inequality: Mechanics of distribution in the U.S. economy.* New York: Basic Books.

Tyack, D., James, T., and Benavot, A. (1987). *Law and the shaping of public education: 1785–1954.* Madison: The University of Wisconsin Press.

Verdier, E. (1990). Pourquoi des entreprises mettent-elles en oeuvre des formations continues diplomantes? *Formation-Emploi, 32* 3–6.

Womack, J., Jones, D., and Roos, D. (1990). *The machine that changed the world.* New York: Ravson-ASS.

10. School-to-work processes in the United States

RAY MARSHALL

This chapter focuses on what has come to be known as the *school-to-work* (*STW*) *transition*, an area where the United States has serious problems relative to most other democratic industrial countries. The United States concentrates more resources, absolutely and as a proportion of GDP, on college and university education but very little on the great majority of Americans who do not intend to pursue baccalaureate degrees. It should be emphasized at the outset, however, that the U.S. economic and learning system's problems are not restricted to STW – they are systemic. Indeed, focusing on the transition from school to work can be misleading because the United States has serious deficiencies in most other learning systems (i.e., families; preschool, elementary, and secondary schools; and workplace education and training) that make it very difficult to establish world-class STW processes. Similarly, the United States is unlikely to create world-class STW systems unless it has much more effective labor market institutions and adopts economic policies that will cause employers to demand workers with higher skills. Major problems for the United States are caused by its past successes with an organization of work that required only a few people with higher-level academic skills; most employees with limited formal schooling could earn relatively high incomes.

A major assumption of this chapter is that the maintenance and improvement of real wages for most workers require much greater attention to improving the skills and knowledge of the large majority of workers who are not likely to be 4-year college graduates. The problem facing the United States is not that we do not have some excellent apprentice, community college, and technical programs for these workers because we do. Our problems are due to a number of factors. First, a relatively small proportion of our workforce receives high-quality training. Second, there are no generally recognized standards for most of

195

these programs (except for our relatively small registered apprentice programs, which do generally have high standards). Third, the United States has no national system to make training, education, and labor market information available to all students and workers.

The recognition of the systemic nature of our problem will prevent two common problems in discussing STW processes. The first is the assumption that marginal programs or those with short durations and limited resources will produce lasting results. Most federal employment and training activities, for example, have had limited impact because they do little or nothing to overcome systemic pathologies or weaknesses in U.S. learning systems. Second, understanding the systemic nature of our problems makes it possible to avoid fruitless debates over whether "education and training" or "economic and social policies" are more important in improving the conditions of workers. Surely no one believes it will be possible to develop a world-class work preparation system if employers do not demand highly skilled workers. By the same token, it is equally misleading – and dangerous – to argue that U.S. workers are likely to continue to command relatively high wages without improving productivity, and therefore skills and the organization of work. There is, in other words, no magic bullet to solve our income problems; we must adopt systematic approaches to educational, social, and economic problems.

Another major assumption of this chapter is that the United States and other industrialized countries are experiencing fundamental structural shifts in economic activity driven by two closely related processes – technological change and intensified national and international competition – which, if we wish to maintain and improve the incomes of most workers, require fundamental changes in education as well as in economic institutions and policies. The establishment of effective STW processes must be based on an understanding of the nature of these structural changes. The first part of this chapter, therefore, outlines the nature of these structural changes and their effect on education and the preparation for work. This is followed by a discussion of some U.S. STW programs. The chapter concludes with some recommendations for improving STW processes.

The context: structural changes in the U.S. economy

America has the worst STW transition process of any industrialized nation (Berlin and Sum, 1988, pp. 22–23; Commission on Skills of the American workforce, 1990, pp. 46–47; Osterman, 1980; Osterman, 1988, pp. 111–114; U.S. General Accounting Office, 1990, pp. 33–41; William T. Grant Foundation, 1988a, pp. 26–28).[1] Put simply, we have no systematic processes to assist high school graduates to move smoothly from school into employment. Our secondary schools and counseling efforts are focused primarily on encouraging youths to continue their education in college and obtain a degree. Yet almost half of each graduating class – roughly 1.4 million young people each year – directly enter the labor market, and only one-quarter of each graduating class ultimately obtains a baccalaureate degree. Most non-college-bound high school graduates are left to sink or swim – without advice or career counseling and without any job placement assistance (Barton, 1991).

The Commission on the Skills of the American Workforce (1990) summarized the problems for youth going to work immediately after high school:

> There is no curriculum to meet the needs of non-college bound youth, no real employment service for those who go right to work, few guidance services for them, no certification of their accomplishments and . . . no rewards in the workplace for hard work at school. (p. 47)

How we got this way

American education and labor market processes are closely related to the factors that made the United States the world's leading industrial economy in the first half of this century. Economic success caused the education and training processes closely associated with the traditional American economy to become institutionalized and therefore very difficult to change.

A basic feature of the traditional American economy was its rapid increases in productivity and standards of living. This was due mainly to an abundance of cheap natural resources, economies of scale, and reinforcing processes whereby market forces shifted resources to higher-productivity uses (e.g., from agriculture to manufacturing) and caused improvements in one industry to lead to improvements in others (e.g., as when reduced steel costs improved automobile and other industries, leading to higher sales and greater scale economies). This mass production system had its problems, but it ushered in the longest period of sustained, equitably shared prosperity in U.S. history – perhaps even in world history (Marshall and Tucker, 1992).

The main forces eroding the mass production system's basic institutions were the closely interactive effects of technology and international competition. Technology reduced the importance of physical resources and changed the nature of mass production processes. Information technology and flexible manufacturing systems allow many of the advantages of traditional economies of scale without large producing units. *Technology*, best defined as how things are done, is basically ideas, skills, and knowledge embodied in machinery and structures. Technological progress, therefore, represents the substitution of ideas, skills, and knowledge for physical resources. Nobel laureate Theodore Schultz demonstrated this process in agriculture, which has experienced great increases in output since the 1920s, despite the use of less land, physical capital, and labor (Schultz, 1981). Moreover, other economists have demonstrated that almost all of the improvements in productivity since the 1920s have been due to factors associated with human capital and technology; natural resources account for none of the increase and physical capital for only 20% or less.

Learning systems for a mass production economy

The bifurcated requirements of the mass production system resulted mainly from the hierarchical, fragmented nature of work (or Taylorism) combined with the assembly line. Although this system required a few educated managerial, technical, or professional employees, most of the work was routine and could be performed by workers who needed only basic literacy and numeracy. Because the system was so productive, workers with limited education could earn enough money to support their families at levels that were relatively high by historical and international standards. This was especially true after the New Deal policies of the 1930s provided safety nets for those who were not expected to work, collective bargaining to increase workers' share of the system's gains, and monetary and fiscal policies to keep the mass production system running at relatively low levels of unemployment.

Learning systems reflected mass production skill requirements. Managerial, professional, and technical families prepared their children for occupations through family information networks and elite learning processes in public or private schools. With some notable exceptions, public schools were organized primarily to provide basic literacy and numeracy skills to lower-income, native, and immigrant students expected to do routine work in service industries, in mass production factories, or on farms. Although the system provided more upward occupational mobility than those in most other countries, especially after the reforms of the 1930s and 1940s, both family and school learning systems basically perpetuated the mass-production, resource-oriented occupational structure. This included education and training for the skilled trades through postsecondary school apprenticeship programs. The STW transition processes were informal and largely family related, but were perpetuated through formal learning systems.

Competing in the new economy

Information technology has combined with international competition to alter the conditions for economic success. In a more competitive, consumer-driven system, *quality*, best defined as meeting consumers' needs, becomes much more important; by contrast, mass-production systems were producer driven and emphasized quantity of standardized outputs, not quality. Moreover, in competitive markets, economic success depends heavily on productivity in the use of all resources, not just economies of scale. Competitive systems thus must be more flexible in adjusting to changing market and technological conditions.

In a more competitive environment, companies or individuals can compete in two ways: They can reduce their incomes or improve value-added productivity and quality. The easiest approach, the one we have followed in the United States, is the low-wage strategy. Most other industrialized nations have rejected this strategy because it implies lower and more unequal wages, with serious political, social, and economic implications (Commission on Skills of the American Workforce, 1990).

Japan and Western European countries take several actions to encourage companies to pursue high value-added strategies. First, they build a national consensus for such a strategy. The essential instruments used to encourage companies to pursue high value-added strategies include wage regulation, relatively generous unemployment compensation and family support systems, universal national health care, full employment policies, trade and industrial policies, and adjustment processes to shift resources from low- to high-productivity activities.

Japan and Western European countries promote various forms of worker participation to encourage companies to organize participative, high-performance organizations (i.e., for quality, productivity, and flexibility) that decentralize decisions to front-line workers as much as possible. In order to encourage worker participation and decentralized decision making, other countries encourage collective bargaining and require or promote worker participation in management decisions at various levels, including boards of directors, but almost always in workplace decisions. Policies in the United States, by contrast, make it very difficult for workers to organize and bargain collectively, and provide little or no requirements for worker participation in workplace decisions.

High-performance organizations likewise develop and use leading-edge technology. Mass-production systems depend on standardized technologies and relatively unskilled labor. As it becomes increasingly clear that this combination is not competitive in high-wage countries, some American companies have attempted to automate by combining advanced technology with unskilled labor, an approach that has rarely succeeded. High-performance organizations require well-educated workers who can adapt and constantly improve leading-edge technology in a process the Japanese call *giving wisdom to the machines.*

Because high-performance organizations give workers much discretion, positive incentive systems are basic requirements for success. The incentives for front-line workers in mass-production organizations are often negative (e.g., punishment for failure) or perverse – penalizing workers for superior performance, as when workers lose their jobs when they improve productivity. Positive incentives include group bonuses for superior performance, participation in decisions, a sense of dignity and self-esteem, internal unity, and employment security.

Above all, high-performance organizations require workers who can analyze data, communicate with precision, deal with ambiguity, learn rapidly, participate in what were considered management decisions in hierarchical management systems, and work well in teams. These have come to be called *higher-order thinking skills,* formerly needed and possessed only by the managerial, professional, and technical elites.

Most industrialized countries have developed policies to ensure that a majority of their workers have higher-order thinking skills. These include high performance standards that all young people are required to meet before they can leave secondary schools. It is each school's responsibility to see that these standards are met. Standards are important because they provide incentives for students, teachers, and other school personnel; information to employers and to postsecondary institutions; and a means for policymakers and the public to evaluate schools. Indeed, by strengthening linkages, standards have helped fashion systems out of disjointed activities.

Standards likewise are important factors in strengthening STW transition systems because students who meet high standards are prepared for work, technical training, or other forms of postsecondary education. Because the United States has no national standards for secondary school leavers, American students in nonacademic tracks too often find their options to pursue postsecondary education and training severely constrained; in fact, this system tracks students at very early ages.

Other countries do several additional things that strengthen their learning systems. First, most have family policies to support children. The United States, unlike many other industrialized countries, has no child support, universal preschool, or paid parental leave programs. The absence of such policies makes many American families, particularly low-income families, very poor learning systems. Many children, therefore, start school far behind their more advantaged counterparts, and subsequently have inadequate learning opportunities at home as well as in school.

Families are not only basic learning systems, but also provide information and services linking young people to labor markets. Families in most industrialized countries have experienced considerable structural change and stress since the 1960s that have reduced their effectiveness as learning systems. However, most other industrialized countries have done much more than the United States to provide public and community processes to help families compensate for these changes (Marshall, 1991).

The problem in the United States is especially serious for inner-city and minority youths and for those in isolated rural areas that lack transportation to available employment or training opportunities. U.S. Bureau of Labor Statistics data on the employment status of recent high school graduates confirm these labor market disadvantages for blacks and Hispanics. Recent graduate unemployment rates for whites, Hispanics, and blacks were 14.9%, 29.1%, and 50.3%, respectively. In addition, more black youths were out of the labor force and thus were not counted as unemployed. Indeed, only 28.5% of black but 53.5% of white male high school graduates had jobs in October after graduation (U.S. Bureau of Labor Statistics, 1989). These data refer to whether or not youths have jobs at all, without reference to the quality of those jobs. The realization that relatively few minority youths obtain any job, let alone a good job, even if they study hard and obtain a diploma, provides little incentive to excel in school.

Problems in making the transition from school to work are not confined to minorities or the poor. Negotiating the labor market is a difficult task for many American youths who have decided not to pursue a baccalaureate degree immediately after high school. In other countries, young people are provided occupational counseling, employment information, and job placement through local schools or labor market institutions, and employers take an active role in youth development activities. The United States, by contrast, has no system for getting youth from school into work, and the employer community takes little responsibility for youths.

America thus is not serving many of its youths well and is particularly neglectful of the needs of the three-quarters of its future workforce who do not obtain baccalaureate degrees. At the same time, it is becoming clear that the new high-performance work organizations require that workers be more highly skilled. Stated another way, in the modern global information economy, few people will obtain a good job that pays well without significant learning beyond high school. The triple demands of efficiency, quality, and flexibility require line workers who have high levels of basic skills and who learn quickly. In short, the quality of America's front-line workers is the bottom line to our nation's economic future. Improving education and labor market systems alone will not solve our competitiveness problems – defined as maintaining and improving incomes for most workers – but our economy is unlikely to remain competitive without more efficient learning and information systems, especially for those who do not pursue baccalaureate degrees.

American employers avoid responsibility for youth skill development

Practices in the United States contrast sharply with those of most other industrialized democracies. Whereas Germany and Japan have systematic incentives and high expectations for performance of their adolescents, and whereas their expectations are generally fulfilled, Americans expect little of adolescents, and our expectations are equally fulfilled (Marshall and Tucker, 1992).

America's preferred employers – those who offer good wages, attractive benefits, and career potential – ordinarily do not hire high school graduates immediately, even if they have good academic records. America's biggest and best corporations avoid hiring youths at all. Only a handful of the Fortune 500 firms hire fresh high school graduates for entry jobs offering career opportunities. Even member firms of the Business Roundtable, which so actively advocate school reform and form partnerships with schools, do not hire teenagers. Although almost all of these firms eventually employ high school graduates, they normally wait until the job applicants are "mature and settled down" in their mid-20s and have accumulated some work experience. Other employers emulate the practices of our largest firms.

Similarly, American apprenticeship sponsors act like any other American employer in a position to be selective about applicants; they choose *against* youth. The average starting apprentice in the United States is in his or her late 20s. This delay in hiring for career-track jobs results in many youths spending 5 or 6 years floundering in jobs that offer neither learning nor advancement opportunities (Osterman, 1980; William T. Grant Foundation, 1988a, pp. 26–28). More important, these conventional American hiring practices have at least four critical consequences for STW transition:

1. The delay in hiring American youths provides German and Japanese youths a 5- to 10-year head start in gaining access to significant occupational skill training.
2. These practices remove some of our best learning systems – our finest corporations – from the processes that develop our youths. By shunning any responsibility for hiring teenagers, the best American employers have effectively disengaged from the process of instructing and socializing their future workers.
3. The delay in hiring high school graduates eliminates a natural communication loop for employers to feed clear information back to schools about what skills are needed in the workplace.
4. Most important, effort and achievement in school are disconnected from rewards in the workplace, thus undermining student incentives to work hard and achieve in school. Improving the STW transition is thus an essential school reform issue.

Recent research by John Bishop (1989) and James Rosenbaum (1989, pp. 193–197, 1990) has demonstrated that effort and achievement in high school are not effectively rewarded for students who do not plan to go to college. Few employers ask for high school transcripts, and most of those that do find that they cannot obtain them on a sufficiently timely basis to make hiring decisions. The high school diploma appears to be valued by employers mainly as an indicator of discipline and persistence rather than as a measure of achievement. Although a high school diploma makes a big difference in earnings over the long run, it appears to make little difference in the type of employment and wages offered in initial jobs after high school graduation. And the gap between those with high school and college training has widened markedly since the 1950s and 1960s, when college graduates earned only about 20% more than high school graduates; in 1979 and 1992 the gap was 49% and 83%, respectively (Mishel and Bernstein, 1994). Because many youths have a short time horizon, near-term employment prospects offer much more powerful incentives than do abstract arguments about lifetime earnings.

American employers currently are not communicating what they need very clearly either to schools or to students. Employers, therefore, must do a better job of identifying the skills they require of job applicants and reach agreement with schools about how to assess and certify those skills. Equally important, employers must act to hire youths with such skills, once certified. Surveying employers to find out what skills they say they need is not enough; the effort must be tied to action. A promising vehicle for achieving employer commitment to action is a formal agreement, an idea that started with the Boston Compact in 1982 and is embodied in legislation passed during the Clinton administration, discussed in the following section.

U.S. STW Programs

The compact

The problem of bridging the transition between school and work requires systematic national, regional, and community responses. One promising approach is to organize job collaboratives or compacts among businesses, schools, and community leaders along the lines of the Boston Compact (Spring, 1987, pp. 4–17; 1989, pp. 3–16). Compacts have been established in several cities, but many are simply unfocused collections of business–education partnership activities. What we have in mind here is a version far more specific, which would be geared to results in integrating school and employment and in creating incentives for learning.

The essential mission of the job collaborative is to stimulate academic achievement and career readiness among students. All of the parties to the compact agree to commit themselves to a set of measurable goals or outcomes and to a system for evaluating each through time. A primary aim is to provide students with incentives to stay in school and perform well in order to be eligible for jobs and financial assistance for higher education. Participating students agree to maintain certain standards of performance. For example, in Boston they must obtain certification from two teachers that they are working hard, must stay out of trouble with the law, and must maintain at least an 85% school attendance level. In return, businesses agree to preferential hiring of students who meet the specified standards. For their part, school authorities agree to make specific improvements in the participating schools.

Begun in 1982 and renegotiated in 1988, the Boston Compact brought together the resources of the public schools, businesses, universities, labor unions, and the mayor's office to improve student academic achievement and work preparation in exchange for increased opportunities for both employment and higher education. This Compact has been most successful in gaining jobs for high school graduates. In 1989, through the Compact, 1,107 graduates out of a class of just under 3,000 found full-time jobs averaging $6.75 per hour in over 900 businesses (Commission on Skills of the American Workforce, 1990). Over 85% of the youths placed are reported to have been satisfactory employees. Perhaps most impressive of all, among high school graduates, employment of blacks reached parity with that of whites at a level substantially above the national average. Youth unemployment rates in Boston were significantly lower than in other places, and the difference between the proportions of black and white unemployed youth were almost negligible, an achievement unparalleled in any other major city (National Alliance of Business, 1989).

Even though Boston's booming economy during the 1980s was a helpful factor, the Compact's accomplishment in raising employment for black high school graduates to the white level was due as much to the efficacy of the concept as to economic conditions. The Boston project focused on a fundamental difference between middle-class white youths and those from poor black families: White middle-class youths have better information and job-seeking networks than do poor black youths. Young people from poor homes lack the networks of employed fathers, mothers, aunts, uncles, friends, and neighbors that smooth the transition for the better connected. The recession of the early 1990s diminished the program's number of placements, but the Compact is still performing and evolving; in 1992, for example, a vocational-technical school was formed to connect to a variety of apprenticeship paths into the workplace, with related training provided by area community colleges.

The Boston experience has taught important lessons that should be incorporated into any program to help young people move successfully from school to work. Youths – especially those from disadvantaged families – must have access to information and job networks in order to find employment. Such networks can be established on an institutionalized basis within the high schools by establishing career services or similar functions. Assistance from an intermediary, including training in effective job search techniques, is an important component. Job-related standards should not be ignored in student recruitment and selection, and special efforts are needed to articulate relevant standards on a clear, objective basis and to communicate those standards to schools, young people, and their families. Reward systems are important for everyone. For students, it must be unmistakably clear that school pays off in terms of economic opportunity and personal satisfaction.

Of course, no uniform prescription is appropriate for all localities. Each process must be adapted to the needs, resources, and circumstances of both the employers and the youths in the community served. Successful compacts are not just single programs; rather, they become frameworks to organize a wide variety of initiatives. Such efforts can refine job entry requirements, foster the availability of effective mentor arrangements between youths and adults, create meaningful training and career paths for youths, improve occupational counseling, and offer training and education on a joint basis between schools and worksites, thereby putting learning into a practical context more likely to motivate students. In short, the process of bridging the school–employment gap must be systematic, focused, comprehensive, and flexible.

Apprenticeships

Conceptually, the apprenticeship model offers many advantages in addressing the employment problems of young people. Indeed, apprenticeship meets most of the requirements of a good learning system. First, unlike most other educational and training processes, apprenticeship provides a built-in opportunity for youths to earn while they learn. Second, its mode of training – practical learning by doing – has natural appeal to many young people who are weary of conventional classroom instruction. Third, learning occurs in a real job setting, in direct contact with employers and older workers who can help socialize youths to the workplace. Apprenticeships thus offer built-in incentives and opportunities for mentor relationships.

The effectiveness of apprenticeship is well documented by research. Studies have demonstrated that craft workers trained through apprenticeship learn new skills faster, are promoted faster and more often, suffer less unemployment, and earn more than their counterparts trained in other ways (Cook, 1989; Hills, 1982; Leigh, 1989; Marshall, Franklin, and Glover, 1975). Likewise, follow-up surveys of former apprentices have indicated that as many as 15% have become business owners themselves (Maier and Loeb, 1975).

Because apprenticeship regulations specify a minimum age of 16 years, it is technically possible for apprenticeship to serve teenagers in the United States. However, there are some impediments to using the American apprenticeship model for youths younger than 18. The child-labor provisions of the Fair Labor Standards Act and insurance regulations, for example, prohibit youths below that age from working in some hazardous apprenticeable job classifications in construction and other industries.

Another impediment is employer reluctance to hire youths as apprentices, especially disadvantaged youths. Sponsors feel that they are making a major investment in apprentices who may leave them before their investments are recouped. Like other investors, apprenticeship sponsors avoid risk. One solution to this problem is to make disadvantaged youths less risky investments for employers, as has been done with a variety of preapprenticeship initiatives such as those provided in the Job Corps, programs registered by the state apprenticeship agencies in North Carolina and Florida, and a wide range of apprenticeship outreach and skill development programs (Tolo, Glover, and Gronouski, 1980). These approaches likewise have done much to increase minority participation in apprentice programs (Marshall and Briggs, 1967).

However, the approach of expanding preapprenticeship programs is limited by what might be called a *funnel problem*. Few apprenticeship positions are available, and competition for many of them is intense. A means of expanding the number of apprenticeships, along with getting more youths into them, is therefore needed. One approach – school-to-apprenticeship linkage – has demonstrated that it can accomplish both. The concept of school-to-apprenticeship linkage is simple. High school seniors are employed on a part-time basis as registered apprentices with transition to full-time apprenticeships after graduation, when they become regular apprentices working full-time while they complete their related training, ordinarily taken through special classes at local community colleges or vocational schools.

Experience to date reveals some weakness with school-to-apprenticeship programs, especially arranging post–high-school-related training opportunities for apprentices with small employers who sponsor only one or two apprenticeships, making it difficult to meet the minimum class size requirements in community colleges and vocational schools.

An ideal solution to this problem is to get employers to join together in associations to sponsor apprenticeships. However, because many school-to-apprenticeship sponsors are new and inexperienced, this is easier said than done. Considerable work is involved in establishing effective programs of related study at the high school level and beyond.

Thanks in part to the work of a number of individuals and organizations, interest in apprenticeship recently has increased dramatically (Hamilton, 1987, 1990; Lerman and Pouncy, 1990; Nordurft and Jobs for the Future, 1991; William T. Grant Foundation, 1988b). In 1991, Arkansas (Jobs for the Future, 1991), Wisconsin, and Oregon established a series of state-funded apprenticeship projects. Several bills have been introduced in Congress to establish a major national demonstration of youth apprenticeship. Forces driving this movement include a new interest in the German apprenticeship system, the rediscovery by cognitive scientists of the effectiveness of learning by doing, work by anthropologists in Third World countries confirming the success of informal apprenticeships, and the reaffirmation of the apprenticeship concept by the U.S. Department of Labor's "Apprenticeship 2000" initiative during 1988–1989 (U.S. Department of Labor, 1989). In order to distinguish them from traditional apprenticeships, advocates usually call their new programs *youth apprenticeship* or *work-based learning*.

Cooperative education

Although apprenticeship is not well established in American high schools, another work-study training scheme, cooperative education, has a better foothold. Approximately 600,000 high school students, nearly one tenth of all students enrolled in vocational education programs, participate in cooperative education.

In contrast to apprenticeship, cooperative education is more school based than industry based; its training typically ends with high school; its workstations are designed to be training stations rather than permanent jobs; and it is best established in a different set of occupations than apprenticeship – primarily in retailing and clerical work. Cooperative education at the postsecondary level has grown significantly over the past two decades, especially among community colleges. Thus, there would appear to be great potential to link the two to offer more advanced training, especially in conjunction with the establishment of tech prep programs (described later). However, at present, there is very little collaboration between cooperative education secondary and postsecondary levels.

Existing evaluations of cooperative education programs have yielded mixed results and incomparable findings, but these evaluations have been methodologically flawed (Stern, McMillion, Hopkins, and Stone, 1990). Clearly, however, most of the programs are more about work experience than about learning. One solution is to tie the programs to a certification scheme similar to the German apprenticeship system, in which the skills and knowledge of the program's graduates are tested in performance and in written and oral tests appropriate to the occupation (U.S. General Accounting Office, 1991).

Academies

Restructuring high school vocational/technical education is a critical component of any system to improve the linkages between school and work. One promising approach is the career academy, originated in Philadelphia and replicated extensively elsewhere, especially in California and New York.

Under the basic academy model, at the end of ninth grade, students at risk of failure are identified and invited to volunteer for a program based on a school-within-a-school format, with a separate team of teachers for a portion of their courses. The resulting cadre of students and teachers remains together for 3 years. Students spend the 10th grade catching up on academics and integrating computers and field trips into the curriculum. In grade 11, every student has a mentor from industry who introduces the student to his or her workplace and joins the student for recreational activities at least once a month. By the end of the school year, the student obtains a summer job with one of the business partners. Students who stay with the program are promised a job on high school graduation.

The academies have worked well because the students have a context for their learning, and they have "found a home" in the small academies (about 100 students or less). Evaluations to date indicate that academies have reduced dropout rates (Stern, 1988; Stern, Dayton, and Paik, 1989). A careful evaluation of the longitudinal effects of career academies using a random assignment design is being undertaken by the Manpower Demonstration Research Corporation.

Partnership academies have been funded in school districts across California, with matching grants from the state. These academies are organized around occupational clusters in hospitality, media, health, or finance, depending on the local economy.

By 1994, the academy movement had spread throughout the United States, especially in growth industries and occupations, which often are specific to particular cities and regions. American Express first developed a Finance Academy in Phoenix, Arizona, to prepare youths for careers in banking and finance. The program has been replicated in other cities in collaboration with other financial service firms. American Express also began an Academy in Tourism. However, some of these examples simply involve adding a few vocational courses independent of academic courses, without attempting academic-vocational integration or establishing multiyear school-within-a-school arrangements.

A private nonprofit organization, the National Academy Foundation (NAF), created by American Express in 1988 has 550 affiliated corporations, civic or nonprofit organizations, and local businesses. In 1993, 6,500 students participated in NAF academies: 4,000 in finance (begun in 1982), 2,000 in travel and tourism (begun in 1986), and 500 in public service (begun in 1990). NAF affiliates provide special teacher training and conferences, field trips, prizes, scholarships, and internships after students complete their junior year. The best of the NAF academies appears to integrate academic and vocational skills very well (Wade, 1994).

The partnership or career academy model offers several advantages over the traditional ways of organizing high school vocational education. First, clustering vocational education by industry rather than by occupation facilitates industry involvement while leaving open a wide array of occupations to which students can aspire. Second, partnership academies are less likely to become stigmatized than vocational education programs organized along occupational lines. An academy in the health occupations, for example, includes students who aspire to be physicians, as well as those who wish to become nurses' aides. Identifying and beginning to work with students as early as ninth grade may prevent some at-risk youths from dropping out. Using the small group school-within-a-school format provides a more personal setting for learning. All of these features make the partnership academy an attractive component of an STW initiative.

Tech-prep programs

Promoted by the Center for Occupational Research and Development (CORD) and the Carl D. Perkins Vocational and Applied Technology Act of 1990, tech prep provides an alternative to the college prep curriculum. The aim is to prepare youths for technical careers by combining school and community college curricula into a coherent, unduplicated set of courses (Parnell, 1985; Parnell and Hull, 1991). These were formerly called *2 + 2 programs* because they combine the last 2 years of high school with 2 years of community college.

Tech prep requires the development of formal agreements between the secondary and postsecondary partners for integrating or articulating high school and postsecondary curricula. Unlike the 2 + 2 program, which could shorten the length of time required to complete work for a certificate or an associate degree because they were designed as a more efficient learning process, tech prep programs intend to provide students with more advanced skills within the traditional time period than those provided by separate high school and community college programs. Students successfully completing the tech prep sequence obtain a high school diploma and a 2-year associate degree or a certificate. Tech prep programs are flexible; they can join components for work-site training with work experience and can even be combined with 2-year apprenticeships.

The Perkins Act of 1990 authorized $125 million annually for planning and demonstration grants to consortia of local education agencies and postsecondary institutions to formulate a 3-year plan for the development and implementation of tech prep programs. The Perkins provisions required federally supported programs to integrate "vocational" and "academic" programs, but provided weak incentives for schools to do so and did not require comprehensive evaluations to ensure high-quality academic–vocational integration.

A major problem with tech prep is limited linkage to employers and work; it is mainly an educational program. Secondary-level vocational education, therefore, should be restructured according to the partnership academy model. High school students would have the opportunity to participate in a compact in which employers promise preferential access to career jobs in return for meeting achievement standards in school. Students not intending to pursue a baccalaureate degree would have a variety of attractive training opportunities, including academies, youth apprenticeships, tech prep, and cooperative education. Adoption of the Commission on Skills of the American Workforce's recommendations to establish high national standards that all high school students would be expected to meet would help keep advanced learning options open for all students, greatly facilitating the transitions to work, technical education, or 4-year colleges.

These tech prep options, therefore, should be presented to students, parents, and employers as high-quality opportunities that do not preclude the possibility of attending college later, especially for students who met world-class academic standards for high school graduation. Students would have to earn admission by achieving certain standards in basic skills and other competencies needed for employment. The training would be competency based, offering a variety of instructional strategies, including an individualized, self-paced mode using instructional materials in a variety of media formats (including print materials, audiovisuals, and computer-assisted instruction). Group work would also be undertaken. The curriculum would need to be substantial and challenging, with a high academic content. For example, knowledge of mathematics (at least through algebra) is required for several apprenticed trades. Competency certification throughout and on the completion of training would be an integral feature.

Conclusions

Fearing for their own survival in an increasingly competitive world, many American businesses are desperately seeking ways to improve public schools. Numerous partnerships and "adopt-a-school" arrangements have been initiated, and education issues are receiving greater attention from business lobbies. A key political theme of business is to make teachers and administrators accountable for student outcomes, but mandating that educators be accountable ignores the fact that learning is a joint enterprise involving both teachers and students.

Unfortunately, businesses often overlook a major lever in their own hands for motivating students; they control the most important incentive for work-bound youngsters – access to jobs – yet most do not use it. In addition, businesses have not articulated clearly to schools their needs in terms of learner outcomes or skills required, nor have they organized to develop a consensus on such standards – even for vocational education students. Within limits, many businesses have simply adjusted requirements to the job applicants available. Further complicating this picture is firms' disparate expectations from schools. Business is highly heterogeneous in terms of management practices and other important dimensions. Moreover, skill requirements change through time, and the demands of the global information economy are raising standards significantly for line workers (Commission on Skills of the American Workforce, 1990).

A primary requirement for success in any STW initiative is getting employers committed to the effort. Business needs to recognize that inadequacies in the preparation of American youth are not just problems for schools. The development of a quality workforce requires active participation of many outside the schools, including parents, public officials, communities, and employers. Ultimately, American employers must shoulder part of the responsibility for the development of youths – their future workers.

It is, however, the responsibility of governments at every level to provide the incentive context within which employers operate. The federal government should build consensus for a high-skills development strategy, and business and labor representatives should be active participants in that consensus-building process. An effective process to facilitate the transition from school to work for the great majority of our young people who do not pursue baccalaureate degrees must be an integral component of any high-skills development strategy.

STW opportunities: Federal efforts

The Clinton administration

The Clinton administration made education, training, and improved STW processes an integral component of a high-wage, high-skills economic policy. Two important components of that policy are the Goals 2000: Educate America Act and the School-to-Work Opportunities Act, signed by President Clinton in the spring of 1994. The Goals 2000 Act built on bipartisan support during the Bush administration, when President Clinton, then the governor of Arkansas, chaired the National Governors' Association Educational Task Force, which adopted the following six goals to be achieved by the United States by the year 2000:

1. All children in America will start school ready to learn.
2. The high school graduation rate will increase to at least 90%.
3. American students will leave grades 4, 8, and 12 having demonstrated competency in challenging subject matter, including English, mathematics, science, history, and geography; and every school in America will ensure that all students learn to use their minds well, so that they are prepared for responsible citizenship, further learning, and productive employment in our modern economy.

4. U.S. students will be first in the world in science and mathematics achievement.
5. Every adult will be literate, and will possess the knowledge and skills necessary to compete in a global economy and to exercise the rights and responsibilities of citizenship.
6. Every school in America will be free of drugs and violence and will offer a disciplined environment conducive to learning.

The Goals 2000 Act has two additional goals – one on parent partnerships and one on the professional development of teachers. The act also establishes several new organizations: the National Education Standards and Improvement Council (NESIC) to examine and certify voluntary national standards; the National Educational Goals Panel (NEGB) to review standards submitted to it by the NESIC, as well as to build public support for and report on programs toward the national goals; and the National Skills Standard Board (NSSB), made up of government officials, business and labor representatives, and educators, to stimulate the development of a voluntary national system of occupational standards and certifications.

The NSSB will accomplish the latter objective by identifying clusters of major occupational standards and certifications. The NSSB and the standards-setting process are designed to improve education and training and to link education more closely to business. Firms and industries can use these generic clusters to tailor more specific standards to their needs.

Another important provision of the Goals 2000 Act allows state education agencies to apply for waivers of certain federal education program requirements that impede state, school district, or school reform plans. The act also allows the U.S. secretary of education to designate up to six states for participation in an education flexibility demonstration program.

Congress appropriated $105 million for Goals 2000 in 1994 and an additional $20 million for an anticrime and drugs provision; $700 million was appropriated for 1995. The act provides for grants to states, local school districts, and schools to develop their own plans to meet the goals by the year 2000; 60% of the funds the first year and 90% thereafter will go to school districts. Most of the school districts' money will go to individual schools – 75% the first year and 85% thereafter. Within the Goals 2000 framework, local schools and communities are encouraged to redesign everything, including curriculum and assessment, instruction, professional development, technology, and parent and community involvement, around clear, high standards.

Goals 2000 is based on the assumption that research and past experience with school reforms provide guidance for the transformation of whole school districts, which has not yet been done anywhere, though many districts are at various stages in the transformation process. The act's basic assumption is that the federal role is not to mandate uniform changes, but to encourage experimentation within the framework of broad federal guidelines. Consequently, none of these activities are mandatory, although the states are encouraged to apply for grants. The administration understands that the goals are very ambitious and will be difficult to achieve, but the objective is to stretch the nation's educational capacity.

The School-to-Work Opportunities Act (SWOA) provides the framework for the creation of a national STW system. The basic objective is to build on the high standards encouraged by the Goals 2000 Act. The SWOA also is based on voluntarism and on a belief in successive demonstrations by states and local areas as the best way to move toward a national system. The act contemplates partnerships between federal, state, and local areas and between business and education at the local level. The SWOA provides $100 million for fiscal year 1994 and $300 million for fiscal year 1995. It also provides $60 million from the Job Training Partnership Act (JTPA) and the Perkins Act to finance planning grants to all states for development and implementation for local partnerships and for urban and rural partnerships. Noncompetitive *developmental* grants were given to all states, the District of Columbia, and Puerto Rico, but *implementation* grants are awarded on a competitive basis, as are those to high-poverty areas and local partnerships.

In July 1994, the U.S. secretaries of labor and education awarded implementation grants totaling $43 million to 8 of the 15 states that applied for such grants during the first year. These eight states (Kentucky, Maine, Michigan, Massachusetts, New Jersey, New York, Oregon, and Wisconsin) were considered to be pioneers in the nationwide effort to prepare young people more effectively for work. The range in the grants was from $2 million in Maine to $10 million in New York. The evaluation criteria used to make these awards included the extent to which states had developed comprehensive STW systems stressing high standards, together with instruction that integrates work and school; the extent of workplace monitoring, effective linkages between secondary and post-secondary schools, work-based learning, the collaboration and involvement of the key partners, state resource commitment, and strategies to involve all youths (including those who were out of school); and the effectiveness of the state's management plan.

The successful states were those that appeared to be making systematic changes in their educational and training systems. All of those awarded first-round grants had clear plans for extending reforms throughout their states, and had succeeded with the critical and difficult process of involving businesses more effectively with educators in reforming school systems. Most of these states already had initiated major educational reforms. Douglas Ross, former assistant secretary of labor for employment and training, emphasized that the administration's STW initiative was "designed to be a new approach to learning. We think it is a better way to prepare most kids for the future. It is not the successor to vocational education. We want to offer an alternative to the various tracking systems for Americans who have high aspirations for their children" (Lively, 1994, p. A-18).

Prospects for a national STW system in the United States

Even strong supporters of a national STW system agree that the establishment of such a system in the United States faces formidable barriers. A study by the U.S. General Accounting Office, for example, discovered numerous obstacles to expanding state STW transition initiatives, including labor laws that make it difficult for students to participate in work-based programs; detailed state regulations mandating courses, making it difficult to tailor programs to the needs of individual students; restrictions on the use of federal funds (e.g., JTPA) for STW activities; the uncertainties of state, federal, and local funding; the reluctance of businesses, particularly smaller employers, to offer work-based opportunities to youths; the unwillingness of universities to grant credit for nontraditional courses; limited business contacts by teachers and school administrators; restrictive school schedules; and parental opposition to nontraditional approaches to education (U.S. General Accounting Office, 1991, p. 10).

Some critics argue that the disappointing outcomes of past federal programs make it unlikely that the Clinton administration's programs will succeed. Some of them state, in addition, that the problem of the youth labor market in the United States is greatly exaggerated because frequent job changes by young people is an efficient way to acquire job information, that "most unemployed teenagers are in school or seeking only part-time work," and that the German apprenticeship and schooling system used as the model for the American proposals is "rigid and unresponsive." In this view, "The real lesson to be learned from the German apprenticeship program is that to promote employment one should reduce regulation in the labor market."[2]

These arguments are surprising because few informed analysts really believe that the job churning of academically unprepared young people is either a desirable or an efficient process. Moreover, because of large externalities and market failures, there is general agreement among economists that competitive markets are unlikely to produce adequate individual or social outcomes. Most proponents of developing market-oriented public–private partnerships believe that interventions can improve the operation of labor markets. Stagnating and declining real wages for young workers and widening income gaps that are more severe in the United States than in other major industrial countries will not be overcome without comprehensive strategies that include more effective STW processes.

It is, however, true that many past public job training programs failed to have much lasting impact because they were not comprehensive enough, which is precisely the reason I advocate systematic changes. I also believe that many lessons can be learned from past failures, as well as successes, about how to design a strategy to make these systems and processes more successful in the future.

More sympathetic critics of STW initiatives appropriately warn of the risks these processes face unless they are properly structured in order to establish strong organic links among schools, labor market institutions, and employers. Norton Grubb (1994), for example, observes:

> The possibilities for school-to-work programs are enormous. They can offer new learning opportunities for young people and stimulate the reform of high schools, including their reconnection to the world outside of school. They can raise larger questions about the responsibilities of employers and programs for out-of-school youth that usually get ignored. But they might also end up as work experience programs for a few at-risk students, or as reforms that generate allegiance only as long as federal dollars last – both implying a life expectancy of about five years. The path to true reform is infinitely more attractive – and also much more work. (p. 54)

Similarly, Robert Glover and Alan Weisberg (1994) are concerned, on the basis of comparisons between U.S. and European STW experiences, that the United States has not given enough attention to building industry-led institutions at the local level, providing adequate incentives for employers, including workers in the process, or developing national frameworks.

> [They] believe that the single most important objective for implementing the . . . School to Work Act should be the serious engagement of industry in setting standards, organizing examinations, advising on curriculum, and providing students with opportunities in the workplace, both paid and unpaid. (p. 31)

These analysts believe, further, that the national skills standards "will take several years to put in place" and are concerned that the STW "effort is being developed outside of the context of broader school reforms and a much stronger alliance with the school restructuring movement is badly needed. Nor are there the connections with efforts to modernize American industry and transform U.S. workplaces into high performance organizations" (p. 31). These writers "also wonder if sufficient attention will be given to the role of our nation's community colleges – the closest thing we currently have to a national system of training both for youths and current workers" (p. 31). They are "suspicious of any broad new system which is specifically geared toward non-college bound students" (p. 31).

Other critics believe youth apprenticeship and STW activities ignore or underestimate the obstacles posed by problems like labor market discrimination and structural problems in the economy. These critics point out that the U.S. and German apprenticeship systems discriminate against minorities and disadvantaged young people. Harvey Kantor (1994), for example, argues that vocational education and other "work-oriented programs" have

> functioned over the years to fragment the curriculum and deepen the division between the college-bound and the non-college bound students . . . Despite the pleas of apprenticeship advocates, there is little reason to think that youth apprenticeship will be much different. (p. 456)

Those of us who support the Clinton administration's efforts to improve the nation's STW and other learning systems should pay close attention to these thoughtful critics, who raise many important cautions. We can safely ignore criticisms suggesting that education or STW systems alone cannot solve all of the country's problems – which I doubt any careful observer really believes – but we must be alert to the interactions between education and other social systems. I believe, moreover, that the Clinton administration's standards-based approach, predicated on experimentation and voluntary incentives, is the next timely step in moving from numerous local programs, some of them exemplary, to larger local, state, and national systems.

There is no denying, however, the obstacles posed by political opposition and employer reluctance to provide training to front-line workers, as evidenced by the business community's solid opposition to the kinds of training obligations used in most other countries and proposed by both the Commission on Skills of the American Workforce and the Clinton administration. Perhaps the voluntary approach or tax incentives will succeed in causing most American companies to provide adequate training and to become effectively involved in reforming learning systems. On this point, however, the critics have history on their side.

Important design features of a community-wide STW initiative

The experience in the United States and elsewhere makes it possible to specify the design features for a successful STW system, whether or not we are able to achieve it. It is clear that the United States cannot simply import the German, Japanese, or West European approaches to American shores, nor should we want to. Each is embedded in its culture and has its own flaws and deficiencies, as well as strengths. Rather, we should learn from the approaches used in other countries and adapt their best aspects in designing our own homegrown solutions.

The design for the systematic yet flexible model envisioned here is based on several principles. *First, achievement in school must be connected with rewards in the labor market.* Incentives are important for everyone. Students must know that achievement in school pays off unmistakably in terms of economic opportunity.

Second, no single program or training approach can meet the needs of all youths or of all employers. Thus, it is important to make available a variety of training and learning services and opportunities, including work-based learning options.

Third, a system needs to be available for all youths rather than a series of short-term demonstrations for special populations. The initiative must be institutionalized, with regular financing, and thus not dependent on ad hoc grants for continued support. It must also have sustained commitment from the business community, which must see that youth development activities are in their own interest. To avoid stigmatizing the participating youths, the initiative must not be reserved exclusively for disadvantaged populations. Of course, helping minority and disadvantaged youths is a key concern, but there are better ways to help ensure their participation than by making poverty an eligibility criterion. Targeting can be achieved by selecting school districts with heavy poor and minority enrollments, and by building in strong recruiting and outreach components to ensure that poor and disadvantaged youths are well served by the system. Also, an integral part of any STW system is to serve those who have dropped out of school and who have enrolled in second-chance learning programs with rewards in the labor market.

Fourth, in several respects, information is a key element of the proposed system. To manage the system properly, accurate feedback is needed about youths after they leave formal learning systems. In order to provide the community with information about its young adults, an information system should be developed to follow young people who have left high school, graduated, and entered the labor market or postsecondary education or training programs. Such data are not commonly available now, but they are essential for accountability and for monitoring progress against goals. Information also is needed on the performance of various public and private training providers, including proprietary schools, community colleges, and other postsecondary training options. In order to make informed decisions about which path to take, youths need to know about the efficacy of various training options after high school. Such information should be collected regularly and made readily accessible to students and their parents, as well as to policymakers and the general public. Finally, graduating youths need a better way to document their competence than conventional school transcripts. Skill certification procedures that are both user friendly and meaningful to employers need to be developed.

Fifth, if adolescents are expected to be in a position to make decisions about careers, providing better and earlier occupational information and guidance is essential. To be successful in the job market, moreover, students need better information on how to get and keep jobs. Students must be able to present themselves on paper and in person; they must have opportunities to practice their interviewing skills.

Sixth, vocational options need to have a strong academic content. Critics of vocational-technical schooling often draw a false distinction between vocational and academic education. Properly taught, technical education always has required considerable academic content – and technical education will contain even more academic content in the future, as higher theoretical and conceptual skills are required. Indeed, most abstract and academic subjects can be taught more effectively through hands-on experience than through classroom lectures. And all students could benefit from earlier and more systematic learning about career options. In fact, learning probably always is more effective with the unity of thought and action. The importance of learning by doing has been rediscovered by much recent research (American Association for the Advancement of Science, 1989; Hutchings and Wutzdorff, 1988; Resnick, 1987). Academic content is also necessary in providing a foundation for adaptability and for learning how to learn. Narrow job training or task learning soon becomes obsolete in the changing world of work. It is essential, therefore, that youths learn how to learn in order to upgrade and improve their skills constantly to match the needs of the workplace.

Seventh, the system should not foreclose the option for higher education. Although students may identify themselves as non-college-bound in high school, many subsequently may decide to pursue further schooling. Attending college is not a one-time-only decision. In view of the need to promote continuous learning as a valued skill essential in almost all jobs that pay well, it is best not to close the options unnecessarily for any youngster. Participation in the program should not preclude college attendance. On the contrary, a major objective of the initiative should be to foster lifelong learning of all types.

Eighth, effective STW systems must be comprehensive. One of the most important weaknesses of American education and training activities is their fragmented, ad hoc, unsystematic nature. If basic learning problems are systemic, it does very little good to take remedial action at the margins of the system. Experience shows such interventions to have temporary and limited effects because they are counteracted by deficiencies elsewhere in the system. If, for example, families are poor learning systems, it is more difficult for children to be successful in school. And if elementary and secondary schooling is inadequate, it will be much more difficult to have successful postsecondary education and training experiences. Effective systems, therefore, must be comprehensive in order to deal with systemic problems.

Ninth, effective STW learning systems need to involve and link all of the principal actors in the system in a community of interest based on positive rewards. Students and their parents must see that the system has positive, accessible outcomes for them, and education and training organizations must see the system as compatible with their basic interests and objectives. It is particularly important for employers to participate in, and have strong interests in, the outcome of school and STW processes. The system likewise needs to be compatible with the interests and goals of incumbent workers and their organizations.

The rewards from education and training are not entirely material. For example, programs that are stigmatized as available only to marginal students or the poor have negative rewards and will be avoided, as will programs that are known to be inferior. Most American parents want their children to go to college, so postsecondary learning systems will be more acceptable if they are open-ended, in the sense that the college option is not foreclosed, and if they carry college credit. Similarly, high standards and credentialing are important parts of the reward system for education and training programs.

For employers, the most important reward will be to consider education and training institutions as valuable suppliers of high-quality human resources, as is the case in Germany and Japan.

Tenth, public and private policymakers must have a strategy for change. By definition, the parts of deeply entrenched systems are mutually reinforcing and therefore do not change very easily. It also must be stressed that a comprehensive approach to establishing an STW system requires an understanding of how learning systems are related to other systems. Learning systems interact, for example, with economic and social systems that can either retard or stimulate learning and learning opportunities. For example, processes to prepare students for work will reflect the organization of work and the demand for skills. If American employers continue the Tayloristic organization of work, as most of them have, there will be less demand for higher-order thinking skills. And if economic conditions are depressed, it will be more difficult for even well-educated, well-trained workers to find jobs. This means, of course, that learning systems *alone* will have only limited impact on productivity and incomes. Human resource and labor market policies are much more effective if they are components of comprehensive economic and social policies or strategies.

Finally, since because STW processes are basically learning systems, they should be based on the findings of cognitive research about effective learning. Most important, they should avoid the popular American myth that learning is due mainly to innate ability, which justifies tracking and the status quo. We know that learning, for people without pathological disorders, is due mainly to hard work and supportive learning systems, not innate ability. Moreover, cognitive research has discovered some important lessons of learning and teaching that many education and training systems seem unaware of. These include the following: Learning is not necessarily the outcome of teaching; what students learn is influenced by their existing ideas; progression in learning is usually from the concrete to the abstract; people learn to do well what they practice doing;

and effective learning by students requires feedback and takes time (American Association for the Advancement of Science, 1989, chap. 13).

Conclusions

Developing effective STW programs should receive very high priority from U.S. policymakers at every level. However, STW systems must be seen as a component of other learning systems linked at both ends (i.e., schools and the preparation for work) by high standards for leaving school and for entering postsecondary education and training. Comprehensive approaches will require larger expenditures than are usually associated with federal employment and training programs, but these should be viewed as investments necessary (but not sufficient) to keep American industry competitive and to maintain and improve the incomes and quality of life for U.S. workers.

Experience demonstrates that macroeconomic policies to maintain employment growth and active labor market and support systems could induce American employers to form more high-performance organizations that require more workers with higher-order thinking skills. Improving learning systems alone will not make it possible for Americans to maintain high living standards and halt the widening income gap that threatens democratic institutions, as well as a prosperous and growing economy. Although improved learning systems are not sufficient, under modern conditions no country is likely to be able to compete on terms that make it possible to maintain and improve high-income conditions unless it has world-class learning systems linked by high standards.

Notes

1. A recent study by Klerman and Karoly purports to cast doubt on the conventional wisdom that "typical high school graduates mill about in the labor market, moving from one dead-end job to another until the age of 23 or 24," as claimed by the Commission on the Skills of the American Workforce (Jacob Alex Klerman and Lynn A. Karoly, "Young men and the transition to stable employment," *Monthly Labor Review*, August 1994, pp. 31–48). Using the National Longitudinal Survey, these analysts found that "the median male high school graduate found a job lasting more than 2 years shortly after his 20th birthday, and a job that would last longer than 3 years while he was 22." However, Klerman and Karoly found considerable heterogeneity. Typical male high school graduates in the first quartile found a "3 year job" when they were 19, but those in the fourth quartile did not find such a job until after they turned 25.

Although this study provides some useful information, it does not disprove the conclusion that U.S. STW processes compare very unfavorably with those of Germany and Japan. Another way to cite the evidence they present is that half of high school graduates do not find jobs that will last at least 3 years by the time they are 22 – 4 years beyond the normal high school leaving age. This is hardly reassuring or evidence of a successful transition, as these authors claim. Moreover, we must assume that a job that lasts 3 years is not a dead-end job – a heroic assumption. We should note, in addition, that by age 22 perhaps 70% or more of all German high school graduates who do not pursue postsecondary education have completed skill training programs that lead either to skilled jobs or in some cases to universities. Contrarians always serve useful functions and often get attention, but they usually overstate their case – which applies to these analysts. Moreover, they render a public disservice by minimizing America's STW problems.

2. James J. Heckman (1994) makes another argument against job training programs, namely, what he considers to be the assumption by proponents of these programs "that investment in physical capital will not aid in promoting productivity in the workplace and in making American firms more competitive in international markets" (p. 115). He reaches this conclusion from arguments by the Commission on Skills of the American Workforce in *America's Choice: High Skills or Low Wages!* that standardized technology *alone* cannot be relied on to establish competitiveness under global market conditions. However, none of us on the commission, which I cochaired and which included the CEOs of some of America's most competitive companies, would deny the importance of capital investment for improving productivity. We believe, however, that skilled workers must develop, use, adapt, and improve technology.

References

American Association for the Advancement of Science. (1989). *Science for all Americans: A Project 2061 report on literacy goals in science, mathematics, and technology* (p. 146). Washington, DC: Author.

Barton, P. E. (1991, Spring). The school-to-work transition. *Issues in Science and Technology, 7*(3), 50–54.

Berlin, G., and Sum, A. (1988). *Toward a more perfect union: Basic skills, poor families and our economic future.* New York: Ford Foundation.

Bishop, J. H. (1989, January–February). Why the apathy in American high schools? *Educational Researcher, 18*(1), 6–10, 42.

Commission on Skills of the American Workforce. (1990). *America's choice: High skills or low wages!* Rochester, NY: National Center on Education and the Economy.

Cook, R. F. (1989, March). *Analysis of apprenticeship training from the national longitudinal study of the high school class of 1972.* Report prepared for the Bureau of Apprenticeship and Training, U.S. Department of Labor, and the National Training Program of the International Union of Operating Engineers. Rockville, MD: Westat, Inc.

Glover, R., and Weisberg, A. (1994, March 23). America's school-to-work transition: The case of the missing social partners. *Education Week, 13*, 44, 31.

Grubb, W. N. (1994, August 3). True reform or tired retread? *Education Week, 13*(40), 68.

Hamilton, S. F. (1987). Apprenticeship as a transition to adulthood in West Germany. *American Journal of Education, 95*, 314–345.

Hamilton, S. F. (1990). *Apprenticeship for adulthood: Preparing youth for the future.* New York: Free Press.

Heckman, J. J. (1994, Spring). Is job training oversold? *Public Interest, 115*, 91–115.

Hills, S. N. (1982). How craftsmen learn their skills: A longitudinal analysis. In R. E. Taylor, H. Rosen, and F. C. Pratzner (Eds.), *Job training for youth* (pp. 203–240). Columbus: Ohio State University, National Center for Research in Vocational Education.

Hutchings, P., and Wutzdorff, A. (Eds.). (1988). *Knowing and doing: Learning through experience.* San Francisco: Jossey-Bass.

Jobs for the Future, Inc. (1991). *A feasibility study of youth apprenticeship in Arkansas.* Somerville, MA: Author.

Kantor, H. (1994, Summer). Managing the transition from school to work: The false promise of youth apprenticeship. *Teachers College Record, 95*(4), 442–461.

Leigh, D. E. (1989, October). *What kinds of training "work" for noncollege bound youth?* Washington, DC: U.S. General Accounting Office.

Lerman, R. I., and Pouncy, H. (1990, Fall). The compelling case for youth apprenticeships. *The Public Interest, 101*, 62–77.

Lively, K. (1994, August 7). 8 states' job-training plans win grants from Washington. *Chronicle of Higher Education*, p. A18.

Maier, D., and Loeb, H. (1975). *Training and work experiences of former apprentices in New York State.* New York: New York State Department of Labor, Division of Research and Statistics.

Marshall, R. (1991). *Losing direction: Families, human resource development, and economic performance.* Milwaukee, WI: Family Service America.

Marshall, R., and Briggs, V. (1967). *The Negro and apprenticeship.* Baltimore: Johns Hopkins University Press.

Marshall, R., Franklin, W. S., and Glover, R. W. (1975). *Training and entry into union construction* (U.S. Department of Labor, Manpower Administration R&D Monograph No. 39). Washington, DC: U.S. Government Printing Office.

Marshall, R., and Tucker, M. (1992). *Thinking for a living: Education and the wealth of nations.* New York: Basic Books.

Mishel, L., and Bernstein, J. (1994). *The state of working America, 1994–1995.* Washington, DC: Economic Policy Institute.

National Alliance of Business. (1989). *The Compact project: School–business partnerships for improving education.* Washington, DC: Author.

Nordurft, W. E., and Jobs for the Future. (1991). *Youth apprenticeship, American style: A strategy for expanding school and career opportunities.* Somerville, MA: Jobs for the Future.

Osterman, P. (1980). *Getting started: The youth labor market.* Cambridge, MA: MIT Press.

Osterman, P. (1988). *Employment futures: Reorganization, dislocation and public policy.* New York: Oxford University Press.

Parnell, D. (1985). *The neglected majority.* Washington, DC: Community College Press.

Parnell, D., and Hull, D. (Eds.). (1991). *The tech prep associate degree: A win-win strategy.* Waco, TX: Center for Occupational Research and Development (CORD).

Resnick, L. (1987). Learning in school and out. *Educational Researcher, 16*(9), 13–20.

Rosenbaum, J. E. (1989). Empowering schools and teachers: A new link to jobs for the non-college bound. In *Investing in people* (Report of the National Commission on Workforce Quality and Labor Market Efficiency). Washington, DC: U.S. Government Printing Office.

Rosenbaum, J. E. (1990, Winter). What if good jobs depended on good grades? *American Educator, 13*, 10–15.

Schultz, T. W. (1981). *Investing in people: The economics of population quality*. Berkeley: The University of California Press.

Spring, W. J. (1987, March–April). Youth unemployment and the transition from youth to work: Programs in Boston, Frankfurt, and London. *New England Economic Review, 6*(10), 3–16.

Spring, W. J. (1989). *From "solution" to catalyst: A new role for federal education and training dollars* (working paper). Washington, DC: National Center on Education and the Economy.

Stern, D. (1988, Summer). Combining academic and vocational courses in an integrated program to reduce high school dropout rates: Second-year results from replications of the California peninsula academies. *Educational Evaluation and Policy Analysis, 10*(2), 161–170.

Stern, D., Dayton, C., and Paik, I. (1989, Winter). Benefits and costs of dropout prevention in a high school program combining academic and vocational education: Third-year results from replications of the California peninsula academies. *Educational Evaluation and Policy Analysis 11*(4), 405–416.

Stern, D., McMillion, M., Hopkins, C., and Stone, J. (1990, March). Work experience for students in high school and college. *Youth and Society, 21*, 355–390.

Tolo, K., Glover, R. W., and Gronouski, J. (1980). *Preparation for apprenticeship through CETA*. Austin: University of Texas–Austin, Lyndon B. Johnson School of Public Affairs.

U.S. Bureau of Labor Statistics. (1989, June). *Nearly three-fifths of high school graduates of 1988 enrolled in college* (U.S. Department of Labor News Release 89–308). Washington, DC: U.S. Department of Labor.

U.S. Department of Labor. (1989). *Work-based learning: Training America's workers*. Washington, DC: U.S. Government Printing Office.

U.S. General Accounting Office. (1990, May). *Training strategies: Preparing non-college youth for employment in the U.S. and foreign countries*. Washington, DC: U.S. Government Printing Office.

U.S. General Accounting Office. (1991). *Transition from school to work: Linking education and worksite training* (GAO/HRD 93–139). Washington, DC: U.S. Government Printing Office.

Wade, B. (1994, August 10). In school: High school students build the foundations of a career while staying in school. *New York Times*, p. B7.

William T. Grant Foundation, Commission on Work, Family and Citizenship, Youth and America's Future. (1988a). *The forgotten half: Pathways to success for America's youth and young families*. Washington, DC: Author.

William T. Grant Foundation, Commission on Work, Family and Citizenship, Youth and America's Future. (1988b). *States and communities on the move: Policy initiatives to create a world-class workforce*. Washington, DC: Author.

11. Finding common ground: Implications for policies in Europe and the United States

RUBY TAKANISHI

Countries sharing democratic traditions all aim to have well-educated individuals who are mentally and physically healthy and who share the knowledge, values, and skills needed to become productive workers, responsible family members, and active citizens (Takanishi, Mortimer, and McGourthy, 1995). However, it is becoming increasingly clear that these countries, specifically those of Europe and the United States, which are the foci of this volume, have far too many young people at risk of not becoming competent adults.

Thus, in working together toward the 1994 Marbach Conference, both the Johann Jacobs Foundation and the Carnegie Council on Adolescent Development shared an interest in exploring ways in which European countries and the United States could better prepare all their young people for the coming century. The chapters in this volume represent the efforts of an interdisciplinary group of educators, health professionals, and researchers in labor economics, cultural anthropology, biology, psychology, and sociology in search of promising approaches. This concluding chapter identifies the common ground reached, the implications for educational and social policies, and the continuing dilemmas facing nations in preparing their young people for adult life.

Finding common ground

Globalization of the risks of adolescence

The experience of adolescence in the United States and in European countries, although different in important ways, is becoming increasingly similar (Chisholm and Hurrelmann, 1995). As Rutter and Smith (1995) document in an Academia Europaea study of post–World War II trends in psychosocial disorders among adolescents in Europe, increasing num-

227

bers of European youth are engaging in crime, abusing drugs, taking their own lives, and becoming depressed. These rates overall are lower than they are in the United States, but the trend lines are all moving in the wrong direction.

The Organization for Economic Cooperation and Development (OECD) reports that 5–30% of the children and youth in its member countries are at risk of failing to complete school and being integrated into mainstream adult life (OECD, 1995a). In the United States, approximately 20–25% of all adolescents aged 10 to 18 are at serious risk of these poor outcomes, as well as teenage pregnancy and delinquency (Dryfoos, 1990; U.S. Congress, Office of Technology Assessment, 1991a–c).

Profound political and economic transformations in Central and Eastern Europe are now affecting the youthful populations in these countries (Csapó, 1992). The pace of change – from long-standing planned to new market economies, from tightly centralized to more open democratic states – offers rich opportunities for naturally occurring longitudinal studies on the effects of these social changes on the lives of adolescents. At the same time, reports from developing countries (World Health Organization, 1993) and from other regions of the world document increased vulnerability in the transition from childhood to adolescence and from adolescence to adulthood.

In the United States and many European countries, adolescents experience stresses that are multiplicative in their effects (OECD, 1995a). The shifts toward a global economy and toward a knowledge elite in postindustrial societies (Reich, 1991) have created wider economic disparities within countries, greater uncertainties about immediate and long-term employment prospects, and pressures for higher academic achievement without the promise of well-paying jobs.

Adolescents are also experiencing changing family structures. Two-earner families are necessary for economic survival, and single-parent families, nonmarriage, and divorce are increasing on both sides of the Atlantic (Hess, 1995). Appropriate replacement structures or supportive workplace policies that provide adolescents with the caring, stable relations they require for healthy development are few and far between. Thus, the family as an important source of social support and as a protective buffer against stress has become progressively weaker just when adolescents need the close relationships often best provided by families (Carnegie Council on Adolescent Development, 1995).

As a result of these related trends, statements about the "globalization" of poor adolescent health and well-being are being heard more often. What is both fascinating and troubling is that no clear, research-based knowledge points to the reasons why the rates of adolescent morbidity and mortality are increasing. The systematic inquiry of the Academia Europaea group (Rutter and Smith, 1995) on causal factors is a significant starting point for sustained efforts to understand what factors contribute to rising rates of psychosocial disorders and poor educational achievement among young people throughout the world.

Common sense points to changes in social, economic, political, and cultural conditions that have occurred simultaneously with these trends. However, although causality may be easily inferred, it is dangerous to do so (see Rutter and Smith, 1995, for a discussion of linking trends in psychosocial disorders to social factors). In the absence of good knowledge about causal factors and how they interact to influence youth outcomes, nations must evolve strategies now on how to prepare their young people for life in the twenty-first century.

As the second millennium approaches, such visioning is occurring at great pace (International Commission on Education for the Twenty-first Century, 1996). What is remarkable about all these studies is the consensus that is emerging about how European and American adolescents can be better prepared to enter the twenty-first century than they now are.

An emerging consensus: Policy implications

In both the United States and Europe, there is common ground to be found in concern about the worsening indicators of well-being, especially in the adolescent population. At the same time, there is a shared sense of what must be done to address the growing numbers of children and adolescents who are at risk for poor outcomes.

A concrete example of an emerging consensus is represented by two reports, one written by the OECD on principles and approaches that must be considered during the first two decades of life and the second by an American intersectoral Carnegie Council on Adolescent Development that focused on early adolescence, from approximately 10 through 14 years. Each study was developed independently with no contact or use of similar documents.

Our Children at Risk (OECD, 1995a) was prepared by the OECD method of conducting country case studies (including the United States) and then evolving cross-cutting principles. The other, *Great Transitions: Preparing Adolescents for the 21st Century*, was based on linking research on adolescent development and program experience, limited to the American scene, to evolve operating principles and recommendations for families, schools, health agencies, community and youth organizations, the media, and government (Carnegie Council on Adolescent Development, 1995).

These two reports, which synthesize experience in both the United States and Europe, have common ideas that can be used by policymakers who are considering ways to improve the life chances of children and youth in their countries:

- *Preventive approaches*, starting in the early years of life and extending through the transition from school into the workplace, must be the guiding principle for public policies in education, health, and social welfare. Such preventive approaches are child and adolescent centered – that is, they meet development needs at each stage and include the provision of social supports, such as strengthening families, improving educational systems, and providing training in social or life skills to enable better coping with and adaptation to current stresses faced by adolescents and their uncertain futures.
- *Effective education* – school organization, curriculum, pedagogy, and teacher education – is central in meeting the social, health, and learning needs of children and their families. A well-educated individual is increasingly being viewed as more likely to be healthy throughout the life span, less involved in problem behaviors including criminal activities, and more active in the civic life of the community and nation. The importance of teacher education, both pre- and in-service, is acknowledged, as is the long-term perspective needed for successful implementation of reforms (Chapter 3, this volume). Within a clear framework of certain operating principles, educators should be given flexibility and autonomy to make changes in their own schools.
- The *coordination of education, health, and social services*, sometimes called *intersectoral cooperation* outside the United States and *comprehensive, coordinated services* in the United States, is necessary to address the multiple risk factors involved in poor educational and health outcomes for young people. Given the interrelatedness of problem behaviors, intersectoral and agency cooperation is necessary to facilitate good outcomes (Dryfoos, 1994). All of the pivotal institutions that affect the life chances of young people – families, schools, health care agencies, com-

munity organizations, and the media – should cooperate to support their optimal development.

- The growing *racial, ethnic, and religious diversity* within countries must be addressed. The search for ways in which the educational system can prepare young people to live peacefully in heterogeneous communities is urgent for social cohesion and economic vitality. In the post–cold war era, when countries can no longer be easily coalesced in common opposition to an external "enemy," and when forces of backlash to the strains caused by a global economy are increasing, political leaders play a crucial role in fostering tolerance and social stability.
- With supportive national and/or state policies and guidelines, *communities* should be enabled to develop approaches appropriate to local conditions to create better schools, stronger families, and networks of community support. The full involvement of teachers, principals, and parents is seen as critical to what is sometimes called *community-based innovation*.

Given this consensus at the level of policy analysis, it is noteworthy that, both in the United States and in European countries, current trends are toward reductions in public expenditures for health, welfare, and social services and the privatization of formerly public services, such as recreation, afterschool activities, and athletics. In the former socialist countries of Central and Eastern Europe, state-supported, nearly universal child-care and youth services have declined. Just as evidence is mounting on the promise of preventive approaches (Carnegie Council on Adolescent Development, 1995; Dryfoos, 1990; OECD, 1995a, 1995b), the fiscal capacity of public and private agencies, both in European countries and in the United States, to address them is in serious jeopardy.

Continuing dilemmas

Social changes have intensified certain dilemmas regarding the preparation of young people for adulthood. Discussions at the Marbach Conference sought to illuminate three of these continuing dilemmas. The first is how adolescents can be encouraged to adopt healthy lifestyles that will protect them from preventable diseases and that foster practices to enhance their health prospects (Chapter 1, this volume). The second is how adolescents can be prepared for life in societies that are diverse in culture, ethnicity, and religious practices. And the third is how to prepare youth for the workplaces of the twenty-first century.

Education for health

A fundamental difference between the United States and the countries of Europe is the health care financing system. In the United States, millions of young people and adults have no health insurance, and thus no preventive care and no easy access to treatment services (U.S. Congress, Office of Technology Assessment, 1991a). Meanwhile, the European countries provide access to health care services for all of their citizens and, in some cases, to immigrants. However, even with this access to health care, European health professionals acknowledge that adolescents do have special needs that require training and sensitivity on the part of their health providers, as well as outreach and health promotion efforts that extend beyond the traditional health care system.

Socioeconomic, gender, and geographic residence factors are related to different rates of psychosocial disorders, even in countries where access to health care is universal (Rutter and Smith, 1995). Thus, although access is a desirable basic requirement, adolescents need more to maintain their health, including timely information about diseases, incentives or motivation to engage in healthy practices, and learning skills in order to practice healthy behaviors (Millstein, Petersen, and Nightingale, 1993).

The role of the schools in promoting health, including health education, is accepted in principle but remains uneven in implementation in Europe (Chapter 4, this volume) and in the United States (Chapter 2, this volume). The European Network of Health Promoting Schools, initiated by the World Health Organization–Regional Office for Europe (1993), and *Turning Points* schools (Carnegie Council on Adolescent Development, 1989) are similar efforts to connect health education, health care delivery, and school-level policies to promote the health of staff and students through smoke-free environments, good nutrition, and access to wellness and physical activity. However, the scale of implementation of these efforts remains limited.

A common challenge faced by efforts to link high-quality, developmentally appropriate education with good health is the burgeoning demands on school curricula and finding the time for health-related concerns, particularly those that compete with other instructional time. Thus, integrated, interdisciplinary curricula such as the HUMBIO program (Chapter 7, this volume) and other similar efforts should be seriously considered by schools with commitments to health promotion for adolescents.

Still, the tension between the academic mission of school and the enhancement of full human development is an enduring dilemma. In authentic *Turning Points* schools, this tension is addressed directly by recognizing that when the academic requirements of schools are matched with and informed by the developmental needs of young adolescents, students are more likely to achieve, behavioral problems are reduced, and teachers feel more satisfaction with their profession (Chapter 3, this volume). Thus, the prospects are indeed promising for linking good education with health promotion, but the widespread implementation of this core principle is far from accomplished (Hechinger, 1993).

Living in multiethnic and multicultural societies

One concrete outcome of globalization is the increased migration of families and youth across national boundaries. Wars and economic instability also contribute to such migrations. Whatever the reasons, adults find themselves living in communities and their children attending schools that are heterogeneous in composition.

It is probably a feature of twenty-first-century life that young people will find themselves living in more multiethnic societies than did their parents. How do schools and other societal institutions prepare young people for living peacefully in such societies? And importantly, how do they do so in a time of economic uncertainty and when some politicians use immigration and bilingual education as emotional issues to divide groups?

As Roosens (Chapter 8, this volume) points out, the issue of language, specifically the maintenance of the language of origin used in the schools, is a particularly difficult one in the education of newcomer or immigrant students. In the United States, there is comparatively less tolerance for languages other than English. In fact, the pressures for legislation of English as the national language are part of the political agenda. This is also the case in France. In other European countries, however, multilingualism is more acceptable and desirable. Under certain conditions, Europeans may be more tolerant of nonnative languages of instruction (Chapter 8, this volume) than persons in the United States, where language is often viewed as a badge of loyalty and assimilation. Even with scientific evidence supporting the value of two-way immersion education in schools with non-English-speaking students, political support for such programs is weak.

Much ink has been spilled on the subject of multicultural education, particularly on the poor state of race relations or intergroup relations in schools and other settings in the United States (Hawley and Jackson, 1995) and in Europe (OECD, 1995a, 1995b; Roosens, Chapter 8, this volume). Institutionalized and self-selected segregation in the schools are common, despite several decades of civil rights legislation. Socioeconomic factors as well as residential patterns are critical factors. As children grow older, friendship and peer groups tend to be more self-segregated even when the school population is diverse.

Adults create environments for young people and thus shape their possibilities. Thus, the state of race relations among adults is often reproduced in the racial and ethnic cleavages among young people, especially as they become adolescents. Schools can do much; in the rather unique circumstances as described by Roosens (Chapter 8, this volume) of the schools created for children of the European Union (EU) employees, young people emerge well prepared to live and work in more than one culture and language, enhancing their considerable social and economic advantages in the international marketplace. But outside such rare and elite circumstances, less economically and socially advantaged children do not have the same experiences. Roosens suggests that EU schools should be considered for adaptation to multiethnic populations in different countries, but the economic, social, and educational barriers to such schools, as he himself notes, are considerable.

In both Europe and the United States, we have rarely successfully addressed how to prepare youth to live in multiethnic societies. This is now more than just an American dilemma. The social consequences of economic globalization and dislocation have already created countermovements in both Europe and the United States (Schwab and Smadja, 1996). An important part of that backlash is the heightening of racial and ethnic tensions within countries, particularly those with immigrant populations. If there is anything to be learned from the past, it will take courageous leadership in democratic societies to create strong ethnically and racially integrated societies. But we must also recognize that the past indicates that such societies are not easily achieved, and that what is achieved can only be sustained through constant vigilance.

Making the transition from school to work

The very expression of the problem, *school-to-work transition*, assumes that a student completes some form of schooling and enters the world of work. Therefore, solutions to the problem focus on how that transition will be made. In an era of uncertainty about the economy of the future, described well by Nadel (Chapter 9, this volume), a central part of the education of all young people must be psychosocial preparation to cope with the inherent stresses of change and uncertainty, fostering intellectual and problem-solving skills that generalize across specialized domains, and developing the capacity for flexibility and innovation. Whether these come under the headings of *life skills education* or *social competency training* would seem to make little difference.

However, the role of the school in preparing young people for such skills in coping and adaptation, and for decision making, problem solving, and negotiating conflict, is being debated on both sides of the Atlantic (Chapter 4, this volume). The problem is that such life skills are not viewed as an essential part of the so-called academic curriculum of schools and, like health education, can take time from teaching other forms of literacy. Whether an integrated approach organized around teaching for higher-order skills in academic subject matter would lead to generalization in these life skills (and vice versa) is an urgent problem for research attention.

Each country has organized connections between its schools and business and industry in different ways (for brief descriptions, see Chapter 9, this volume). However, even these long-standing relationships are in flux as national economies move into the global economy. In the United States, the business community, except in limited instances, has not established the working relationships with the schools that have characterized Germany and Japan.

Unless there is a change in the free-market orientation of American companies, workers in the United States will continue to find themselves competing in an open, highly competitive international market. At the same time, American students currently have few incentives to ensure that their performance in the K-12 grades increases their chances for decent employment (Chapter 10, this volume). Even the recent momentum toward national standards, which are viewed as a corrective to employers' lack of recognition of levels of educational achievement in hiring, seems to have faltered with declining congressional support. Thus, more than in other industrialized economies, American young people face the greatest stresses and uncertainties about how they will make an orderly transition from school into the workplace. This source of stress may be an important contributor to the high levels of psychosocial disorders among American youth, and may be a factor in rising rates in Europe as the economic rules change there as well (Chisholm and Hurrelmann, 1995).

The two chapters in this volume addressing the school-to-work transition exemplify, on the one hand, the more optimistic, can-do approach of Americans (Chapter 10) and, on the other, the more pessimistic, realistic approach of the European continent (Chapter 9). Taken together, however, all countries could benefit from stepping back and acknowledging that highly touted, well-paid, knowledge-intensive workers will likely be a small part of the workforce in industrialized countries (Reich, 1991). More serious attention must be focused on the large parts of the workforce that will be displaced by technology and downsizing in a postmanufacturing society. What role, if any, will the schools have in preparing a wide range of young people for futures in which even the well educated may not be adequately compensated for their knowledge and skills?

This disturbing scenario returns us to our starting point: How will nations prepare their young people for life in a new economic order? This economic order will undoubtedly have social and political ramifications. Although a certain base of literacy – knowledge, analytic and social skills – is necessary for all (OECD, 1995b), not all students will win in the economic race. Schools must play a role, supported by relevant social policies – particularly in education, worker training and retraining, job creation, and social safety nets – to deal with the effects of globalization (Friedman, 1996; Schwab and Smadja, 1996). Addressing the impact of economic globalization and its ramifications on preparation for adulthood should be placed at the top of educational and social agendas immediately.

Conclusion

The chapters in this volume attest to the necessity and the value of cross-national conversations about how nations prepare young people for a new century. Opportunities for these exchanges will no longer be limited to printed works and face-to-face conferences, but will be expanded to the information superhighway of the near future. This will likely create even more common ground rather than less as individuals are exposed to the ideas and experiences of a wide range of people who are attempting to address similar concerns.

These are indeed exciting times to be engaged in thinking about the prospects for children and youth worldwide. Building from common ground, we have our best chance to apply existing research and experience to address enduring human dilemmas in preparing youth for adult life.

References

Carnegie Council on Adolescent Development. (1995). *Great transition: Preparing adolescents for a new century.* Washington, DC: Author.

Carnegie Council on Adolescent Development, Task Force on Education of Young Adolescents. (1989). *Turning points: Preparing American youth for the 21st century.* Washington, DC: Author.

Carnegie Council on Adolescent Development, Task Force on Youth Development and Community Programs. (1992). *A matter of time: Risk and opportunity in the nonschool hours.* Washington, DC: Author.

Chisholm, L., and Hurrelmann, K. (1995). Adolescence in modern Europe: Pluralized transition patterns and their implications for personal and social risks. *Journal of Adolescence, 18,* 129–158.

Csapó, B. (1992, Summer). Educational testing in Hungary. *Educational Measurements: Issues and Practice, 11* (2), 5–8, 15.

Dryfoos, J. G. (1990). *Adolescents at risk: Prevalence and prevention.* New York: Oxford University Press.

Dryfoos, J. G. (1994). *Full-service schools: A revolution in health and social services for children, youth, and families.* San Francisco: Jossey-Bass.

Friedman, T. L. (1996, February 7). Revolt of the wannabes. *The New York Times,* p. A19.

Hawley, W. D., and Jackson, A. W. (Eds.). (1995). *Toward a common destiny: Improving race and ethnic relations in America.* San Francisco: Jossey-Bass.

Hechinger, F. M. (1993, Spring). Schools for teenagers: A historic dilemma. *Teachers College Record, 94* (3), 522–539.

Hess, L. E. (1995). Changing family patterns in Western Europe: Opportunity and risk factors for adolescent development. In M. Rutter and D. J. Smith (Eds.), *Psychosocial disorders in young people: Time trends and their causes* (pp. 104–193). New York: Wiley.

International Commission on Education for the Twenty-first Century. (1996). *Learning: The treasure within.* Report to the United Nations Educational, Scientific and Cultural Organization (UNESCO). Paris: UNESCO Publishing.

Millstein, S. G., Petersen, A. C., and Nightingale, E. O. (Eds.). (1993). *Promoting the health of adolescents: New directions for the twenty-first century.* New York: Oxford University Press.

Organization for Economic Cooperation and Development. (1995a). *Our children at risk.* Paris: Author.

Organization for Economic Cooperation and Development. (1995b). *Literacy, economy, and society.* Paris: Author.

Reich, R. B. (1991). *The work of nations: Preparing ourselves for 21st century capitalism.* New York: Knopf.

Rutter, M., and Smith, D. J. (Eds.). (1995). *Psychosocial disorders in young people: Time trends and their causes.* New York: Wiley.

Schwab, K., and Smadja, C. (1996, February 1). Start taking the backlash against globalization seriously. *International Herald Tribune,* p. 8.

Takanishi, R., Mortimer, A. M., and McGourthy, T. J. (1995, May). Positive indicators of adolescent development: Redressing the negative image of American adolescents. In *Indicators of children's well-being conference papers. Volume III: Cross-cutting issues; Population, family, and neighborhood; Social development and problem behaviors* (Special Report No. 60c, pp. 149–162). Madison: University of Wisconsin Institute for Research on Poverty.

U.S. Congress, Office of Technology Assessment. (1991a). *Adolescent health: Volume 1: Summary and policy options* (OTA Publication No. OTA-H-468). Washington, DC: U.S. Government Printing Office.

U.S. Congress, Office of Technology Assessment. (1991b). *Adolescent health: Volume 2: Background and the effectiveness of selected prevention and treatment services* (OTA Publication No. OTA-H-466). Washington, DC: U.S. Government Printing Office.

U.S. Congress, Office of Technology Assessment. (1991c). *Adolescent health: Volume 3: Crosscutting issues in the delivery of health and related services* (OTA Publication No. OTA-H-467). Washington, DC: U.S. Government Printing Office.

World Health Organization, Regional Office for Europe. (1993, May). *European network of health-promoting schools*. Denmark: Author.

Author index

Subject index